WITHDRAWN

UNIVERSITY OF CALIFORNIA
PUBLICATIONS IN HISTORY

VOLUME XL

THE GEORGIA-FLORIDA FRONTIER
1793–1796

Spanish Reaction to French Intrigue
and American Designs

BY

RICHARD K. MURDOCH

UNIVERSITY OF CALIFORNIA PRESS
BERKELEY AND LOS ANGELES
1951

University of California Publications in History

Editors (Los Angeles): J. W. Caughey, D. K. Bjork, R. H. Fisher

Volume 40, pp. X + 1–208

Submitted by editors December 5, 1949

Issued June 15, 1951

Price, $2.00

975
M949

University of California Press

Berkeley and Los Angeles

California

◇

Cambridge University Press

London, England

28486

Feb 53

PRINTED IN THE UNITED STATES OF AMERICA

TO

JOSEPH BYRNE LOCKEY
SCHOLAR—TEACHER—GENTLEMAN

PREFACE

THE EFFORTS OF numerous agents of the French revolutionary government to persuade the citizens of the United States to coöperate in projects directed against the New World possessions of England and Spain have been explored in great detail by several generations of historians. These investigations have produced a fairly detailed picture of official reaction of the federal and state governments to French intrigue. Little attention has been accorded, however, to the measures taken by England and Spain to prevent violations of their colonial possessions. This account deals primarily with Franco-American designs against the Spanish in East Florida and with the plans adopted for the defense of that province.

This study is, I believe, the first attempt to examine in detail the reaction of the Spanish authorities in St. Augustine and Havana to the so-called "French schemes." I have endeavored to explain the countermeasures taken both to drive the invaders from East Florida and to frustrate attempts at internal revolt. I have relied on Spanish documentary sources wherever possible, particularly in those parts of the study concerned with activities in and around St. Augustine. As far as I know, no previous use has been made of many of these documents. They throw additional light on certain aspects of Spanish colonial policy during the critical years of the French Revolution. This study reveals that although procrastination may have appeared to be Spain's first line of defense, when finally aroused to action, her colonial administrators could and did make effective use of their limited military resources.

Among my obligations, the deepest are to the late Professor Joseph Byrne Lockey, of the department of history of the University of California at Los Angeles, who originally inspired the undertaking of this study. I am especially grateful for the assistance rendered me by the Department of Archives and History of the State of Georgia in examining their documentary collection, and to Julien C. Yonge for permission to make use of the materials in the P. K. Yonge Library of Florida History in Gainesville, Florida. I am indebted to the following societies, libraries, and institutions for many services: the Manuscript Division of the Library of Congress; the Georgia Historical Society; the Charleston Library Society; the National Archives of Cuba; the Florida Historical Society; the St. Augustine Historical Society; the South Carolina State Historical Commission; the Library of the University of Chicago;

the University of California at Los Angeles; the Boston Public Library; and the Carnegie Institute of Technology.

Finally, I would like to express my gratitude to Professor John Walton Caughey of the department of history of the University of California at Los Angeles for his many suggestions in the completion of this study. I am directly responsible, however, for any technical errors and shortcomings that may appear.

R. K. M.

Pittsburgh, Pennsylvania

CONTENTS

CHAPTER I

EARLY HISTORY

THE LONG STRUGGLE for the possession of Florida, from its discovery early in the sixteenth century to its transfer to the United States in 1821, was one for strategic geographic advantage, rather than for potential wealth. Its position at the southeastern extremity of the North American continent, its proximity to the rich islands of the Caribbean and to the British continental colonies, and its importance as a "window" on the Atlantic made it valuable both to Spain and to England, and in lesser degree to France. This struggle can be divided roughly into three phases: the race between France and Spain to establish a successful colony; the attempt of England to wrest the colony from Spain during the eighteenth-century wars; and the frontier difficulties resulting from the American and French revolutions, when France once again had designs on certain of the North American colonial possessions of Spain. This study makes no attempt to embrace this vast field, but rather is restricted to an account of events during a short part of the third phase of the struggle.

Although Spain claimed legal possession of Florida by right of discovery and exploration, she made no successful settlement until driven to do so by the encroachment of France. Jean Ribault, the leader of a party of French Huguenots in search of a new home, reached the mouth of the Rivière de Mai in 1562,[1] and laid claim to the entire region in the name of Charles IX of France.[2] Two years later, another party of Huguenots, under the leadership of René de Laudonnière, succeeded in establishing a small settlement at the mouth of this river, giving it the name of Fort Caroline. The reaction of the Spanish to this encroachment was swift and terrible. In the next year, a sizable expedition under the command of Pedro Menéndez de Avilés reached Florida, attacked Laudonnière's establishment, and put all the Protestant members to the sword.[3] In addition, the Spanish built a small fort a few miles south of the former French settlement to protect their interests in this region. This marked the origin of St. Augustine, the first permanent European settlement within the present bounds of the United States.[4] As the religious wars in France rendered the royal government powerless, and as Laudonnière's venture was of private origin, there was little official reaction to this abrupt termination of French attempts to colonize Flor-

---

[1] For notes to chap. i, see pp. 147–149.

[1]

ida. When, however, half a century later, French colonial interest was
revived, turning first to Canada and then to Louisiana and the Gulf of
Mexico, exploration in the Gulf region brought the French once again
into close contact with the Spanish in Florida. Rumors of French plans
for settlement in this region reached Madrid in 1697 and 1698. This
renewed threat of French encroachment led to the establishment of a
military post, the presidio of San Carlos de Austria, on Pensacola Bay
in 1698, to serve in part, as an outpost for the old Spanish settlement
at St. Augustine, and in part to forestall French settlement in West
Florida.[5]

After the founding of a permanent settlement, Spanish control over
eastern Florida was not seriously threatened for nearly one hundred
and fifty years, although St. Augustine was the scene of attacks by
English freebooters, Sir Francis Drake in 1586 and Captain John Davis
nearly a century later.[6] There were minor frontier skirmishes with the
British far to the north in the Carolinas, over the question of harboring
pirates, hiding runaway slaves, and inciting the Indian tribes to war.[7]
However, in the first three decades of the eighteenth century there was
constant expansion of the southern frontier of the English colony of
South Carolina, a threat regarded seriously by the Spanish officials in
St. Augustine. A thoroughly unsuccessful attack by the British on St.
Augustine in 1702, led by Governor James Moore,[8] was followed in the
next year by a more successful attack on the Indians in central Florida,
who were under Spanish protection.[9] The Spanish, supported by a
French fleet under LeFebvre, retaliated in 1706, making a futile attack
on Charleston.[10] The founding of the colony of Georgia in 1733 caused
renewed anxiety in Florida, for now the southern outposts of British
rule were moved more than one hundred miles closer to St. Augustine
and into a region still claimed by Spain. The outbreak of the War of
Jenkins' Ear[11] gave Governor Oglethorpe an opportunity to renew the
attack on his neighbors to the south, once in 1740 and again in 1743.
Although these expeditions were large and expensive, the results were
meager, and disease proved to be a more deadly enemy than the Spaniards.[12] The Spaniards retaliated by attempting to attack Savannah in
1742, using both the overland and sea routes. After an unsuccessful
attack on Frederica, Governor Manuel de Monteano and his forces fell
back to St. Augustine.[13] The Treaty of Aix-la-Chapelle brought a temporary halt to hostilities, although frequent Indian raids along the
frontier forced the local settlers to maintain a constant vigil.

The Seven Years' War brought disaster not only to France but also to her ally, Spain, for the latter was forced to cede Florida to England in order to ransom the city of Havana, which had fallen to the British in 1762. The treaty of 1763 marked the physical transfer of Florida to England and also the beginning of a short but highly prosperous period for this colony. In the twenty years of British rule, the colony of Florida was transformed from a single sleepy province into the two thriving and industrious provinces of East and West Florida. There was a rapid increase in population and a marked development of the economic structure.[14] Because of this prosperity, the two Floridas remained staunchly loyal to the mother country during the American Revolution.[15] In 1778, East Florida served as one of the bases for a successful attack by the British against Savannah and the rest of Georgia. But the entrance of Spain into the war of the American Rebellion on the side of France resulted quickly in the loss of West Florida. The Spanish capture of Pensacola in 1781 marked the end of this short campaign. At the conclusion of the war, England was forced to retrocede both provinces to Spain, in spite of certain vague claims to this territory put forward by the state of Georgia.[16]

This change of masters was a disastrous blow for East Florida, for it saw the virtual end of the period of prosperity, and a return to the economic status of the years before 1763. Whereas in 1783, the year of the transfer to Spain, the population of the two Floridas was seventeen thousand, by 1785 only four hundred and fifty whites and two hundred Negroes remained. The Catholic population of the New Smyrna colony accounted for the majority of these.[17] In a few short years, practically all the progress made under British control was lost, and St. Augustine gradually returned to its former position as a small, obscure frontier outpost of the Spanish colonial empire.

However, troubles north of the frontier were not brought to an end by the disappearance of England from the colonial scene. The new state of Georgia was expanding rapidly because of a constant flow of new settlers from Virginia and the two Carolinas. These new settlers were hungry for free land and eyed with great interest the fertile regions south and west of the Altamaha River.[18] It meant little to them that these were Indian lands, guaranteed by treaties with the state of Georgia. The Indian frontier had been pushed back toward the northwest and the southwest by treaties in 1733 and 1763, the latter ceding a narrow strip of land along the coast south to the St. Mary's River. In 1773, the treaty of Augusta, between Governor James Wright of Georgia and some of the Cherokee and Creek chieftains, had more than doubled the area of the colony. As each cession of land was made reluctantly by the Indians, the frontier was pushed that much farther to the south and west. Finally, in 1785, by the treaty of Galphinton, the small number of Creeks who held the land from the confluence of the Oconee and Ocmulgee rivers to the southernmost bend of the St. Mary's River ceded it to Georgia. After a brief period of hostilities which resulted from the refusal of a larger number of Indian chiefs to recognize the validity of this treaty, the cession was reaffirmed in the following year by the treaty of Shoulderbone.[19] Now the frontier of Georgia for the first time abutted on the northern frontier of East Florida, from the depths of the Okefenoke Swamp to the mouth of the St. Mary's River. Since the Spaniards claimed to be the protectors of all the Creek people, they refused to recognize the validity of this cession by some of them.

Although there had already been some scattered settlement in this area south of the Altamaha River, the first permanent townsite was not laid out until 1788, on the northern bank of the St. Mary's River at a place called Buttermilk Bluff. The new town was given the name of St. Patrick and was recognized almost immediately as the seat of Camden County government.[20] Four years later, as a result of a petition from the local inhabitants, the state legislature changed the name to St. Mary's, the name it still bears.[21] Throughout this period, the Spaniards insisted on calling it New Town or Newton. In a few years, the population along the northern bank of the river had increased to several hundred. As the best lands in the newly opened areas of southern Georgia were taken up, later settlers found themselves forced to homestead undesirable locations on the outskirts where the land was less fertile and the threat of Indian attack very real.

Yet when these discontented settlers looked across the St. Mary's River to the Spanish province, they saw an abundance of fertile land stretching to the south. Much of this region had once been dotted with prosperous plantations, but the exodus of British settlers had brought the population practically to the point of extinction. Few Spanish settlers had come to take over the necessary burden of growing grain and raising cattle to supply the needs of St. Augustine.[22] Some American settlers wished to cross into Spanish territory, even at the risk of losing their citizenship, but the restrictive colonial policy of Spain forbade the admission of aliens, unless a permit was obtained from higher authority. Governor Vicente Manuel de Céspedes suggested in 1787 that a policy be established which would permit the settlement of some industrious Americans in East Florida.[23] It was pointed out that it might assist the poverty-stricken provincial treasury if a few carefully chosen settlers were admitted to aid in growing vital crops; this might well result in an economic and agricultural revival for all the province. Eventually, a royal order was received in 1790 inviting aliens to come to East Florida at their own expense. Although they were forbidden to practice openly any religion other than Roman Catholicism, they did not have to forego their own religion, nor were they required to attend Mass. They were required to swear an oath of allegiance to the crown, thus becoming Spanish subjects. Lands were to be granted to the head of each new family; 100 acres to the head of the family, 50 for each white member, and 50 for each slave. The settlers were required to build adequate houses and to cultivate the fields for a period of ten years, at the end of which time an outright deed would be granted to all the land.[24]

As a result of this very liberal policy on the part of the Spanish government, a number of settlers crossed to the south bank of the St. Mary's River in 1790 and 1791. Most of them came from Virginia and the Carolinas, though many had lived a few years in southern Georgia. Among the new settlers were found such family names as McIntosh, Atkinson, Hollingsworth, Lang, Cryer, Raines, Blunt, Hogan, Ashley, and Plummer. These families figured prominently among those to whom Governor Juan Nepomuceno de Quesada made temporary grants of land in the years following the royal order of 1790.[25] At least three of these families, McIntosh, Atkinson, and Ashley, came from the new settlement at St. Patrick.[26] These grants of land lay for the most part in the region between the St. Mary's and St. John's rivers, although a few were along the southern bank of the latter. Few were in the immediate vicinity of St. Augustine, for it appeared to be the policy of the authorities to keep these new settlers at a distance from the town and fort. Nevertheless, some were granted permission to settle in the town itself, although they were kept under close watch and were forced to obtain a bond from an established Spanish citizen as a guarantee of good faith whenever the purchase of a house or lot was made.

Thus it was that the Spanish authorities permitted fairly large numbers of Americans to settle in East Florida, little realizing that in so doing they were preparing the way for serious difficulties in the future.

The new settlers soon found that the very liberal terms under which they were allowed to come into the province were in reality merely a ruse to get them to establish themselves there. Restrictive measures placed on business enterprise made everyday life more difficult than it had been at home even under British rule. There were restrictions on commerce, on buying and selling necessities, on raising certain crops, on traveling within the province, on public assemblage, and on many other things. In addition, foreign trade was strictly limited, and the price of American goods in East Florida was very high. This encouraged illicit trading back and forth across the St. Mary's River, even though the penalties for such violations were severe.[27] The language barrier caused dissatisfaction and inconvenience, for it meant the employment of translators who often turned a pretty penny by incorrect rendering of contracts from one language to the other. And finally, complaints by the new settlers against what they considered to be abuses of their liberties received but scant attention in St. Augustine. It seemed to them that the governor and his council studiously avoided giving them fair hearings. All in all, the new settlers were thoroughly discontented with their lot and anxious to do something about it, although most of them did not want to move away and abandon the fertile lands given them by the Spanish government.[28] Most of them cherished the freedom so recently won from England and were willing to take part in any move to overthrow the government of the province if this would result in union with the United States and in further distribution of fertile lands. A few of the settlers may have come to East Florida with this in mind, but this number must have been small.

The majority of the citizens of Georgia were in sympathy with those American settlers in East Florida who were ready to take up arms against their new masters. Ever since the founding of Georgia there had been constant friction along the border over the recovery of runaway slaves, and no satisfactory solution had ever been reached. This question grew more serious as more settlers entered the area and became the source of much correspondence between the United States and Spain.[29] Negotiations were of necessity protracted, and often years elapsed between dispatches, with the result that redress was sought by the aggrieved parties through retaliatory raids across the border. On the whole, the government of Georgia refused to listen to complaints from citizens of East Florida since, it declared, the Spanish authorities in St. Augustine refused to acknowledge the receipt of American complaints.

Furthermore, the citizens of Georgia were unwavering in their belief that most of the troubles with the Creek and Cherokee Indians resulted from the evil machinations of Spanish officials. Whether this was actually true or not did not matter, for the rank and file of Georgians firmly believed it, and this belief was shared by many of the officials in Augusta. Even as the frontier was pushed farther back, as the Indians were deprived of their homes and hunting grounds, the frontier settlers still believed that the ensuing troubles came from Spanish interference. They claimed that the Indians were armed and fed by the Spanish in New Orleans, Pensacola, St. Mark's, and St. Augustine. The Georgians welcomed each new land cession and forged ahead, always eager to cross the newly established boundary, treaty or no treaty. The vast land concessions made by the Indians to the state in 1785 and confirmed the next year momentarily sated the land-hungry settlers, but a serious Indian war broke out when Congress declared these treaties to be null and void.[30] When, in 1790, the news of the treaty of New York between the federal government and the Creeks reached Georgia, popular indignation knew no bounds. By this new agreement, the federal government declared that all treaties between the Indians and the state of Georgia were invalid, and thus a large tract of land across the Oconee River reverted to the Creeks. Many settlers refused to recognize the validity of the retrocession and were determined to remain west of the new line. They were supported in this decision by most of the state authorities, who either refused to carry out the orders of the federal government or did so in such a way as to render them ineffective. As a result, frontier warfare raged during the three years following the new treaty. An extract from a letter written in Knoxville summed up the situation very succinctly:

Excursive parties of horse, well directed, laying waste their Creek towns, stock and grain, would shortly teach these too faithless nations, to seek safety on the west sides of the Mississippi, in the bosom of their friends the Spaniards, and it would not be very difficult to send the Spaniards of East and West Florida apacking with them; for the frontier people are highly exasperated against them, and it is well known here, that many of the inhabitants of their two provinces are earnestly wishing for, and ready to lend their will to, the completion of so desired an event.[31]

The Indians applied for and obtained some aid from the Spaniards. A regular military campaign was planned by Georgia against the Creeks in 1793, but Governor Edward Telfair postponed the departure of troops at the direct request of President Washington.[32]

It was not surprising that the Spanish authorities gave aid to the Indians. The most disastrous blow that could befall Spain would be the defeat and dispersal of the southeastern Indian tribes, who served as a buffer between the land-hungry Americans and the weak Spanish settlements in the Mississippi Valley.[33] Thus, while the Georgians desired to see the elimination of the problem created by the presence of the Indians on the frontier, the Spaniards were anxious to have them remain in order to hold the attention of the United States and to prevent further growth of interest in the area south of the Ohio River, in the general direction of New Orleans. The correspondence of Francisco Luis Héctor, Baron de Carondelet, governor of Louisiana,[34] shows the importance that he placed on the maintenance of good relations with the Indian tribes. These could be maintained only by constant payment of subsidies, presentation of gifts and arms, and granting concessions, which could be done only if the colonies were accessible to Spanish ships. As the governor pointed out, there was an unofficial race between the governments of the United States and Spain to see which could outbid the other for the favor and support of the Indians.

Interest in western lands was not confined to settlers on the frontier, for there were people in the United States deeply involved in various schemes of land promotion and speculation. There had long been interest in the region south of the settlements along the Tennessee River, and west of the farthermost outposts in Georgia. Much of this area was still in dispute between the United States and Spain as a result of the vague terms of the treaties of 1783. The attempt of the South Carolina Yazoo Company to obtain and dispose of a large part of this region had focused the attention of many people on the attractiveness of this area, still occupied by the Creeks and Cherokees.[35] Although this particular attempt came to nothing, it did succeed in planting an idea in the minds of many Georgians, which later resulted in such things as the Pine Barren Speculation scheme and the scandalous Yazoo sales in 1794 and 1795.[36]

Linked with the problem of the Indians and the question of expansion into more fertile lands was the desire of the commercial interests in Savannah and Charleston to extend their business into fields hitherto closed to them. They were jealous of the degree to which the Spaniards monopolized the lucrative trade with most of the southeastern Indian tribes and looked with disfavor on the Spanish policy which forbade free trade by foreigners. They saw in the Floridas and Louisiana a ready market for many sorts of American products. The chief obstacle to American participation in this trade appeared to be the royal monopolies of certain items and the favored position of the trading-house of Panton and Leslie.[37] This Scottish trading-house had long been under attack by the American settlers, who charged that through this organization the Indians were supplied with food, clothing, arms, and ammunition in exchange for their entire annual production of handiwork and furs.

If the United States wanted to get Spain out of the Floridas, the situation in 1793 along her southeastern frontier presented plenty of causes for a quarrel. The temper of the frontier people was roused over recent Indian depredations; the more conservative landowners were crying out for the restoration of their runaway slaves; many of the new settlers wanted access to more free land; and the commercial interests sought new outlets for their trade both in the Indian lands and in East Florida. Furthermore, most of the new settlers within that province were dissatisfied with their lot under the Spanish flag and were willing to support any action that might lead to a change in government. The sympathies of a large part of the American public were with the frontier people and with those living under the authority of Spain. The government of the state of Georgia was in the hands of a group of men either generally partial to such action or so involved in various land schemes as to be indifferent to affairs outside the state. To turn to Philadelphia for guidance and aid was unavailing, for the federal government was either unable or unwilling to give assistance in any of these issues. As has been pointed out previously, negotiations with Spain for the granting of commercial concessions were getting nowhere; little progress was being made in the matter of the return of runaway slaves; the policy of the new government was opposed to land speculation, particularly if it involved areas not definitely belonging to the United States; and finally, the federal government and the state of Georgia were deadlocked over the question of the validity of treaties with the Indians.

This was the state of affairs when Citizen Genêt arrived in Charleston as the new French minister plenipotentiary to the United States.[38] He was given a tumultuous reception, partly because of the popularity of some of the changes made during the early stages of the French Revolution, partly because of what it was hoped his mission might accomplish, and partly because of the strong anti-English sentiment in South Carolina. His instructions bristled with hostile declarations against the possessions of Spain, even though they were drawn up at a time when France and Spain were still at peace with one another.[39] Although French interest seemed to be concentrated on Louisiana and Canada, it was easy enough to stretch the meaning of these instructions to cover almost any eventuality. To many of the frontier people, the arrival of Genêt with instructions to begin hostilities against the possessions of Spain appeared to be the opportunity for which they had been waiting.

Small wonder that such men as George Rogers Clark[40] of Kentucky, Governor William Moultrie[41] of South Carolina, and Elijah Clark[42] of Georgia were immediately attracted by his schemes. To these three revolutionary leaders, the plans of the new French minister seemed to offer the opportunity to serve their country by putting an end to the Spanish and Indian problems. It is unlikely that any one of the three envisioned himself either as the founder of a new nation or as the vassal of France. But each saw an opportunity to use the forces and finances of France to accomplish something that the federal government was unable to do. These men were but three among a large number who quickly understood what the aid of France could accomplish along the frontier. Once their enthusiasm was kindled, it took but little effort to convince the frontier people, many of whom had followed these military leaders into battle against the English and the Indians, that their future happiness and welfare would be insured by the success of Genêt's schemes. In a short time, a number of hardened fighters were ready to take up arms under the flag of France. This study will follow one part of Genêt's plan—the raising of forces in South Carolina and Georgia to form the nucleus of an expedition against the province of East Florida—and will describe the events which followed immediately after the failure of the original project. These events occurred in the years 1793–1796 and formed an episode in the vast westward surge of the new American nation.

CHAPTER II

MANGOURIT'S PREPARATIONS IN
CHARLESTON

THE ARRIVAL OF Citizen Genêt in the United States was eagerly awaited
by those with active French sympathies, and it needed only his personal
magnetism to launch the events which followed with bewildering rapidity. Genêt was convinced that the United States felt herself bound
forever to her benefactress because of aid given in the American Revolution and because of the terms of the treaty of alliance of 1778. He felt
that as a minister of France, concerned with his country's welfare, his
duty was to secure American aid for his plans. Confident of success,
Genêt stepped ashore at Charleston, quite prepared to make the United
States the scene of undeclared warfare against both England and Spain.
His arrival in Charleston rather than Philadelphia was in itself an indication of his unorthodox approach to the duties incumbent upon an
accredited representative of a foreign power. Washington's neutrality
proclamation, issued almost simultaneously with Genêt's arrival, did
little to dampen the ardor of the new minister[1] and was probably un-
connected with his anticipated arrival, for it was customary for a neutral
nation to make known its stand upon the outbreak of an international
war.

Genêt had four important factors in his favor: his cleverness in preparing the way with flattery and promises caused many friends of
France to listen; the unbridled enthusiasm shown him upon his arrival
in the United States indicated the temper of the average American
toward the new French Republic; the unconcealed interest that Jefferson
took in the ideals of the French Revolution made it seem probable that
the secretary of state would favor the French cause in preference to that
of England or Spain; and it was clear from the very outset that there
would be no difficulties encountered in crystallizing the dislike and distrust of Spain into active support of a French attack on the former's
colony of East Florida.

Awaiting Genêt's arrival in Charleston was Citizen Mangourit,[2] the
French consul accredited to the states of North Carolina, South Carolina, and Georgia,[3] and a man well qualified to spread the doctrines of
the French Revolution and to gather about him eager converts, ready
to assist its cause. Early in October, 1792, Mangourit had been ap-

---

[1] For notes to chap. ii, see pp. 149–153.

proached by a Major Tintiniac,[4] a former officer in the American Revolutionary army, who proposed a scheme to raise a force of frontiersmen to be transported to Europe to aid in the war against Austria. According to the major, it would be a simple matter to raise a corps of expert riflemen from among the French refugees from Haiti living in and around Charleston. All that was needed was the approval of the French minister of foreign affairs and the allocation of sufficient funds to defray the expenses of the voyage to Europe. As requested by Tintiniac, Mangourit wrote to Paris on October 14 seeking permission to assist in the formation of this group, which he suggested might be known as the Legion of South Carolina.[5] The minister of marine sent an affirmative reply on February 11, declaring that the Convention had discussed the matter at great length on the third and had given its approval to the scheme.[6] This occurred just after Genêt's departure from Paris, and it is perfectly possible that the Ministry of Foreign Affairs hoped that the new minister might be able to use this favorable situation in South Carolina as a sort of trial balloon to measure the temper of the American people. When the news of this favorable decision reached Tintiniac, he expressed his gratification and announced his intention of commencing his recruiting scheme among his old comrades in arms then living along the upper reaches of the Edisto River.[7] A week later, he was reported to be busy with this project in the "upper country."[8]

The project was short-lived, however, for on August 6 Mangourit had to inform Genêt that Tintiniac had abandoned his scheme and had assumed an air of offended dignity, accusing him of having failed to supply the necessary funds. According to Mangourit, Tintiniac had had the effrontery to demand a reasonable retirement pension. The consul hastened to deny that the Republic had lost a single penny supporting the unrealized project of this "Don Quixote." Besides, Mangourit asserted: "I knew very well that 200 men coming to France from Carolina could be only a burden to the Republic which already has plenty of men; but I realized the value of the enthusiasm of these backwoodsmen who would be crossing 1400 [sic] miles of stormy seas to France...."[9]

Although this episode in itself may be regarded as an isolated event of no great importance, it proved to be the first step in the scheme to obtain tangible American assistance in the war against Spain and England. It certainly afforded Mangourit an excellent opportunity to study the possibility of recruiting armed men within the United States.

The second step led to the rapid increase in the number of violations of American neutrality by armed French merchantmen and ships of war. Not only were the port facilities being used, but the ship captains purchased arms, ammunition, and supplies, sold prize goods at auction, and finally began replenishing their crews and building up new crews for prize ships. Recruiting of both French and American sailors was carried on openly in nearly all the ports of the United States. Many of the blank letters of marque that Genêt had brought with him to the United States were soon issued to willing sea captains, both French and American.[10]

Although a great many diplomatic notes were passed back and forth between the representatives of the United States, France, and England over the question of privateers making use of American ports, no definite solution to this problem was reached during this period.[11] This is shown by the fact that nearly a year later, Mangourit was bold enough to order Captain Branzon of the French warship *Las Casas* to recruit sailors along the water front of Charleston, assuring him that he would always find a safe haven for his ship in that American port.[12] Spain's representatives in Philadelphia became alarmed over the number of armed French vessels using American ports, and their correspondence with the governor of East Florida and the captain general in Havana contained long accounts of what they considered to be American indifference to the violation of her neutrality. By December, the Spanish ministers had received orders to protest directly to Congress.[13]

A third plan for using American assistance, this time for an attack on East Florida, was a combination of ideas based on the two earlier steps. The idea of recruiting soldiers from among the frontier population sprang from the earlier scheme to enlist soldiers to go to the Continent to fight. The plan to assist the land forces with a naval force and to supply them with arms and ammunition by ship from Charleston and Savannah, involved the continued use of American harbors by French privateers and warships. This projected incursion into East Florida was but a small part of the much larger scheme to revolutionize all Spanish and English territory in North America, as visualized in Genêt's instructions.[14] Plans were already under way for such projects as General George Rogers Clark's attack on Louisiana and West Florida, the sea-borne attack on New Orleans, the invasion of English Canada from New York and the northwest settlements, and the liberation of Mexico by way of Texas and the Provincias Internas.[15] The anticipated attack on East Florida was to be coördinated with these other plans in order to bring about a concerted drive against the colonial possessions of Spain and England.

When Genêt departed for Philadelphia, he left the preparations for the attack on East Florida entirely in the hands of Mangourit, whom he regarded as a capable and enthusiastic agent.[16] In writing to the minister of foreign affairs concerning the French consul, Genêt declared: "Citizen Minister, Citizen Mangourit, consul in Charleston, is a devoted patriot. He has prepared the ground very well, and I have left him all the instructions necessary to direct his zeal toward the goal that the council set forth in the various instructions given to me."[17]

It is not known just what these instructions were, but later events showed that they must have included a general outline of the projected attack on East Florida. It is probable that the consul received additional instructions to attempt to raise a sizable force of men in the Carolinas to assist in the projected attack from the Ohio River area on New Orleans. This secondary force was to march west to act as a supporting group, with the task of capturing Pensacola and the rest of West Florida.[18] Mangourit selected William Tate of South Carolina to be leader of this expedition.[19] He was commissioned a colonel by Genêt and was given instructions to recruit men for the Revolutionary Legion of America.[20]

As soon as Genêt left Charleston, Mangourit began to lay plans for the expedition against East Florida. It was fairly evident that one of the first steps must be a visit to Savannah. Here he hoped to induce local sea captains to accept some of the letters of marque that Genêt had left with him for distribution. These blank commissions included the interesting order: "In case the ports of Florida are attacked, the aforementioned vessel will come to render common cause against the enemies of the French Republic."[21] Besides issuing letters of marque, Mangourit hoped to be able to select dependable men as leaders for the projected expedition. He held a lengthy conversation with Governor Moultrie of South Carolina, who gave him letters of introduction to leading military and political figures in Savannah.[22] A few days after this interview with the governor, the consul had the opportunity of meeting and conversing with a captain of the federal militia, on leave from his post on the Georgia frontier. From this discussion, Mangourit got the impression that most Georgians were ready to fight against Spain because of the assistance they claimed that the Spaniards were giving the Indians. According to this officer, the fact that Spanish officials were paying the Indians a bounty for each American scalp brought in was enough to turn all the frontier against Spain. The captain promised to send

Mangourit a detailed map of the frontier region, an item long desired by the consul.[23]

Although there is no definite evidence that Mangourit did in fact go to Savannah, there was a significant lapse of six weeks in his official correspondence which would have afforded him ample time to make such a trip. His meeting with the captain from Georgia must have increased his desire to hasten preparations for the attack in order to take full advantage of the favorable conditions along the frontier. His next dispatch to Genêt gives the impression that he had been in Georgia. The reference to Samuel Hammond,[24] the man selected by Mangourit to be the leader of the expedition, indicates a meeting between the two men. It is possible that at this time Hammond was given his official commission appointing him "Colonel in command of the Revolutionary Legion of the Floridas."[25] In the summer of 1793, a savage war was being waged with the Creeks, and Samuel Hammond was in the field at the head of a small detachment of state militia. This prevented Mangourit from carrying out that part of his plan which called for an alliance between the French and the Indian tribes in the southeast. But he was nevertheless determined that several such alliances should be consummated before the departure of any force to attack East Florida. The duties of second in command were handed over to a Major Bert[26] who, like Tintiniac, had been a French officer aiding the cause of the American Revolution. The faith that Mangourit placed in Bert was shown by the decision to employ him as the official go-between to carry messages between Charleston and Savannah, as well as to Philadelphia.

Mangourit understood his own limitations, as far as decisions on the details of the plans were concerned, for he knew nothing of the local frontier conditions. He left these details to be worked out by Colonel Hammond and Major Bert, urging them to communicate with him frequently. On his first trip north, the major brought a proposal from Colonel Hammond that the two of them should attempt to raise 300 to 500 frontiersmen to form a force for an attack on St. Augustine. Bert was emphatic that there would be no difficulty in recruiting such a force, as Colonel Hammond's popularity in Georgia was very high. The question of commissions for the officers was discussed, although Mangourit could make no final decision without the approval of Genêt.[27] It is likely that the final plans for the proposed attack were discussed during the long conversations between these two men. When the major left for Savannah, he carried an authorization from Mangourit which entitled him to carry on "the plan," after consultation with Colonel Hammond. In part, this authorization read:

By virtue of the powers granted us, we authorize Citizen Major Bert to confer with the Colonel [Hammond] about the best and quickest means to use to ensure success of the enterprise; to communicate to him the advantages that the Republic will accord to the friends of Liberty and Equality who devote themselves to her service; and to inform us of their decisions by means of expeditious and energetic correspondence.[28]

Obviously the plans were well under way as far as Mangourit was concerned.

It is possible that French attempts to issue letters of marque in Georgia had already been made even before Bert was able to return to Savannah to deliver Mangourit's suggestions to Colonel Hammond. In July, two French agents were reported to have been arrested in Savannah, although the charges against them were not clear. Mangourit sent an official protest to Governor Telfair demanding their release. The seriousness of the case was shown by the decision of the governor's council to send the entire matter to the president for his immediate attention.[29] This may well have added one more count to Washington's indictment of the activities of Genêt in the United States, since the French minister was already the center of a storm over the violation of American neutrality by the warships of France.

After a lapse of several weeks, Mangourit found it necessary to defend his activities to Genêt, possibly after the latter requested an explanation of certain expenditures made in Charleston. The influx of refugees from Haiti put a strain on the sums available to Mangourit. There were many who suspected that the consul was showing partiality to refugees of antiroyalist leanings, and many complaints were sent to Genêt in Philadelphia. The consul denied that he had squandered any of the Republic's funds on worthless schemes, but insisted, instead, that he had carried out all Genêt's instructions as far as the expedition against East Florida was concerned. A full and useful report would be forwarded to Philadelphia in a few days, since he had just returned from a visit to Georgia.[30] It may be that this report was sent to Genêt at the same time that Bert traveled to Philadelphia to discuss matters of the East Florida expedition with the French minister. When the major returned to Charleston about November 1, he brought back certain important instructions from Genêt. Among them was a copy of one of the many dispatches that Genêt had written to Paris on October 7, when he made a sweeping defense of all that he had done since his arrival in the United States.[31] In this dispatch, he spoke of the East Florida expedition as a vital part of the larger plan to attack the Spanish in Louisiana. In addition, he emphasized the important part that the navy was to play in the attack on St. Augustine, since the volunteers from Georgia were to be transported by sea.[32] While Bert was bringing this dispatch to Charleston, one from Mangourit was on its way north urging immediate preparation of such a fleet, so that a rendezvous could be set for the end of the year. The consul expressed great worry over Genêt's delay in acting on these matters, particularly the sending of arms and ammunition as well as food and clothing. He declared, also, that he awaited the final order from Genêt to put the force in motion against St. Augustine. He closed this dispatch with the usual request for money, pleading, "Send me funds. I swear to you that they will be more respected than the Golden Madonna of the superstitious Spaniards."[33] It would appear that Mangourit was attempting to emphasize the fact that his plans for the attack on East Florida were completed. Yet the consul was continuously short of funds and was burdened with debts. The French minister's suspicions were aroused at this strange combination of facts.

Although the dispatches brought by Bert cheered Mangourit, they made no mention of the transmittal of vital funds. This prompted another appeal on November 3, which accompanied an account of the latest news from Charleston. The consul had become alarmed over the increasing amount of criticism leveled at Genêt and himself for their continued activities against both England and Spain. In order to defend the French position, he had taken the liberty of publishing part of a letter that Genêt had sent to Governor Moultrie protesting against the "dark and perfidious intrigues" that were being spread abroad.[34] Mangourit expressed the hope that Genêt would approve of this step.[35] But the French cause was already going into eclipse in South Carolina, and the activities of William Tate and his friends were causing the governor much worry.[36] The close connection between the Girondin government of France and the *Société des Amis des Noires* was being used to great advantage by the foes of the Republic. Any government that recognized the equality of Negroes and permitted them to send representatives to a national assembly was regarded with the utmost suspicion and disrespect by the slaveholding society of South Carolina. Although fairly small in number, this group nevertheless controlled the politics of that state and could count on the support of the governor. They were aided by the activities of the French royalist refugees who had fled from the horrors of the civil war in Haiti. These people were showering the executive with petitions and charges aimed at Mangourit. Finally, on December 9, at the recommendation of the state legislature, Governor Moultrie issued a proclamation in which he ordered the immediate suspension of all recruiting within the state for the cause of France.[37] A legislative investigation was launched to determine whether or not several important political figures in the state had accepted large sums of money from Mangourit and Genêt, in exchange for the promise to assist in recruiting men.[38] After months of idle bickering, the entire matter was dropped, but not until the schemes of Mangourit had been effectively halted. A copy of the proclamation, together with a full account of Mangourit's activities, was forwarded to the governor of Georgia in an effort to forestall any trouble within that state. The text of Governor Moultrie's proclamation was printed in full in the Augusta newspapers on December 21, but there was no editorial comment, nor was any immediate reaction audible in the statehouse.[39] The action of the South Carolina legislature angered but did not worry Mangourit. He declared, "It is a pustule of federalist virus which was pierced in the legislative chamber, and all the servile and niggardly men applauded."[40]

However, in spite of the proclamation of December 9, there is sufficient evidence to show that Governor Moultrie had no intention of causing the French supporters much embarrassment.[41] He made a special visit to Mangourit's quarters a month after the issuance of this document, and the consul had the following to say about this meeting:

Our old friend [Moultrie] came to see me this morning. He has seen Tate. He chides you for having left me without money, and I do likewise. He told me that several officers of general grade, formerly in the American army, are demanding more than commissions as lieutenant colonels. But I told him that once the conquest was over, they would receive in honors that which their military talents warrant. He is content. He knows nothing of Florida.[42]

If, as Mangourit wrote, Governor Moultrie knew nothing of the projected expedition against East Florida, he could not have warned the governor of Georgia about such a plan. As far as the consul was concerned, he had no fears about the future of his Georgia schemes. Once again he urged Genêt to hasten the departure of the all-important naval force which was to act in conjunction with the land forces under Colonel Hammond and his associates.[43]

Late in 1793, a copy of a document of uncertain authorship bearing the title "Proposals for enlistment in the French service" fell into official hands in Charleston.[44] The document opened with the words: "In consequence of instructions and authorization from Citizen Mangourit of the French Republic, I, the subscriber, have set down the following proposals for the consideration of Colonels. . . ." This wording indicates that the original proposals were the work of Mangourit for the future consideration of Colonel Samuel Hammond and his friends. The document bore the name of Major Bert as the official copyist. It purported to be the guide for all French agents recruiting soldiers along the frontier of Georgia. An attempt was made to prepare for every eventuality that might develop during and after the expedition. It was stated that once the volunteers had reached East Florida, they would swear allegiance to France. The commander and all his officers would be commissioned only after becoming French citizens. If the scheme failed, the participants were guaranteed ample reimbursement from booty taken by France from the English and Spanish West Indies. But the most interesting paragraph was the one which declared:

East Florida will be considered as a part of the French Republic during the continuation of the war, and as such remains under its immediate protection. At the conclusion of the war, the said country is to become independent to all intents and purposes, with the proviso of adopting a strictly democratical republican government, and the Rights of Man to form the basis of their constitution.[45]

The entire document breathed the advanced political and humanitarian theories of the French Revolution.

Shortly after this document appeared, Mangourit decided that the time was auspicious to renew his efforts to get the Creek Indians to come to terms with France. Time was running short, for he had already set April 10 as the date of the rendezvous on the south bank of the St. Mary's River for all forces involved in the expedition.[46] A lengthy "Plan for a treaty with the Creeks" had been prepared, perhaps as early as December.[47] The inclusion of several clauses dealing with the mutual return of prisoners, hostages, and property was intended to appeal to the frontier people. In addition, it was stated that the terms of the treaty were not to go into effect unless the Creeks remained at peace with the United States. The wording was typical of the French Revolution, and it must have sounded strange to the Indian chiefs. Article eleven read: "And in an effort to spread the principles of virtue, humanity, and morality which alone can result in true human goodness, the French nation promises and agrees to send to its brothers in the Indian towns and straggling villages, men whose sole purpose will be to teach and make these virtues understood."[48] But the concluding paragraph contained the true motive lying behind the desire to conclude a treaty: to alienate the Creek Indians from their earlier treaties with Spain.

Mangourit sent drafts of this proposed treaty to both Samuel Hammond and William Tate, as the latter was to attempt to reach similar agreements with the Cherokees and the Choctaws. Short but comprehensive instructions for handling the actual negotiations with the chiefs were sent them with the treaty drafts. These instructions concluded with a bit of advice that was to be given to the Indians:

> The French have guaranteed the security of persons and property to all free men. They invite you to join in this solemn treaty. They sincerely desire that your quarrels with the United States cease, and that a perpetual peace replace these deplorable differences. They desire that you unite with them against the monarchs who are guilty of so many crimes against the human race. It is for these reasons that the French nation offers you the following treaty. I have spoken.[49]

To insure the success of the Creek treaty, Samuel Hammond was authorized to purchase a large selection of gifts for the chiefs, in accordance with his earlier suggestions to Mangourit. The consul urged Hammond to observe the greatest secrecy in carrying out these negotiations, lest an inkling reach the ears of the Spaniards, and possibly of the federal government. Mangourit had to appeal to Genêt for additional funds to enable Samuel Hammond to pay for the suggested purchase. According to the consul's accounts, approximately $3,300 was needed to defray the cost of Indian gifts, and only $1,000 was then available in Charleston and Savannah.[50]

The need for Indian support appeared greater to Mangourit after he had received letters from Colonel Hammond and Major Bert late in February. In each of these dispatches, the writer indicated that the element of surprise had been lost, as the Spanish were hastily preparing St. Augustine for an assault from the north. Hammond enclosed a copy of a report on the size and distribution of the forces that would be encountered in East Florida. According to his dispatch, the attacking force could expect to encounter approximately 1,040 of the enemy in East Florida, of which only 510 were infantry. He pointed out that the Spanish forces were widely scattered in the area between St. Augustine and the St. Mary's River.[51] But Mangourit had already been warned that the Spanish knew there was some sort of expedition being prepared to attack East Florida. The privateer *Sans Pareille* had just captured the Spanish vessel *Santa Isabella* carrying more than thirty soldiers from Havana to join the garrison at St. Augustine. One of these captured men had revealed that another vessel carrying one hundred and thirty soldiers was on the way to that port.[52]

When this news reached Charleston, the consul renewed his urgent appeals for armed vessels to support the planned expedition. He ordered Captain Branzon of the privateer *Las Casas,* which was operating out of Charleston, to arrange to be back in port by March 31, in order to reach the mouth of the St. Mary's River by April 10.[53] According to Mangourit, all that was now needed to put the expedition under way was the arrival of Genêt's long-promised fleet of warships.

Unknown to Mangourit, the continued presence of Genêt as French minister had become intolerable to the government of the United States. In August, a demand for his immediate recall had been sent to Gouverneur Morris in Paris, although Genêt did not learn of this action until the middle of September.[54] The Committee of Public Safety, already occupied with a witch-hunt for all former Girondin sympathizers, acted at once on the request from Jefferson and issued the necessary recall orders late in October. Genêt was to be replaced by a group of four commissioners, headed by Jean Fauchet.[55] However, circumstances prevented them from leaving France until late in December, and this permitted Genêt to remain in his position as minister until their arrival in February.[56] All other French diplomatic representatives appointed before the fall of the Girondins were recalled by the same series of orders. The letter recalling Mangourit was dated November 19,[57] and notice of it reached him about February 10, although it did not cause him to deviate in the slightest from his prepared plans. Adopting an offended attitude, he wrote Genêt:

> They announce here that we have been arrested by order of a new minister. They know nothing except that the enemies of the Republic have made a terrible move. I have not written to the new minister. The innocent man does not make the first move; such a step bespeaks either fear or sycophancy. I shall demand that they send someone here to make a survey of my actions.[58]

Nevertheless, Mangourit redoubled his efforts to complete the preparations for the expedition, lest something occur to frustrate his entire plan. His letters to Genêt expressed growing concern that the rumors of his recall might be true. Any alarm that he may have had concerning the future of the expedition against East Florida was dispelled on March 15, when André Michaux, the botanist, arrived in Charleston from Philadelphia with letters and information from Genêt. Michaux visited Mangourit's office immediately upon his arrival and informed the anxious consul that when he had left Genêt on January 10 the French minister had been enthusiastic about the projected attack on St. Augustine.[59] The scientist remained nearly ten days in Charleston, dining with Mangourit on the sixteenth and holding a long council with him and some of his trusted agents on the twenty-second. During this conference, Michaux revealed all that Genêt had told him about the French fleet and other assistance that could be expected to reënforce the East Florida venture.[60] Relieved by these reassuring reports from the French minister, Mangourit virtually ignored the news of Fauchet's arrival in the United States and Genêt's recall, when this news reached Charleston the very next day. In a letter to the former minister he declared: "As the republic desires only to replace one virtuous man with another virtuous man, I am consoled."[61] The consul's next dispatch was directed to Fauchet, and it contained a short account of the proposed expedition against East Florida as well as the usual request for Genêt's promised warships. He indicated that according to Frémin, the French vice-consul in Savannah, everything was ready for the attack on April 10.[62]

What Mangourit had really dreaded occurred on March 27. At Fauchet's request the Charleston papers published his proclamation of March 6 which revoked all commissions and letters of marque granted by French consuls under the signature of Genêt.[63] Now thoroughly aroused, the consul called a meeting of all his agents then in the city, including Bert, Tate, and Captain Branzon, to discover their reaction to the new events. After a lively discussion, Mangourit succeeded in convincing most of the men that as he had received specific orders from Genêt to carry out the expedition against East Florida, and as the proclamation of Fauchet did not specifically mention this expedition, the proper course was to go ahead with their plans.[64] Although Bert did not agree with the consul's stand, he nevertheless decided to obey orders as a good soldier. He expressed the opinion that men would always be easy to get, but that they were useless without a good fleet to back them up. Samuel Hammond disagreed with this view.[65]

Mangourit decided to send Tate to Philadelphia to lay the whole matter before Fauchet. He then wrote a long and impassioned plea for his cherished plan.

Make no mistake, Citizen Minister, if these useful projects are destroyed, confidence in the Republic and her agents will be destroyed with them. We will not find a single friend, all will be lost to us forever. I do not believe that these projects are to be upset. You certainly are going to send a trustworthy man to give me some advice. You will save me from the most cruel of uncertainties. To serve my country is my only desire. My blood, all my affections are hers and are for her alone. Citizen Genêt put the sloop *Las Casas* at my disposal with the other armed vessels in this port. They are all requisitioned. Two transports are to leave on

April 4 for St. Mary's. The food, the arms are ready. A treaty with the Indians is on the stocks. The presents collected should cement it. They are ready for the 10th. We wait only for the fleet and Florida is ours, and the tree of liberty will grow everywhere. And they come from everywhere to get commissions for the excursion to St. Mary's. Ah! Citizen, if only you will send a fleet . . .[66]

The letter continued in the same vein and ended with another of Mangourit's frequent requests for the much-needed and much-promised fleet.

Apparently a night's sleep revived Mangourit's spirits, for the next day he sent a second letter to Fauchet which gave no indication of his earlier fears. As a matter of fact, he completely disregarded the new minister's proclamation. To all practical purposes, the preparations for the expedition were completed, and Mangourit was certain of success. He urged Fauchet to grant him permission to expend all of the $8,000 in specie and the $10,000 in credit that Genêt had deposited in Charleston. The rumors of war between England and the United States were driving commodity prices up, and the consul recommended immediate purchase of arms and supplies.[67] Writing to Colonel Hammond four days later, he sent a proclamation to be published to the Floridians once the frontier had been crossed.[68] His attitude was one of high anticipation, although tinged with apprehension.

This was destined to be his last dispatch to Georgia, for the new vice-consul, Fonspertius, appointed by Fauchet on March 7, finally reached Charleston in the first few days of April. When Fonspertius informed Mangourit of his orders to halt the East Florida expedition, the former consul attempted to convince him that it was already too late for such action. Undeterred by Mangourit's hindering tactics, Fonspertius sent a small sloop posthaste to the St. Mary's River to order immediate cessation of all hostile preparations within the United States and the return of French warships, including the *Las Casas,* to Charleston.[69] The impact of this order on the forces collected along the St. Mary's River will be discussed in the following chapter.

After the final collapse of his plans, Mangourit hurried to Philadelphia to beg Fauchet for some sort of assistance, but the new minister refused to heed his urgent request. Fauchet's dispatches to Paris, however, showed that he really regretted the necessity of putting an end to these plans:

The attack on Florida was next; all that was lacking for its execution was a naval force and the money that Citizen Genêt was to give out. We would have been embarrassed whichever course we took. On one side, considerable expenses had been made and were going to be wasted, the brave men who had given up everything for our cause were going to be sacrificed if we broke our word to them . . .[70]

After a short stay, Mangourit sailed for France and an uncertain reception. That he was willing to return to his native land and face the new minister of foreign affairs showed his belief in his own innocence. He was exonerated of any connection with the so-called crimes of Genêt, and he remained in France to render long and faithful service in the diplomatic corps under Napoleon.

CHAPTER III

SAMUEL HAMMOND AND FRENCH PREPARATIONS IN GEORGIA

WHEN THE FIRST rumors of Mangourit's projected attack on East Florida reached Georgia in the summer of 1793, the frontier population was in a most receptive mood. Preparations for a war with the Creeks were under way along the entire frontier. A feeling of uncertainty prevailed because of continued disagreement between the state and federal governments over which had the ultimate authority to make permanent treaties with the Indians. The refusal of the Georgians from the first to respect the terms of the treaty of 1790 enraged the Indians and caused some of them to turn again to the Spaniards for aid. By the spring of 1793, both sides were making ready for a long struggle. Nearly every hamlet, from Camden County on the south to Greene and Franklin counties on the north, was ready to supply its quota of mounted militia. A general order was issued on April 11 requiring all divisions of the local militia to remain in constant readiness for the anticipated assault.[1] Reports reached Governor Telfair in the summer that Spanish agents were at work stirring up trouble among the Creeks.[2] Late in September, both sides carried out extensive raids along the banks of the Oconee River. It was during this period of the fighting that Samuel Hammond commanded a small detachment of state militia. Finally, stern representations from President Washington convinced the governor that his contemplated attack on the Creeks would result in federal intervention within Georgia. This brought a short respite in the frontier struggle with the Indans.

It was at this time that certain influential Georgians became interested in the plans of Mangourit as a possible means of ending the problem of Spanish interference in Indian affairs. There was a general feeling of frustration within the state because of the stand taken by the federal government on the punishment of hostile Indians. This was sufficient to cause many to turn a receptive ear to the French schemes. In addition, some of the leading military and political figures may have seen in this situation an opportunity to enhance their personal stature with the people of the state. Finally, Samuel Hammond, his brother Abner, and their uncle LeRoy Hammond[3] had personal reasons for throwing their support behind the plans of Mangourit. Abner was a

---

[1] For notes to chap iii, see pp. 153–155.

partner in the firm of Hammond and Fowler, a commercial house which carried on extensive trading within the state of Georgia. For some time these merchants had been attempting to break the monopoly of Creek trade enjoyed by the firm of Panton and Leslie, which received the military protection and active support of the Spanish government and was therefore in a very favorable position. An expedition against East Florida to destroy Spanish control would also bring about the downfall of Panton and Leslie. In addition, the preparation for an expedition would entail large expenditures for an assortment of supplies of food, clothing, and arms, items that were stored in the Savannah warehouses of the firm of Hammond and Fowler. Hence the great interest shown by the three Hammonds in Mangourit's schemes.

In spite of the French consul's report to Genêt, it is unlikely that many Georgians were attracted to the French cause by a desire to participate in the further extension of the principles of the French Revolution. Selfish interests drove these frontier people to take up the cause of France, and when it became apparent that these interests were not being served, they were prompt in withdrawing their support. Although Mangourit failed to do so, later French representatives to the United States realized the true motives that caused people like the Hammonds to support his plans. Fauchet was distressed by the general failure of all French plans in the New World, and he wrote: "Everything goes wrong for us; the distance between places; circumstances; perhaps the ill will of some people, the personal interests of certain others, for among the strangers who have dedicated themselves to our cause, there are but a few who have not done it for their own advantage."[4]

The exact moment when these plans received active support is not known, but it is probable that the Hammonds became interested in November. During the next month, many rumors circulated about so-called "French agents" holding secret meetings along the frontier. One of these "agents" was Citizen Frémin, the French vice-consul in Savannah, who spent much time cruising about the St. Mary's and St. John's area in a small vessel, trying to learn the whereabouts of Spanish forces. He was aided by a rather mysterious person named Mouchet, who later was supposed to play an active part in the attack on East Florida.[5] Such activities soon attracted the attention of the local press, and letters and editorials on the subject began to appear in December. In the middle of the month, a letter was printed in a Charleston newspaper which gave the impression that the formation of military units was already well under way in Greene County. In part, the letter follows in part.

A spirit of recruiting prevails here to a great degree, for an expedition, under French authority, against Augustine, West Florida and New Orleans. It is said Colonel Kerr is to have a command of a legion, and Colonel Philips of a battalion. Captains Oliver and Cook are to be captains in Colonel Philips' battalion. Several men in this part of the country have already been enlisted.[6]

Simultaneously, there appeared in a Boston newspaper an article based on the same letter and containing additional information on the number of recruits already attracted to the cause of France. According to this report, things were going well in upper Georgia where more than thirty members of the mounted militia had enlisted.[7] This solicitation of recruits from the state and federal militias was soon to attract the attention of the authorities in Augusta and Philadelphia.

It is difficult to ascertain just what part the Hammonds played in the early stages of the recruiting program. Samuel was freed from his duties in the state militia early in the fall when the projected attack on the Creeks was postponed. He was in Augusta or Savannah early in November when Bert was ordered to deliver to him the latest news from Genêt.[8] At first it seemed that Samuel Hammond considered the defenses of East Florida too weak to necessitate a large attacking force. Perhaps for this reason, he took no very active part in the recruiting plans, although he did make an extensive journey through the back country in order to see some of the recruiting officers and arrange for the date of the rendezvous.

In addition to this inspection tour of the frontier region, Hammond turned his attention to the possibility of reaching some sort of agreement with the Creek Indians. He wrote to Mangourit:

I am convinced that not only is it easy to induce the Creeks to aid us in our operation to the south, but also that the safety and success of our enterprise depends on this. For if we are not at peace with these savages, the establishment of a government will be very difficult and hazardous to such a degree that vital emigration will be halted.[9]

He assured the French consul that his influence among some of the chiefs, augmented by the good will that his brother had built up through gifts and trading, would be sufficient to draw a number of the Creeks away from their adherence to the Spanish cause. He emphasized the need to destroy the stores of Panton and Leslie along the St. Mary's and St. John's rivers as the first step in supplanting Spanish with American influence over the Indians. To do all this, he appealed for money and a large supply of Indian gifts, which, he indicated, could be purchased from the firm of Hammond and Fowler. Mangourit hastened to reply, sending Bert to Savannah with $1,500 to be used in buying the necessary articles to be presented to the Creeks.

While Samuel Hammond was conducting his inspection trip, he received additional information about the arrival of troops in St. Augustine to enlarge the local garrison. According to this report, the total number of men under arms in the Spanish province had been increased to more than one thousand.[10] Thoroughly alarmed, he hastened to inform Mangourit that the original estimate of the forces needed would have to be increased. Such a change of plans would mean a postponement of the rendezvous until a general council of war could be held, at which time all the recruiting officers could make full reports of their progress. Samuel Hammond decided to hold this meeting in Washington on February 10,[11] although this date was later changed to February 20.[12] According to his reorganized plan, ten battalions of 120 men each would be needed. Some of these would be cavalry and others infantry. By the beginning of February, the total number of men already recruited was said to have reached approximately 750. This figure presumably represented the number of men who had been approached on the subject and who had indicated their willingness to participate directly or indirectly in the adventure. It is doubtful that such a large number could actually have been enlisted in the French cause.

What really alarmed Samuel Hammond, even more than the news of Spanish military preparations, was the rumor that his brother Abner had been arrested in East Florida at the order of Governor Quesada. Abner Hammond had departed early in January, ostensibly to visit his wife, who was then living with her parents on a plantation on the St. John's River. It was the news of his arrest on January 14 that caused Samuel Hammond to falter in his resolve and to forward a pessimistic letter to Mangourit. He reported that the seizure of his brother made necessary a new plan of attack, one not dependent upon the support of the local Indians. This indicates that his brother's visit to the Spanish province might have been for the purpose of negotiating with some of the Indians living in East Florida. A more detailed account of Abner Hammond's visit and subsequent arrest will be given in the next chapter, when the countermeasures taken by the Spaniards are discussed. His capture removed him from any further participation in the planned assault on East Florida.

This turn of events put Samuel Hammond in a very ticklish position, for, as he wrote Mangourit: "If I should suspend my activities, as it appears necessary for the present, I shall remain fixed irrevocably on

April 10 ... and if you should be disposed to attempt this plan while we are inactive, I shall employ my efforts to aid it. ..."[13] In other words, he hesitated to take too active a part in the preparations, lest the Spaniards retaliate against his brother. He wrote a few days later from the St. Mary's region that his brother's seizure had been confirmed. He suggested that the crossing of the two rivers in East Florida would now necessitate the use of heavy artillery and a large additional naval force. In other words, the element of surprise had been lost, and the planned Indian attack had been rendered impractical. As events turned out, Samuel Hammond's hesitation because of fear for his brother's safety was of short duration.

Bert also showed alarm and annoyance at this turn of events, blaming the arrest of Abner Hammond on the work of Spanish and English spies who had been instructed to discover the true identity of all the leaders of the projected attack. In addition, he found fault with the measures used to recruit troops in South Carolina and Georgia. Writing to Mangourit he declared:

In my last letter I had the honor of telling you of the measures taken by the Spaniards in Florida as a consequence of the alarm caused by the failure of the recruiting officers in the back parts of Georgia and Carolina to take the necessary precautions. I complained about it at the time, and I informed you of the several indiscretions of T[ate], and I sent you an article from the Augusta newspaper of last October which must naturally have alarmed our enemies. From that time the spies of the English and American governments must have redoubled their activities and they must have discovered a portion of the plans. ...[14]

He went on to advocate immediate action as soon as the promised fleet arrived. Once adequate bases had been established on Amelia Island and along the southern bank of the St. Mary's River, it would be an easy matter to cross the St. John's River and march on St. Augustine. He was certain that a successful crossing of the St. Mary's River was necessary in order to offer a place where American merchants could trade outside the United States, and to provide a rendezvous for American volunteers who might be attracted by the success of the first step in the conquest of East Florida. "Land forces will not be lacking after we have taken possession of the St. Mary's," he wrote. "Americans will come from all directions to join us as well as the inhabitants of Florida, who recently have been forced to leave that province. All will depend on a naval force sufficient to act and to inspire confidence in the adventurers."[15]

When the council of war was held at Washington on February 20, the decisions reached apparently were in accord with the plans outlined by Bert. It was now generally accepted that a French naval force was to proceed to the St. Mary's region to establish a base in East Florida where French warships and corsairs could find a safe haven. Once this had been accomplished, American volunteers could cross the river and accept commissions in the French army. The training of a regiment of infantry and of a small body of dragoons was to be undertaken by a group of French officers sent there by Mangourit. According to his report, four of these officers had once served in the 48th Infantry Regiment, and a fifth had been associated with the dragoons.[16]

Samuel Hammond now plunged into the recruiting program in earnest, and when the next council of war was held at Washington on March 14, he was able to write Mangourit that all was going well. At this meeting, he gave the orders necessary to bring the recruits together, fixing the last day of the month as the date for the general assembly. For the first time, he divulged some of the details of his future plans. As he wrote the French consul:

All those residing in the upper district have received the order to assemble on the 31st of this month on the south bank of the Oconee River opposite Greensborough, and those in the middle district on the south bank of the same river opposite Kerrs Bluff. The latter will be a little less than 90 miles distant from the former in their march to St. Marys, and four days will be required to come from the first rendezvous to the second. All the companies in the lower district will begin to march for St. Marys as soon as they are ready without waiting for the others. Two companies will leave Burke County about the 25th or 26th of this month. The inhabitants of this place [Augusta] and the vicinity will leave by water as soon as Mr. Course, the bearer of the presents for the Indians, returns; and they will join with another company about 90 miles from this place.[17]

As to the total number of recruits involved in this plan, Samuel Hammond wrote:

It is impossible for me to be certain of our exact number prior to setting out, but I am convinced that it will approach, and possibly surpass 1500. There will be many that we may expect at the end of next month. They will follow us at the expiration of their term of enlistment with the United States, which terminates about then.[18]

The conclusion of a treaty with the Creek Indians also occupied his attention. A trusted agent had already been sent with a supply of gifts to arrange a meeting with some of the chiefs, at which time Samuel Hammond hoped to be able to get them to ratify the treaty draft that Mangourit had sent him.

Colonel Hammond was able to forward another bit of news that may have pleased Mangourit. During the second council of war, General

Elijah Clark, one of the ablest and most respected of Georgia's revolutionary heroes, announced his desire to join the East Florida expedition.[19] According to Clark's most recent biographer, he had attended a banquet in December, held in honor of the French Republic, and at that time "became convinced that he could be of greater service to his state by joining the French to go against the Spanish in Florida, than by remaining with the state troops."[20] Possibly as the first move to join the French cause, he informed Governor Mathews on February 18 that it was his intention to resign his commission as major general in the state militia, giving as the reason his advanced age and declining health.[21] Mathews and his council read and accepted Clark's letter of resignation on March 22.[22]

According to Clark's own correspondence, he had attended the first of Hammond's councils of war on February 20, just two days after writing his letter of resignation to Mathews.[23] It is of interest to note that neither Samuel Hammond nor Bert made any mention of Clark's presence at the first council of war, nor is there any evidence that Hammond mentioned the general's interest in the French schemes during his subsequent visit to Charleston. Nevertheless, Clark wrote to William Tate of South Carolina expressing his hope of receiving some sort of commission in the expedition. He showed some apprehension at Colonel Hammond's plan to attack St. Augustine by way of the St. Mary's River, declaring that he and the majority of the officers preferred the more inland route through the Indian country.[24] The old general had been in command of part of the state militia in 1793, during the preparations for the attack on the Creek villages. After that venture had been postponed, he had conducted a tour of the temporary forts along the southwestern frontier, keeping himself and some of his followers in readiness for any eventuality. He was thus able to offer considerable information as to the location of Indian forces.

According to his letter to Tate, he alone was responsible for preventing a hasty and foolish departure of the expedition. He seemed convinced that there would be no difficulty in collecting a large force, drawn primarily from his former comrades both in the Revolution and in various Indian campaigns. Already in the early steps of the planned attack, Clark appeared to be attempting to assert his leadership.

Although there is no direct evidence that either Mangourit or Genêt issued a commission to Clark, he nevertheless associated himself with the recruiting plans.[25] From the very first meeting with Samuel Hammond and the others, he seemed to consider himself to be the leader of the entire expedition. As far as the Spaniards were concerned, Clark's name appeared to carry a great deal more weight than that of Samuel Hammond. This may have been due, in part, to a report which reached St. Augustine early in February that General Clark was to lead a force against Pensacola, with Samuel Hammond in command of a cavalry troop.[26] But in spite of this, as has been pointed out, the name of Elijah Clark does not appear in the dispatches of Mangourit.

Clark began gathering his old friends about him even before sending his resignation to the governor. It may be that these men represented a part of the Greene County militia which had been under arms the previous fall. Early in March, the suspicious activities of certain local residents caused some of the citizens of that county to feel increasing alarm. A band of forty or more armed men traveled through the country attempting to enlist recruits either by persuasion or by physical force. Some of the more stubborn citizens were threatened with whipping or shooting if they revealed what had taken place in their presence. Six of these outraged citizens appeared before the local justices of the peace and swore to affidavits divulging all that had occurred. One of the justices, Thomas Houghton, wrote a letter to the governor revealing what had taken place and enclosing a long list of names of the men supposedly involved in the recruiting program. Although Houghton was not able to name the leader of the group, he was able to locate the future assembling place as Phillip's Fort on the Oconee River.[27] He pointed out to the governor that these armed men were being assembled without the authority of Georgia or of the United States, and that they were planning some adventure that would endanger the peace of the whole country.[28]

This letter from Houghton was not the first information that Governor Mathews had received concerning the activities of Americans serving as French agents within the state. For many months there had been an ever increasing accumulation of evidence in the governor's hands. As early as October, William Tate had inserted an advertisement in the Augusta newspaper seeking recruits for his West Florida venture.[29] Moultrie's letter with an account of events in Charleston had been received in December. Mathews had acknowledged its receipt and had sent a copy to the Georgia legislature. In late January or early February, letters had arrived from the governor of East Florida containing charges that an attack on St. Augustine was being prepared by French agents with the assistance of certain citizens of Georgia.[30] The Augusta and Savannah newspapers had printed several letters and editorials on the subject of recruiting for the French service.[31] Armed privateers were a common sight in the port of Savannah, and prize cargoes were being sold openly in the streets. Finally, the grand jury of Burke County forwarded presentments to Mathews dealing with the issuance of commissions in a foreign army.[32] Yet, in spite of this accumulation of evidence pointing to the illegal activity of certain citizens of Georgia, the governor chose to ignore the entire affair. He was much troubled by the attitude of the federal government toward the Indian problem. In a letter to the secretary of war, he complained about the recent order from Philadelphia forbidding the Georgia militia to cross the "temporary line" in pursuit of plundering Indians.[33] No mention was made of any unusual military activity within the state. It is possible that he believed that a successful venture against the Spaniards might remove one of the causes of Indian unrest.

Public opinion against unrestricted recruiting became so pronounced that the governor felt required to take a stand. After careful consideration, he sent a message to a joint session of the legislature in which he informed the lawmakers that "the Spaniards are much alarmed at the reports that are in circulation, to wit, that French commissions have been distributed to the citizens of this state with a view of raising men to carry on operations against St. Augustine."[34] This information had been contained in two letters from the governor of East Florida to Mathews. The legislature was, however, not asked to take action, and the matter was dropped. The governor forwarded a similar message to the adjutant general of Georgia requesting him to apprehend anyone attempting to raise an armed force, before such activity might embroil the United States in a war with Spain. He pointed out that because of the geographic position of Georgia, the state would bear the full brunt of such a war.[35] On March 5, he issued a short proclamation warning the citizens of Georgia against joining any group of men who might offer commissions in the armed forces of a foreign power. He urged the law officers to do their utmost to prevent any rupture of the peace.[36]

Nothing was done to enforce the terms of the proclamation beyond forwarding copies to all parts of the state. The governor failed utterly in his duties by permitting recruiting to continue, particularly in Greene, Burke, and Camden counties. When Mangourit was informed of Mathews' proclamation, he apeared quite unconcerned. A few days later, he wrote Hammond: "The governor of Georgia whose proclamation has been inserted in our newspapers is a good republican. But his proclamation affects neither the independent Indians, nor the others who join the French at St. Mary's after we have taken possession of it."[37] Many of the state officials followed the governor's example, and nothing was done to prevent the continued activity of the friends of Clark and Hammond.

As the date set for the rendezvous on the St. Mary's River drew near, an increasingly large number of armed men were to be seen along the southwestern frontier of the state. Armed strangers appeared in the western part of Camden County late in March, near the villages of Coleraine and Temple.[38] The arrival of these armed men created a noticeable disturbance, as the entire population of the county in 1791 numbered but 305.[39]

It is impossible to give the exact number of men involved. Actually there were several separate groups, one in Camden County under Samuel Hammond's command, one in Burke County, and one in Greene County, supposedly raised by friends of General Clark. As had been arranged by Mangourit, several small French and American vessels began to arrive off the St. Mary's River late in March. These vessels brought supplies of food and ammunition that had been purchased in Charleston and Savannah. The stores were landed near the village of Coleraine. The *Las Casas* and a small schooner anchored off the town of St. Mary's on April 9 and apparently brought orders from Mangourit.[40] However, April 10 came and went without a move having been made to cross to the south bank of the river. The expected French fleet was not yet in evidence, and it was decided that no move against East Florida could be made without it.

Most of April was spent in watching and waiting, with the spirits of the men gradually sinking. The leaders themselves either departed or traveled about attempting to sustain the flagging enthusiasm of the disappointed recruits. One of the younger and more enthusiastic members of Samuel Hammond's party wrote to a friend describing conditions at Fort Independence near the village of St. Mary's.

We have about fifty men at this station, with a large store of provisions, and expect Colonel S. Hammond on in ten days, when we expect something capital may terminate. The spirit of party work since your departure from this country, has been extreme; numbers have been killed, the laws openly violated and trampled on, and what is to be more lamented, the violations have been committed by those persons who have been appointed by our legislators to distribute justice and the benefits of our laws to the people.[41] Squire Fleming, John Houston, and a number of others, have been killed by the Indians. A few days ago, they killed a woman at Coleraine Fort, a few miles above us; in short, we have been in a continual state of war ever since you left this country, and now it has got to a higher pitch than ever; our fort is in a manner surrounded by enemies, the Indians on one side, the Spaniards on the other, and the deluded people under the direction of J. Seagrove,[42] and Old King,[43] on the other two; but we flatter ourselves we have fortitude enough to carry ourselves safe through the impending dangers.[44]

Things were not going well for the projected expedition, as public opinion was now definitely against the continuation of such an enterprise. The citizens of Savannah held a public meeting to decide on the course that would most quickly conclude the whole affair. Every attempt was made to prevent further recruiting or forwarding of supplies to Hammond's forces.[45] In addition, the federal government was becoming troubled by reports from Georgia dispatched by Henry Gaither, commander of all federal troops in the state, who wrote:

The French are going on with an expedition against the Floridas from this place, and appear to have many friends in this undertaking among the inhabitants of this place. There is now at anchor within musket shot of my fort the sloop of war *Las Casas* of eighteen guns,[46] with two hundred men, most of them French, and one company of them infantry; they are last from Charleston.[47]

He went on to report that thirteen more ships were on their way, and that the rendezvous was at Temple, where some eighty men were already collected.

Additional information was sent to the secretary of war by Constant Freeman,[48] who described the preparations under way near the Oconee River. He was certain that popular opposition to recruiting was so great that the expedition would come to naught. However, it was the frequent desertion of members of the federal militia that finally caused Freeman to request the secretary of war to take drastic action. Many of the militiamen were attracted to the French expedition by the promises of adventure and substantial loot. There appeared in a New York newspaper a letter from a member of the Georgia militia, expressing concern over these desertions and declaring: "If any more of the federal troops should desert, with an expectation of being received as one among the adventurers against East Florida, they will be mistaken by being sent back to their quarters."[49] He went on to explain the stand taken by Clark in the matter. The old general promised that if any of his friends attempted to persuade a member of the federal militia to desert, he would take immediate action and would return the culprit to his commander. Without doubt, he expected to be able to recruit sufficient men from the state militia without running the risk of becoming embroiled with federal authority.

The official reply to Freeman's letters did not reach Augusta until after the conclusion of the St. Mary's episode, and Governor Mathews hastened to point out to the secretary of war that the successful termination of the affair was due largely to the efforts of the Georgia authorities. The tone of the secretary's letter carried an implied warning that the federal government was determined to take a firm stand against any further violations of American neutrality.[50] Unfortunately, Governor Mathews did not take this warning seriously, and this was to result in further difficulties with the federal government later in the year.

The final blow to the hopes of the leaders of the expedition, then gathered near the St. Mary's River, fell on April 24, when a fast dispatch boat from Charleston appeared off the town of St. Mary's with the fatal letters from Fonspertius, announcing the recall of Mangourit and the withdrawal of official French support from the East Florida expedition. The captain of the *Las Casas* was ordered to embark all French forces that had come to the St. Mary's region on his vessel and then to set sail at once for the north. Obeying these orders, the captain of the warship made ready to depart, but not until he had landed a small group of French agents and a large quantity of supplies on Amelia Island.[51] An earthen fort was constructed at the northern tip of the island, and these men prepared to hold their position indefinitely. The departure of this warship and the smaller auxiliary vessels hastened the complete collapse of the plans of Samuel Hammond and his supporters. Apparently both Hammond and Bert left hurriedly for Savannah, and the assembled men broke up into small parties, some returning home and some remaining to join the forces under Clark.

While these events were taking place in Camden County, Clark was occupied with his preparations farther north. He appeared before his men early in the month, possibly at the time that Samuel Hammond's forces were collecting in the vicinity of Coleraine and Temple. From this evidence, it may be assumed that Clark had not agreed to bring his men to the St. Mary's River by April 10, or, if he had, he now had no intention of so doing. According to contemporary accounts, his men gathered in the vicinity of Phillip's Fort. The exact date when this force began its southward march is somewhat uncertain, although it probably was about April 15. Among the men gathered along the Oconee River were some of questionable character who had joined Clark's expedition in order to carry out certain illegal activities. Among this number were two men known to be active in a counterfeiting ring which was trying to distribute worthless notes drawn on the United States Bank. No doubt they intended to pass some of these forged notes after Clark's force had taken possession of East Florida. The apprehension of these two men by the state authorities embarrassed Clark considerably, as it directed unfavorable criticism against his command. It required strenuous efforts on his part to disassociate himself from the activities of the counterfeiters.[52] The disgraceful manner in which the pair of criminals were allowed to escape justice no doubt caused people in Greene County to hesitate in their intention to support Clark's plan.[53]

The march to the St. Mary's River was made down the west bank of the Oconee River through the Indian country. This was done to avoid any clash with state or federal forces. Apparently Clark and his men arrived at their destination at about the same time that the dispatches from Fonspertius were handed to Samuel Hammond and the captain of the *Las Casas*. A report from Savannah, dated April 26, placed Clark and approximately 150 armed men in the neighborhood of Temple. Some of these men were doubtless former members of Samuel Hammond's party who had remained behind after the majority had headed back toward Augusta and Savannah.[54]

With the withdrawal of French support, the collapse of Samuel Hammond's plans, the increasing hostility of the local population, the preparations of the Spaniards in East Florida, and the threatened intervention of the federal government, the prospects for the future of Clark's small force were very dim. He realized full well that it would be impossible to carry on without a French fleet and without a continued flow of supplies of food and ammunition. But as he looked about him, he could see all his faithful followers who had given up their homes and families to accompany him to East Florida. He was acutely conscious of what he considered to be his duty to them, and during the next few days he spent his time in consultation with the other leaders of the expedition in an attempt to find some way in which to employ these forces to their own advantage, as well as to his own, and to that of Georgia. It was the sudden renewal of Indian attacks on the western border of the state that gave him the idea that was soon to develop into his Trans-Oconee scheme.

CHAPTER IV

COUNTERMEASURES IN EAST FLORIDA

ALL MANGOURIT's admonitions to his agents to cloak their preparations in South Carolina and Georgia with secrecy were needless, for the Spanish authorities in East Florida, Louisiana, and Cuba were already in possession of sufficient information to put them on their guard. In March, 1793, the governor general in Havana, Luis de Las Casas y Aragorri,[1] had received from Spain news of the impending rupture of relations with France and had sent a warning to Louisiana and East Florida, ordering the two governors to make the necessary preparations against a possible French assault.[2] A month later, the viceroy of Mexico acknowledged the receipt of the news of the actual declaration of war, and he informed the Spanish government that he anticipated an attempt on the part of France to seize certain of Spain's possessions in North America.[3] These bits of information increased the feeling of uncertainty that had gripped East Florida during the past year, ever since the outbreak of the undeclared war between the state of Georgia and the Creek Indians. The rumored movement of American settlers into the Cumberland region and the presence of suspicious persons along the northern bank of the St. Mary's River caused Governor Quesada to request further orders from Havana. At the same time, he reported that an American merchant ship with a French privateer's commission was anchored off the town of St. Mary's.[4] The governor was prompted to write to the Spanish representatives in Philadelphia, requesting that they protest to the federal government over this breach of American neutrality.[5]

Although there was as yet no indication of any activity in the United States aimed at East Florida, the governor felt insecure since his military force was far from sufficient to ward off a serious assault from the sea, from Georgia, or from the Indian country to the west. An insufficiency of well-trained officers was in some measure responsible for a steady decline in the general level of morale among the soldiers. This had necessitated the temporary appointment of several officers of very poor quality to positions far exceeding their abilities. In addition, the soldiers of the 3d Cuban Battalion had not been paid in over a year, and this increased the widespread discontent in the garrison of St. Augustine. Desertions to Georgia were fairly common, and on March

[1] For notes to chap. iv. see pp. 155–158.

[38]

13 there had been a concerted movement bordering on rebellion when eleven soldiers fled to the cathedral and claimed the right of sanctuary.[6]

A further cause for worry appeared in July and August, when the new commander of the frontier, Colonel Carlos Howard,[7] reported that there were signs of growing unrest among the settlers recently arrived from the United States. It had been brought to Howard's attention that several of these people were carrying on illegal trading activities with their friends on the northern bank of the St. Mary's River. These people had never pretended to abide by Spanish laws regulating commerce. As Howard pointed out to Quesada, these settlers of American origin comprised most of the border militia and could be counted on in the event of an Indian campaign, although they could not be expected to remain loyal if there were difficulties with the United States.[8]

The recognized leader of the citizens of Anglo-Saxon origin living between the St. Mary's and St. John's rivers was Richard Lang,[9] who had been appointed temporary justice of this region by Quesada, after the unfortunate murder of the previous justice. In addition, Lang was a captain in the local militia, and was said to be one of the wealthier of the newly arrived citizens. Although he was not suspected at this time of having any connection with the plans of the French agents in the United States, he was known to have had knowledge of illegal trading with Georgia, particularly the purchase of herds of cattle to be used as fresh meat for the garrison and population of St. Augustine. Howard characterized Lang as being a typical American, ambitious and grasping.[10] On receiving this information from Howard, the governor wrote to Havana and requested reinforcements from Cuba, pointing out that East Florida would not long remain Spanish if her arms were not sufficient to enforce her laws. He indicated that the total effective force then available to him amounted to one battalion of infantry, one company of dragoons, one company of artillery, and a few sailors, all of "notoriously bad quality."[11] With these forces scattered along the frontier and in various little posts, and with the majority of the local militia unreliable, Quesada felt that the situation could easily become very dangerous. With this information the governor also enclosed certain letters which showed to what extent the French agents in Charleston were attempting to gain American support in their war against Spain.

When this news reached Havana, the governor general forwarded copies of Quesada's letters to Spain and enclosed a few of his own observations on the probability of a French attack on East Florida.[12] In replying to Quesada, he ordered that all public assemblies be prohibited and that proclamations be posted to inform the newly arrived citizens of the penalties that would be inflicted on anyone carrying on trade in violation of Spanish law. In conclusion, he said that although the situation in the province did appear to be grave, he was unable to send a single soldier to East Florida.[13]

In spite of the fear of an assault upon the province expressed in his letters to Las Casas, Quesada did not appear to be greatly concerned over the activity of French corsairs. He informed his superior in November that the province was in a state of complete tranquillity.[14] Even the news that a large French fleet under the orders of Genêt was about to sail from New York did not appear to cause him much concern.[15] But this calm was shattered a few days later when a letter from Charleston reached East Florida, enclosing a clipping from a local newspaper which revealed the extent of the activities of Mangourit and his agents in both South Carolina and Georgia. "Among the various plans and expeditions which the French in America are planning," the newspaper reported, "one is mentioned against the Spanish port of St. Mary's. It is said that it is indispensable for them to hold a port in North America where they can collect their corsairs, send their prizes to arm, and sell them."[16] Once again the governor found it necessary to write to Havana to emphasize the vulnerable condition of the province's defenses. He requested that he be sent additional naval forces, as there were at his disposal but one sloop armed with two guns, and one small gunboat. He said that Howard had been instructed to begin a complete reorganization of all military forces along the defense line of the St. Mary's River.[17] In this way, the governor hoped to be able to use his small military force to the best advantage.

In the meantime, Abner Hammond had decided to make a trip to East Florida. He sent a letter to Colonel Howard requesting a temporary permit to enable him to cross the St. Mary's River and reach the home of his father-in-law, William Jones.[18] The actual motive behind the visit to the province has never been fully established. More will be said later about this very controversial point and about the various views taken on the question.[19]

Besides the request for a permit to visit East Florida, Abner Hammond urged Howard to allow him to bring certain trade goods to sell in St. Augustine. The colonel refused the second request, and he issued the travel permit only on the condition that Hammond go at once to St. Augustine to obtain the governor's approval of his visit. Instead of obeying Howard's order, Hammond went directly to the home of his father-in-law, where he arrived about January 8.

Howard had had an excellent reason for ordering Hammond to see the governor at once. The news of Moultrie's action in preventing further development of the plans of Mangourit and Tate had arrived in East Florida at the very end of the year. However, of much greater significance was a letter containing several startling revelations that Richard Lang sent to Howard on December 30. Included with this letter was a sworn declaration from one Reuben Pitcher,[20] which revealed the major part of Mangourit's plans to attack the province and which purported to give the real reason for Hammond's visit. According to Pitcher, the leader of the entire expedition was Samuel Hammond, who intended to lead a small force from Camden County into East Florida in order to loot the plantations along the St. John's River. In addition to Abner and Samuel Hammond, Pitcher implicated several other persons, including John McIntosh,[21] William Plowden,[22] and John Peter Wagnon.[23] His reason for betraying the scheme was probably fear that his plantation would be sacked.

Howard's scheme was to permit Abner Hammond to enter the province and then inform the governor of Lang's letter. Thus, if Quesada chose, he could lay his hands on the American. When Howard's letter did reach the governor, he acted at once and ordered the arrest of Abner Hammond. He called a special junta on January 14, at which time it was decided to arrest McIntosh, Plowden, Wagnon, and several others suspected of having taken part in negotiations with Samuel Hammond and his agents or of having expressed sympathy for the French cause. To be on the safe side, the governor ordered the arrest of Lang and Jones.

The arrest of Abner Hammond was made at the home of his father-in-law, and the others were rounded up at their respective homes. They were brought to St. Augustine where each was interrogated separately before being shut up in the castle of San Marcos. All protested ignorance of any French plans to attack the province. However, on January 20 Lang agreed to inform on the others in return for a promise of leniency. According to his story, Samuel Hammond was the leader of the expedition with the rank of brigadier general; Abner Hammond held a commission as colonel in command of six hundred cavalry; and three frigates with fifteen hundred recruits then in the ports of South Carolina were to land these forces at the mouths of the St. Mary's and St. John's rivers.[24] It is unlikely that Quesada would have put much faith in Lang's story, if it had not been for a packet of papers found on the person of Abner Hammond at the time of his arrest. It is hard to understand why a person in his position should have been so imprudent as to carry such incriminating material with him into Spanish territory.

The packet was forwarded to Quesada who went over each document carefully with the aid of an interpreter. Among these papers were found copies of Genêt's commissions to both Hammonds,[25] as well as Samuel's commission appointing his brother chief quartermaster of the expedition. Other documents showed that Samuel had told his brother about the entire plan and had made arrangements to use one of the warehouses of Hammond and Fowler to store sufficient supplies for six hundred men. Complete plans for the formation of Abner Hammond's cavalry force were also found. According to these, several groups of fifty horsemen each were to be formed near the Great Satilla and Altamaha rivers. Several letters from Mangourit and other French agents were found in the packet, as well as a copy of the outline for recruiting for the French service.[26] According to one citizen of East Florida, the real reason for Abner Hammond's visit was to use a large sum of money to bribe the Creek Indians in an effort to obtain their active support for the French plans.[27] If this was so, Quesada made no mention of finding a large sum of money on the prisoner or a copy of any proposed treaty with the Indians.

After examining the other men, all of them citizens of East Florida and former citizens of the United States, Quesada decided that only John McIntosh had communicated directly with the French agents. Among McIntosh's possessions were found four letters from Samuel Hammond with some very embarrassing information, including instructions on what to do in the event of an assault on the province. As McIntosh held a rather important position in the provincial government, his crime therefore appeared to be fully as serious as that of Abner Hammond, who was not a Spanish subject. After brief questioning, both men were placed on board a small armed sloop for the voyage to Havana.[28] Quesada forwarded a complete account of all events concerning the two prisoners, as well as another appeal for additional troops to reinforce St. Augustine. The two prisoners reached Havana on February 5, and after a brief questioning were placed in the same cell in Morro Castle.[29]

A junta had been held in Havana on February 1 and 2 to discuss the matter of sending troops to St. Augustine, as requested by Quesada in his letter of January 3.[30] As the governor's demand seemed urgent, it was finally decided to send three companies of line infantry and one company of grenadiers from the Mexican Regiment, amounting to 187 soldiers. These men had been selected earlier to reinforce the garrison at Santo Domingo and were preparing to depart when the junta decided to send them to East Florida. The two prisoners and Quesada's request for additional military aid arrived while preparations for the departure for St. Augustine were under way. A second junta was held immediately, at which time Las Casas pointed out that Quesada's new request for a battalion of line troops, a battalion of infantry, and ten four-inch cannon was far greater than could then be fulfilled. After a short inquiry, it was found that there were no available cannon in Havana, nor was there a single auxiliary war vessel. It was therefore decided to expedite the departure of the 187 infantry soldiers under the command of Colonel Sebastian Kindelan, together with twenty-four convicts, one hundred and fifty tents, a small supply of food, and a chest of medicine.[31] As Las Casas had expressed a desire for speed, the force was ready to depart on February 8, but because of the absence of a large armed merchant vessel it was found necessary to embark the soldiers on two smaller vessels, the *Santa Isabella* carrying thirty-two, and a large brig taking the remainder. Unfortunately, one of Genêt's privateers, the *Sans Pareille*, intercepted the smaller vessel, and brought it into Charleston as a prize, together with the thirty-two soldiers.[32] As was mentioned earlier, it was the capture of the *Santa Isabella* that gave Mangourit warning that the Spanish in East Florida were already on the alert. The larger vessel reached St. Augustine promptly.

After the arrest of those suspected of having active sympathies with the French cause, most of the loyal population of East Florida heaved a sigh of relief, believing that the worst was over. As one of them wrote to his family: "We have been a little alarmed here but are now well prepared for any enemy that can come from Georgia. I am very anxious to see you all as you may suppose which I believe will be when this alarm is totally vanished, and I hope that will be in a short time."[33] A few, however, were not so certain that the danger had been eliminated. They feared that their former friends, now in hiding, would retaliate against them for their refusal to join in the French schemes. Some of the settlers armed their Negro slaves and organized them into small parties to maintain a constant patrol in the region lying between the St. Mary's and St. John's rivers. The large Fatio plantation was put in a state of readiness for any sort of attack. Both Howard and the governor gave their approval to these measures.

Interrogation of the other prisoners continued, and on February 6 Quesada obtained a lengthy affidavit from Jones, which not only confirmed the charges against Abner Hammond but also convinced the governor that Lang had been fully aware of the real reason for Hammond's visit to East Florida. The facts uncovered during these examinations decided Quesada to take a drastic step that he had contemplated for several weeks. Immediately after the arrest of Abner Hammond and those citizens of the province suspected of complicity in the schemes of Mangourit, the governor had concluded that some strong measures had to be taken to protect the northern frontier. After some discussion with the members of his council, he now decided that the newly arrived settlers must be removed from the region along the two rivers, either back to Georgia or farther south near St. Augustine. In this way they would be either removed or under closer surveillance, and thus unable to assist an invading force. Acting against the advice of several members of the council, including Howard, the governor issued orders to burn the homes of some of these settlers and to destroy their crops standing in the fields and stored in barns. This would prevent an attacking party from finding shelter or food. In addition, this move would certainly serve as a warning to any of the settlers considering adherence to the French cause. Obviously Quesada's plans did not embrace holding the defense line of the St. Mary's River. Apparently he preferred to rely on the wider and deeper St. John's River as a protection from attack. When the governor's decision was made known, Howard expressed reluctance to carry it out, as he foresaw considerable trouble. The anger of the new settlers was certain to be aroused, valuable crops would be lost, and a large section of Spanish territory would be abandoned. However, he ordered one Augustin Byck to carry out the order, and a number of homes were burned, after the residents had been given a few hours to collect their belongings and retire either to Georgia or to St. Augustine.

According to certain newspaper accounts, several families decided to return to Georgia, some filled with the desire to exact retribution from the Spaniards.[34] The Augusta newspaper reported: "We hear from St. Augustine, that the Spaniards have broken up and destroyed all the settlements on the rivers St. Johns and St. Marys; they gave the American settlers the option of retiring with their goods, to St. Augustine in eight days, or of returning to the United States in three days. Many chose the former and about 40 families adopted the latter alternative."[35] A Charleston paper reported that Quesada had driven out all the white population in order to turn the region over to a band of five hundred

Creek warriors who would patrol the area and keep out any intruders from the north.[36] This rumor gained great credence throughout the frontier region, although there actually was no evidence to support such a report.

At a later date, certain of the dispossessed settlers, including Artemas E. Ferguson, made an attempt to collect damages by petitioning the governor. He, however, refused to listen to their complaints, declaring, "There is no time or justification for such inquiry since the reasons for government orders cannot be revealed, and it was all done for the defense of the province."[37] Among those who lost their homes, furniture, and personal effects was Timothy Hollingsworth,[38] a captain in the rural militia. He remained silent, however, and returned later to rebuild his home, once the unrest in the province was at an end. But later events were to prove that his loyalty was severely shaken by Quesada's drastic action.

When the governor was called upon to make a full report of the threatened French invasion and his countermeasures, he referred to the removal of the settlers as a voluntary move on their part, a falling back to Howard's prepared line of defense. He included several letters from the colonel as evidence to support his contention that this drastic step had been necessary. Actually these letters showed how much suffering had been caused by the destruction of the grain crops. According to Howard, Quesada's orders had rendered some one hundred and twenty-five people homeless and had made them completely dependent upon the government for all food supplies. In defending his position, Quesada claimed that all this distress had been caused by the subversive activity of the "adherents of the National Assembly," in conjunction with their American friends and supporters.[39]

Once this withdrawal had been completed, Quesada ordered Howard to establish his first line of defense along the south bank of the St. John's River and to maintain only a few scattered patrols north of the river.[40] All his forces were ordered reorganized on February 26, in an effort to eliminate every soldier whose loyalty was suspected. The entire militia was to undergo an investigation to determine their attitude toward fighting for Spain. As a result, only a few were found to be acceptable.[41] Members of the militia who were innocent of complicity in the French schemes, and who were deprived of their positions in the military forces, were naturally deeply offended. It is likely that in the light of Quesada's stern measures, some of these men reconsidered their earlier decision not to support any move against the Spanish authorities.

As the defense of St. Augustine also was a vital matter, Quesada next turned his attention to this task. A few inquiries proved that the defenses of the town and fort were in need of considerable repair. As Colonel Kindelan, who had come to St. Augustine from Havana in command of the reinforcements, was a member of the Royal Engineers, he was delegated to carry on an investigation and to report on the condition of the important defenses. After a month's work, he produced a lengthy report dealing with all phases of the problem, including what he considered to be the best plan of defense against a surprise attack. Kindelan's plans included several extensive drawings of the fortifications with his suggestions for rebuilding parts of the fort.[42] The governor sent a copy of this report to Havana with a request for necessary building materials and a supply of labor.

In order to complete the defense plans for the province, it was necessary for the governor to ensure the maintenance of Spanish control over the Creek Indians. To do this, he decided to obtain renewed promises of loyalty from certain of the chiefs. It was agreed at the junta held on January 14, that letters should be forwarded to some of the Creek chiefs known to favor the Spanish cause in preference to that of the United States. As this was a very important mission, it was necessary to select an agent capable of conducting the delicate negotiations with patience and adroitness. John Hambly, a trusted agent with a record of faithful service among the southeastern tribes, was finally selected. He was ordered to deliver letters to various chiefs and to Pedro Oliver, a Spanish agent living among the Creeks. Hambly's precipitous departure from St. Augustine on January 18 indicated the importance of speed in these negotiations. Upon the completion of his mission, Hambly returned to St. Augustine where he received the commendation of the governor.[43] At a later date, Quesada declared that the successful defense of the province and the continued loyalty of many of the Creek chiefs were due in no small part to Hambly's courage and enterprise.[44] The measures taken by the governor to ensure the support of the Creeks were given unqualified endorsement by the governor general at the same time that he approved all the measures taken for the defense of East Florida.[45]

But it is not to be supposed that Quesada confined his activities to defensive measures alone, for he carried on quite a vigorous diplomatic offensive, in the hope of preventing the threatened expedition from becoming a reality. He tried, through correspondence with Governor Mathews of Georgia and the Spanish representatives in Philadelphia, to keep the issue of the expedition constantly before official eyes.

But he was hampered in forwarding dispatches to Augusta and to the American capital by the dearth of Spanish consular agents accredited to the United States. It was often necessary to employ the services of British consuls in such places as Savannah, Charleston, Norfolk, Baltimore, and Boston.[46] The presence of several privateers with French letters of marque had driven most of the Spanish vessels to shelter, and the resulting delays in the transmittal of important messages were very annoying. At times, Quesada was forced to rely on British and American coastal vessels to carry his dispatches to Savannah and Charleston, and even to Havana. Nearly all his letters to the north passed through the hands of the British consul in Savannah.

His first official protest against American aid to the French cause was directed to the governor of Georgia. It was of a general nature, since no definite information about Samuel Hammond's activities had as yet reached St. Augustine. The suggestion was that Mathews make a complete investigation of affairs in Savannah and in Camden County and take the necessary measures to suppress any move contemplated against East Florida. Although Quesada named Samuel Hammond specifically, the letter was couched in polite and friendly terms.[47] At the same time, a similar note was dispatched to Philadelphia, to be brought to the attention of the Congress.[48] In discussing these letters with his council, Quesada intimated that the suppression of the projects of Mangourit by the governor of South Carolina would mean that the same course would be followed by the governor of Georgia, as soon as he was in possession of the necessary evidence.

After the arrest of Abner Hammond and the others suspected of similar intentions, Quesada decided to send a second protest to Augusta and Philadelphia. In these letters, he employed some of the knowledge gained from the papers of Abner Hammond, although he did not send copies. It was evident from the way in which he wrote that he felt certain of his stand.[49] A short time later, he once again wrote to Philadelphia, enclosing copies of many of the incriminating documents. He pointed out that there could be no doubt as to the guilt of Abner Hammond.[50]

When Quesada's first dispatch to Mathews reached Savannah on January 26, John Wallace, the British consul, forwarded it to Augusta with a covering letter of his own. After waiting for a reply for nearly three weeks, the consul addressed himself to Quesada, saying that since the entire French scheme had failed in South Carolina, and Mathews had not deigned to reply, it was safe to assume that the plans for the projected assault from Camden County were in the process of dissolution.[51]

When an answer did come from Mathews on March 6, Wallace hastened to forward it to St. Augustine. In this letter, Mathews expressed great surprise at Quesada's statements and pointed out that since no evidence had been sent him, he was in no position to take legal action, for such an unwarranted step would violate the spirit of the United States Constitution. He requested copies of all documents mentioned by Quesada and a more thorough investigation of the part that Georgians were supposed to have played in the French plans.[52] In forwarding this letter to Quesada, the British consul expressed his reluctant agreement with Mathews' contention concerning the lack of evidence. He attempted to clarify Mathews' stand, writing, "Your Excellency will perceive from Governor Mathews' letter to me that he will take no measures in regard to arresting the persons of those who it is said are under the authority of French commissions, enlisting men in this state with an intention of invading your province, without the stronger proofs than I am yet possessed of."[53] But Wallace had by this time changed his views on the possibility of an attack from Georgia, for, as he wrote: "I am sorry to inform Your Excellency that the report of such enlistments going on, gains ground daily, and I now believe they are but too true. Yet I have not been able hitherto to prevail on any individual to step forth to prove it."[54]

These letters reached Quesada on March 26, and after reading them carefully, he apparently became convinced that nothing could be gained by further correspondence with Mathews. However, he did prepare copies of all incriminating documents at hand dealing with Abner Hammond and the projected expedition. These were sent to Wallace with a request that they be forwarded to Augusta. The consul sent them to Augusta, but he directed the letter to the attention of the attorney general of the state, rather than to the governor, in the hope that more attention might be given the matter. When acknowledging the receipt of Quesada's letter, Wallace revealed that all was not well with Samuel Hammond's plans, since the respectable people in the city were now openly hostile to such an expedition.[55] And on the same day, Wallace received a letter from Colonel Howard addressed to Samuel Hammond, with a request that it be forwarded to him by way of his wife who would probably know his whereabouts.[56] This letter was in reply to one addressed to Howard in February, in which Samuel Hammond protested bitterly against the arrest of his brother. A similar protest had been voiced in Mathews' letter of February 21, in which he demanded the release of the prisoner.[57] But Quesada gave this protest as little consideration as the governor of Georgia had given those directed to his attention by the authorities in East Florida.

Once Quesada had completed his defense plans for the province, he followed a policy of watchful waiting. He expressed the hope that a change in the policy of the United States toward France would end the threat against East Florida. On April 28, he received the news of the arrival of the *Las Casas* in the St. Mary's River and of the imminence of Samuel Hammond's attack on St. Augustine.[58] In his letter to the British consul in Charleston, Quesada expressed "great consternation" at the absence of any Spanish vessels in Florida waters to carry the vital news to Havana. He was considering the seizure of the American ship, *Uxbridge*, which lay at anchor off the fort.[59] However, two days earlier, Wallace had sent a letter by special courier to inform Quesada of the departure of the *Las Casas* and of the complete collapse of Hammond's plans. According to this report, the followers of the French cause were now streaming back to Savannah in a disorganized state.[60] This was most welcome news to the governor, and it prompted him to express the opinion that the entire expedition had been nipped in the bud, largely through his efforts and those of the British and Spanish agents in the United States. He associated the dismissal of Genêt with the decision to recall the *Las Casas*. He was able to assert that East Florida had been saved from an invasion without the loss of a single life and without the expenditure of a vast sum of money.

All that was true, but there were other factors involved, not immediately evident, which boded ill for the future peace of the province. The American settlers who had been driven from their homes but had remained in East Florida, were in a resentful mood. The men who had been held in custody by the governor during the months of February and March still protested their innocence and were ready to lend a willing ear to future schemes against the government of the province.[61] But a much more immediate threat to East Florida was the continued presence of Elijah Clark and his small band of faithful followers along the southeastern frontier of Georgia. As long as these men were under arms and in the neighborhood of the St. Mary's River, there could be no true security for East Florida. However, when Clark marched his men away to the northwest and to the Indian lands, the threat to Spanish security was lessened although not entirely dissipated.

CHAPTER V

TRANS-OCONEE AFFAIR

THE ABRUPT ABANDONMENT of the plans of Mangourit and the Hammonds did not end the troubles generated by French intrigue along the Georgia-Florida frontier, for there was still a small body of armed men encamped north of St. Mary's River. The leader of these men, General Elijah Clark, was of no mind to send his men meekly home with empty hands and pockets after having brought them all the way from central Georgia. For a few days, however, he chose to bide his time, apparently waiting for a sudden change in the attitude of Fauchet or for the arrival of the promised fleet from France.[1]

While Clark was hesitating about what course of action to pursue, events were taking place which influenced his subsequent actions. Indian depredations along the western frontier of the state were increasing, and his son, Brigadier General John Clark, was on the march with his division of the state militia. Although the movements of these forces across the Oconee River violated the treaty of 1790, Governor Mathews was enthusiastic in his approval. He wrote John Clark, "I am so well persuaded by your attention to the protection of the frontier that I have the greatest confidence of your zeal on this occasion."[2] It was only natural that Elijah Clark should take a keen interest in the activities of his son. In addition, he was acquainted with many of the settlers who were suffering from the Indian raids. He called a meeting of his men near Temple and told them they were free to return home, or they could join him in an attempt to aid the frontier settlers by carrying on a struggle against the Creeks in their own lands. Nearly all his men agreed to follow him to the upper waters of the Oconee River, not far from Greene County.[3]

It seemed only right to Clark that the men and the supplies already at hand for the French plan should be utilized in another scheme which he hoped would benefit the state of Georgia. He also was determined to make use of the commissions issued by Genêt and Mangourit and, in this way, keep his expedition under the technical protection of the French Republic. His plans, already well laid, involved the establishment of a settlement on the west bank of the Oconee River in the lands guaranteed to the Creek Indians by the treaty of 1790. Being a typical frontiersman, he was undeterred by the fact that both the United States

---

[1] For notes to chap. v, see pp. 158–161.

and Spain laid claim to this region. An old Indian fighter like Elijah Clark felt no compunction at seizing lands belonging to his old enemy, particularly as he intended to carry out this act under the protection of the French flag.

The move to the northwest probably took place early in May, for in the middle of the month General Jared Irwin was sent by the governor to investigate a rumor that a small band of armed men, levied in the name of the French Republic, was skulking about in the woods west of the Oconee River.[4] Irwin later reported that he had talked to these men and had extracted their promise to return home peacefully, once their livestock had been rounded up.[5] It is extremely doubtful, however, that these men had the slightest intention of obeying Irwin's orders. A short time later, two Indians paddling down the river reported seeing signs of a large settlement. There were several loaded wagons and a large herd of horses. The presence of several women indicated that the settlement was at least a semipermanent one. According to the Indians, armed sentries were in evidence at all times. They identified Elijah Clark as the leader, although they did not claim to have seen him at that time.[6]

All this information was known to Mathews. From various sources he had learned that Clark and his men were carrying out extensive plans for the construction of small towns and forts. A lengthy dispatch from Thomas Houghton of Greene County[7] described the development of Clark's plans as well advanced and declared that the leader showed no apprehension lest the governor or the federal government take action to break up the settlement. Houghton had seen the activity himself, and he urged immediate action before the number of settlers involved became larger and thus form a definite threat to the peace of Georgia and the United States. He indicated that many of Clark's followers were men of ill repute, asserting that, "All of these things may alarm Your Excellency, as it does me, sure to engage us in war, infest us with thiefs, weaken if not destroy our reputation as people, that we can wink at people violating the laws of this and the United States, and I believe the laws of nations."[8] Houghton reported that the settlement covered an area ten miles wide on the west bank of the Oconee River, and that a chain of small forts was being built, each fort ten miles from the next, all facing toward the river. A second chain similarly laid out was planned farther to the west, to act as a rear guard for the settlements. Other blockhouses were being erected, one at the site of each settlement. The two largest forts were named Defiance and Advance, and the main settlement was laid out about the latter. Land was being parceled out in lots of 640 acres to each settler who agreed to cultivate it and erect a suitable dwelling. An additional 400 acres would be granted each settler who remained a full year on his original grant. Every man in the expedition who was able to supply four additional men fully armed and equipped was automatically a member of the Committee of Safety.[9] From these facts, it is evident that the plan of settlement was well drawn up, and that rapid progress was being made in getting the newcomers established on the west bank of the Oconee River.

Of far greater importance was Houghton's report that plans were under way to draw up some sort of legal document, possibly a constitution. A few days earlier, Clark had written a friend in the state militia, trying to interest him in taking part in the new venture. As the general wrote, "There are a number of gentlemen engaged preparing a plan for the support of the measure and reducing everything to method."[10] A few days later, a second report reached Augusta that Clark's forces were actually preparing to make a permanent stand across the Oconee River. According to the writer of the report, "Major-General Clark with his party is now building forts on the Oconee. They are now building one at the Trading Ford just above Fort Twiggs[11] and say in a few days that they will be building one opposite Mount Pelier."[12]

Finally, an official report of Clark's activities reached Augusta, enclosed in a message from the commander of all federal troops in the state. He reported the presence of Clark and a party of men on the west bank of the Oconee River, nearly opposite the federal post at Fort Fidius.[13] The governor was urged to take immediate action to recall Clark and his men from the lands belonging to the Indians, before the latter decided to take matters into their own hands and begin a general attack on the western frontier of Georgia.[14] According to the author of the letter, this would mean the intervention of federal troops, something that Mathews always tried to avoid. The governor was well aware that if the Spanish in Pensacola and St. Augustine became alarmed at what they might consider hostile troop movements, they, too, might send an armed force into this disputed territory.

However, the governor hesitated to take any action whatsoever, partly for fear the state militia, always loyal to Elijah Clark, might follow him, and partly because of a desire to see Clark settle the Indian problem while he, the governor, watched from a safe distance. But the proddings of the federal government, the letter of Houghton, and the dispatch from the federal troop commander forced Mathews to admit the need for action. It was pointed out to him by members of his council that he could not afford to allow public opinion to turn against him, as it certainly would if Clark really had any intention of setting up an independent state. Realizing that there was a close bond of friendship between Irwin and Clark, Mathews wrote to Irwin requesting him to visit the settlement across the Oconee River and then to report to Augusta, saying, "You will be pleased to continue to exert yourself in preventing these illegal settlements which are making on the southwest side of the Oconee from being carried into effect."[15] However, he did not authorize Irwin to use force if Clark refused to listen to reason.

As was mentioned previously, Mathews' indecisive stand was interpreted as approval of Clark's activities. Public opinion was pretty evenly divided between defense and criticism of Clark. A long editorial appearing in the *Columbian Centinel* of Boston accused Mathews of gross partiality to the French schemes against East Florida, assuming that Clark's new activities were a part of the former plan. The editorial stated: "If this principle is admitted, the greatest object of all government, security of person and property, are entombed to the citizens of Georgia, for, at least, a period of 16 months and 12 days."[16] Another editorial accused Mathews of secretly desiring an Indian war, declaring, "The Georgians seem determined on a war by some means or other."[17] Part of the bitterness of these comments could be attributed to the general attitude in Georgia toward the matter of Indian treaties—views not shared by the northern states.

To many of the frontier settlers, Clark's activities appeared to be directed toward establishing a strong barrier against further attacks by the Creek Indians. Since the established view had long been that the frontier settlers had to protect themselves, they naturally looked with favor upon his schemes. The renewal of Indian assaults in May in the central part of the state and in August in the northern part made the need for protection all the more evident. There was always the threat that the Creeks under Spanish instigation might attack the southern fringe of the state. It was rumored in August that such an attack was about to take place.[18] Expressing great alarm that the Spanish would favor such a scheme, the governor advocated an all-out attack first, for, as he wrote, "There is also reason to believe they [Indians] must be chastised before a peace will have any permanency."[19] The governor believed that a carefully planned and skillfully executed attack on the hostile Indians was bound to receive the applause of the entire border citizenry, although it might well bring down the wrath of the federal government, which was trying through its Indian commissioners to draw the Creeks and other southern tribes away from any steadfast alliance with Spain. If Clark were successful in crushing the Indians, Georgia could breathe freer. If he failed, then he alone would bear the brunt of President Washington's anger.

Nevertheless, Mathews was determined to prevent Clark from creating a separate government, lest the federal officials insist on intervening. He sent several letters to the Wilkes County officials,[20] declaring, "Some stop must be put to such unwarranted proceedings, and I think the civil authority the first proper step."[21] The justices of the peace were ordered to issue the necessary warrants for the arrest of any person suspected of giving aid to Clark's plans. On July 26, Mathews issued an executive order condemning the reported move of Clark on the grounds that such a settlement violated the integrity of the territory of Georgia. Two days later, this order was reissued in the form of a public proclamation. All citizens were forbidden to give succor to Clark's friends, and all law enforcement officers in the state were ordered to assist in apprehending the members of the expedition.[22] Two days later, Mathews issued orders to Captain Jonas Fauche[23] to call out one-third of the state militia to hold themselves in readiness to protect the person and property of all Georgians along the east bank of the Oconee River. Fauche was given additional orders to prevent reinforcements and supplies from reaching Clark and to cut off the channels of communication between the settlement and the source of supplies near the St. Mary's River. The captain was given explicit orders not to try to cross the Oconee River, and he was admonished to conduct himself "with the greatest circumspection, and, in no instance to commit an act of hostility, unless in self-preservation."[24] Mathews was loathe to permit a step being taken that might lead to bloodshed.

When Clark was informed that the governor contemplated issuing a proclamation containing a sweeping condemnation of the settlement scheme on the grounds that it was illegal, he determined to clear his name before the courts of Georgia. He chose to appear before Judge Stith in Wilkes County where he knew he would receive a favorable hearing. By appearing voluntarily, he hoped to steal a march on the governor and present his side of the argument first. After a hurried examination by Judge Stith, Clark was turned over to a board of four justices of the peace,[25] all friends of his. A proclamation was issued stating that, as far as could be ascertained, the general had not violated or contravened any statute or treaty of the federal or state governments. With this finding, the defendant was summarily dismissed.[26] The complete absence of hostile witnesses and tangible evidence made the verdict a foregone conclusion. No member of Clark's expedition could be found to testify against his leader.

The findings of the Wilkes County justices of the peace were reported to the governor on August 19, and he expressed dismay at the news. It was painful for him to learn how popular Clark was and how far some state officials would go in open defiance of the executive's orders.[27] But the chief cause of Mathews' worry was his fear that the federal government would interpret the justices' pronouncement as a sign of the inability of the state government to control the situation. On the very day that Mathews issued his proclamation against Clark, the secretary of war had sent a letter to Georgia informing the governor of President Washington's extreme displeasure at the news of Clark's flagrant violation of the terms of the treaty of 1790. It was suggested that Mathews either call out the state militia to suppress the expedition or else request the assistance of federal troops.[28] The governor had attempted to forestall such a move by writing to Philadelphia to inform the secretary of war of his proclamation and his order to Fauche, both dated July 28.[29] As it turned out, Mathews' explanation of his activities apparently satisfied Washington, for on September 25 Alexander Hamilton[30] reported that the chief executive had expressed gratification with the governor's actions.[31]

While Mathews was hesitating to put the terms of his proclamation against Clark into force, he received a rather peremptory demand from certain of the Creek chiefs that he remove all members of the expedition from the lands guaranteed to the Creeks by the treaty of 1790.[32] He replied on August 11, declaring that such troubles as the Creeks were then experiencing were no fault of the Georgia administration. He wrote:

> The fort you complain of over the Oconee, is not built by my orders, nor your father, General Washington; it is done by men that are acting without authority. I am informed they intend to rent the land of you; but if you don't choose to let them live on it, and you will comply with your treaties by giving up our prisoners, and returning our property, you need not be uneasy about them.[33]

It is doubtful that this statement did much to reassure the Indians, for here was Mathews urging them to abide by their treaties when he gave no indication of abiding by them himself. It is interesting to note that in spite of the rumors that the Spaniards were encouraging the Creeks to attack Clark's settlement, the Indians remained relatively quiet during the short existence of the settlement. One of the federal Indian commissioners expressed great surprise at the peaceful state of

Indian affairs during the late fall of 1794.[34] Those who have attempted to defend the activities of Clark claim that the Indians really welcomed his arrival west of the Oconee River. According to one author, "Clark was actuated less by the prevailing land-greed than by sagacious states-manship, and he looked to a permanent preservation of peace with the Indians."[35] As a result of this peaceful policy, the Indians did not mani-fest "any hostility toward the adventurers, for they were ancient friends of the French...."[36] Be that as it may, Clark's difficulties all came from the eastern side of the river and not from the Indian country at his back.

Uncertainty and procrastination continued to mark Mathews' policy toward Clark's settlement. This attitude bothered several of the leading legal authorities in the state, and some were determined to take matters into their own hands. Judge Walton,[37] one of the most learned jurists in the state, charged the grand jury of Richmond County,[38] then about to issue warrants for the apprehension of some of Clark's followers. The judge declared that Clark's activity constituted an encroachment on the legal property of the Indians in direct violation of a state law of Feb-ruary 17, 1783. In addition, it violated both the law of February 22, 1785, which forbade any sort of survey across the Indian Line, and the law of February 10, 1787, which reaffirmed and restated the earlier law. Finally, it was in direct violation of a federal statute of March 1, 1793. He pointed out that under a state law of 1791, local justices of the peace were empowered to issue warrants for the arrest of anyone violating these laws, in order to preserve the integrity of Indian lands. He went on to attack the proposition that Clark's men, functioning under French commissions, had automatically expatriated themselves and were there-fore under the protection of the French Republic. He asserted that as long as these men remained on the soil of Georgia they were citizens of that state, and if they claimed to have established an independent state, then they were insurgents. He concluded his charge with the hope that Governor Mathews would employ the legal machinery of the state to suppress Clark's expedition, before the federal government decided to intervene in the matter.[39]

Emboldened by Judge Walton's charge, the governor requested the attorney general of the state to give him an opinion on the Clark case. When the requested report reached Mathews, he found that the attorney general had leaned heavily on Judge Walton's charge. The attorney general used bitter words in discussing the findings of the Wilkes County justices. He declared, "The proceedings of the justices in Wilkes County appear to me altogether prejudicial, and a violation of both constitutional and legal principles."[40] In the final paragraph, the report of the attorney general read:

Your Excellency is appraised of the Provincial Act of Georgia, on the subject. It appears to me that this act is in force and that a criminal prosecution might take place under its authority. The Act of 1787 is also applicable, tho perhaps under that act, the proof required might be more difficult. The law of the United States passed March 1, 1793, no doubt comprehends the case as clearly and positively as words can make it. I shall with cheerfulness exercise the duties of my office so far as may be in my power for the purpose of prosecuting and punishing a measure so fraught with illegality and injustice as the attempt of General Clark and his adherents. Unjust it certainly must be considered besides its illegality. The territory is unquestionably the right of the State of Georgia. Under what pretext then, can any particular set of individuals lay hold of it in exclusion of the citizens at large.[41]

The governor's plan now was to send General Irwin, armed with these documents, to hold a final conference with Clark and his followers in an attempt to persuade them to give up their illegal project and return to their homes before it became necessary to use the state militia. He later changed his mind and ordered General Twiggs,[42] another old friend of Clark's, to go to the settlement to read the various legal documents to the assembled members of the expedition.[43] In order to avoid any family complications in routing out General Clark, the governor wrote John Clark, "Delicacy forbids any ordering you to take command of the men in the Greene County militia."[44]

While Mathews was making up his mind to send Twiggs on this mission, the local newspapers began printing a series of letters representing both sides of the argument. Editorial comment became heated and bitterly pointed, with the governor frequently the butt of unflattering remarks. The charge of Judge Walton received widespread attention and became the center of heated arguments. An interesting letter, signed "Oconee," blamed the entire Clark episode on President Washington, claiming that if he had used the "same coercive spirit" against the Creeks as he had employed to force Mathews into action against Clark, then Clark and his men would still be at home tending their farms.[45] A second letter, printed on the same day, signed "Cato," defended Walton's charge:

The public is extremely anxious to see the opinion which the attorney-general has given the governor respecting the legality of General Clarke's settlement on the Oconee, because it is secretly whispered in town, and openly declared in the country, that the first law officer in the state declared to the magistrates of Wilkes County, before whom General Clarke was brought for examination, that he had offended against no existing law of this state. Should this be the case, Good Lord deliver us![46]

A few days later, a letter signed "Harbinger" declared that any inter-ference on the part of the federal government would be a coercive act against the sovereign rights of the state of Georgia.[47] "Cato" and "Oconee" continued their journalistic battle long after the collapse of Clark's expedition across the Oconee River.

Clark had returned to his settlement after the Wilkes County hearing, convinced that his activities were above official censure. With this legal carte blanche, he was certain that the governor could cause him no further trouble. In addition, the general believed that the majority of the citizens of the state were in favor of his plans. He counted on pop-ular support in any contest of strength with the chief executive. Thus temporarily freed from the fear of official interference, Clark went ahead with the formation of a permanent settlement. A council of leaders was held at which it was decided to continue with the plan for an independent state under the direction of an elected Committee of Safety, with Clark as the elected military and political leader with vir-tually dictatorial powers. Joseph Phillips was appointed as the general's chief aide and second in command. Colonel Gains and a Mr. Griffin, who had been appointed in May to draw up a constitution, were urged to hurry their work.[48] On September 3, Clark accepted command of the settlement with full powers. He wrote a letter to be read to every mem-ber of the expedition, in which he assured them that nothing was to be feared from Mathews and the militia. He urged his men to stand firm, admonishing them, "If you are summoned to surrender in the garrison, you must refuse."[49] He pointed out that the orders of the secretary of war were unconstitutional and that the proclamation of the governor was illegal, as he, Clark, had set up an independent government on lands seized from the Indians.[50] He set the first official meeting of the Commit-tee of Safety for the first Monday in October, as established in the constitution.

When Twiggs, carrying out Mathews' instructions, held a long meet-ing with Clark and his leaders and read the necessary documents, he was unable to convince the old general of the illegality of his stand. The failure of Twiggs' mission made it imperative that the militia be called out to enforce the governor's orders. Twiggs was ordered to call out 600 members of his division, to prevent reinforcements from reach-ing Clark. He was left free, however, to carry out his own plan of strategy, since the governor realized that Twiggs knew Clark and his peculiarities better than he.[51] Irwin was to call out his division and to proceed to the Oconee River to support the detachment under Fauche that had been there since early in August.[52] The governor ordered a third division of the militia to stand by in Augusta, until a battery of heavy artillery could be moved overland from the new fort at Savannah.[53] The militia under Irwin camped directly across the river from Fort Advance, thus blocking the only usable ford on this part of the river.

A final effort was made to induce Clark to surrender peacefully. Mathews requested General James Gunn[54] and Thomas P. Carnes[55] to hold a conference with Clark, for he believed that the arguments of a senator and a representative of the United States Congress might convince the general of the futility of his stand. The meeting was held at a hamlet in Greene County, some thirty miles from Fort Fidius. Although Clark listened politely, he did not deviate from his previous decision to carry on until the bitter end. The two congressmen gave up and returned to Augusta to report the failure of their mission to the governor.[56] Clark returned to his settlement convinced that he was involved in a real struggle with the Georgia authorities. He held a meeting of his leaders on September 22 and decided to abandon all outlying forts. All his men and supplies were withdrawn to the protection of Fort Advance. In the next few days, several members of his party were captured while scouting along the east bank of the river. All were released to go home on parole, a clear indication that the governor had no intention of doing more than break up the settlement across the Oconee.[57]

Irwin's strategy was to surround Clark's forces and to send a small force of cavalry to the south to prevent the arrival of supplies from the French stores along the St. Mary's River. A cavalry force under Colonels Melton and Lamar crossed the river south of the fort and invested all the outlying works. By the morning of September 27, the forces under Clark found themselves cut off from the Indian lands and facing the main militia force across the broad river. Irwin had already issued a proclamation guaranteeing the safety of person and property to each member of the expedition who crossed the river to surrender.[58] Many of Clark's men now realized that he had misled them with his assurances that Mathews would not employ military force to dislodge them. The threat of federal intervention, the presence of large militia forces, the lack of supplies and building materials, and a general suspicion that Clark's motives might be selfish caused his men to express willingness to come to terms with Irwin. Some began to slink away and cross the river under cover of darkness.

Clark met with his leaders who advised him to come to terms with

Irwin. Complying with their request, he sent a letter to the militia general in which he wrote:

Inclosed you receive the conclusions of the captains present, who will direct their several companies to collect horses, cattle, etc., and abdicate their stations as nearly to the time agreed on as possible. Relying on this measure coming fully up to the idea and wish of government, depend on the troops ordered here, to be dispersed. The people belonging to each station to return with their property without molestation. If a known law is violated, every man will cheerfully submit to a verdict of his fellow citizens. You will please inform me if the measures are fully satisfactory.[59]

Two days later, in spite of a reassuring dispatch from Irwin, Clark addressed three additional letters to him requesting further clarification of his status after surrendering. Early on the morning of September 28, Clark quietly passed over the river into Irwin's camp, where he gave his parole to the militia general before departing for his home in Greene County. As soon as the surrender was completed, Colonel Gaither and Captain Fauche were ordered to destroy the buildings in Clark's settlement. In short order, all of the blockhouses, forts, and farmhouses were consigned to the flames. All the members of the expedition who had surrendered were released on their parole.[60] It is of interest that not a single member of Clark's party ever faced trial for violating the laws of the state.

When news of the destruction of the Trans-Oconee settlement reached Augusta, Mathews hastened to send congratulations to Generals Twiggs and Irwin. He forwarded a complete account of the whole affair to Philadelphia, hoping to head off any further bitter criticism from the secretary of war. As he informed Knox, there was no need to begin prosecution of Clark's adherents, as the entire affair had been terminated without the loss of a single life.[61]

It is doubtful if General Clark fully realized how fortunate he was to escape court action of any sort, even after his obviously treasonable acts against the state of Georgia. A few months after his return home, he wrote an old friend in Kentucky, saying that he was contemplating moving to that state because, as he wrote, "I am disgusted with this state, and intend to visit yours in the spring."[62] Certain accounts of the general's life, written by fellow Georgians, tend to attribute his activities in connection with the French and Oconee schemes to a desire to expand the frontiers of his state. There is some ground for such an assertion, although a biographer such as Chappell goes too far in trying to forgive all of Clark's faults on this basis.[63] Without a doubt, if the nascent federal government had been a little surer of its position, it would have intervened more forcibly and probably chastised Clark. As it was, President Washington was satisfied to have the affair concluded so quickly and without bloodshed.

Although Clark's venture across the Oconee River left no lasting trace, it did at least succeed in concentrating federal attention on the need for a settlement of the frontier problems. It is too much to say that the Trans-Oconee affair was the cause of the settling of the boundary line with Spain in the next year, but it did add one more argument for the need of such an agreement. In addition, the Spanish authorities in St. Augustine and New Orleans were kept constantly on the alert, lest Clark's adherents spread out to the south and southwest. Quesada was forced to keep his troops in a state of readiness, which enabled him to meet a new threat to his province which developed the following year.

CHAPTER VI

SPANISH REACTION

Although the Spanish authorities eventually learned of the Trans-Oconee scheme and expressed some interest in the outcome of the struggle between General Clark and the state of Georgia, they took no active part in the suppression of Clark's enterprise. The seeming indifference of the Spaniards early in the summer of 1794 to Clark's venture was, in fact, ignorance resulting from poor land communications and delay in the dissemination of news. The expedition was virtually abandoned and the settlements in the process of breaking up before definite news of the start of the venture reached St. Augustine. Even then, Quesada was more alarmed by the possible effects of Clark's residence in the Indian country on future Indian relations than he was by the indirect threat to the safety of East Florida. The Indian hunting grounds west of the Oconee River and beyond the frontier settlements were still regarded as an integral part of the Spanish domain, American claims to the contrary. The removal of the general from this region was, in Quesada's opinion, a matter of necessity in order to maintain friendly relations with the various Creek chiefs.

When the news of Clark's departure from the St. Mary's region reached the governor, he expressed relief, although he did not indicate that the danger to the province had been completely removed. After all, there were still several scattered caches of arms and supplies near Coleraine and Temple which the retiring expedition did not attempt to remove. It was rumored that the men landed from the *Las Casas* on the northern end of Amelia Island had every intention of remaining there. Quesada told his council that the departure of Clark for the northwest did not necessarily mean that the old general had given up all hope of an eventual attack on East Florida. Because of these facts, he was determined to keep constant guard along the St. Mary's River, and to hold all his armed forces in the province in readiness for any eventuality.

The departure of Clark virtually coincided with the news that the month-long federal embargo on American shipping had been raised. The shortage of food in St. Augustine resulting from the embargo had alarmed the governor, for the grain supply of the province had been greatly diminished by the burning of the crops along the St. Mary's River at his own orders. Quesada's correspondence with Spanish and British agents in the United States was devoted more to this problem of food than to the possibility of an attack from Georgia. Conversely, dispatches from the north were filled with expressions of sympathy for the shortage of supplies and with promises of future provisions as soon as the embargo was lifted.[1] The British consul in Savannah wrote to the governor that a sizable cargo of flour was waiting to be dispatched at the first opportunity. A few days later, the embargo was lifted, and Wallace sent a small vessel to St. Augustine with a cargo of flour. The governor expressed his gratitude for this gesture on the part of the British consul.[2]

In a letter to Philadelphia, which included a long account of the collapse of Hammond's plans, Quesada expressed complete satisfaction with the way in which his defense policy had functioned. He declared that through his personal efforts "friendship and harmony" had been maintained with the United States.[3] All reports from the north tended to corroborate the governor's statement on the conclusion of the danger from Georgia. Dispatches indicated that the French threat was at an end and that the federal government had given assurances that no further hostile preparations against Spanish possessions would be tolerated within the boundaries of the United States.[4] In a letter to his partner, William Panton, the merchant John Leslie declared that "the Spaniards were beginning to be eased of their apprehensions of an invasion from the Sans Cullottes."[5] Panton was glad to receive this news for it meant that there was less danger to the monopoly of Indian trade enjoyed by his partner and himself. However, he warned Leslie that the threat of Indian troubles would not be eliminated as long as there was the slightest chance of an invasion from the north. He believed that the peace of the frontier depended on the settlement of the Indian problems.[6] The governor of Louisiana had frequently voiced the same sentiment in his letters to Spain.[7]

Although Quesada was fairly certain that he had heard the last of a French-inspired assault on his province, he was perturbed by constant reports of American activity near the mouth of the St. Mary's River. News reached him late in May that some unidentified project was being carried out on the southern end of Cumberland Island.[8] Suspicious that this might be the continuation of the earlier schemes of Clark and Hammond, the governor wrote Howard for information, saying that he awaited a reply with great impatience. After some delay, Howard sent an account of a recent meeting between Captain Andrew Atkinson of the Florida militia and Mathews, when the governor was visiting a plan-

---

tation near the St. Mary's River.[9] According to Mathews' secretary, the governor was taking a vacation, although it was fairly evident that he was in reality inspecting the frontier establishments. In the course of this meeting, Mathews informed the Spanish militia officer that he had just received orders from the War Department to build a stockade fort on Cumberland Island to protect the mouth of the St. Mary's River. According to Atkinson, a member of the governor's party had told him that it was rumored that the federal government intended to build a large arsenal on Cumberland Island, at a spot only two miles distant from Amelia Island.[10] This information presumably referred to the plan of the War Department to erect permanent fortifications at Charleston, Georgetown, Savannah, and St. Mary's.[11] The fortifications at Savannah and St. Mary's were under way early in May, and in July Knox asked Congress for an appropriation of $1,500 to complete the work at St. Mary's.[12] However, this part of the coastal defenses was not completed until the very end of 1795.[13]

This information did not please Quesada, who was suspicious of any American move along the frontier. He could see no reason for fortifying the mouth of the St. Mary's River unless the move was directed against Spanish use of the river. At the meeting between Atkinson and Mathews, the governor admitted that General Clark had actually crossed the Oconee River with a force of a thousand men, a figure far in excess of the actual number but possibly used by Mathews to impress the Spaniards. Although he identified this movement as the first phase of an attack on the Creek Indians in retaliation for their recent forays in Greene and Franklin counties, he was forced to confess that it was being carried on in direct violation of both his and Washington's orders. In his estimation, a war with these Indians was inevitable. After prolonged conversation, Atkinson forced the governor to admit that Clark had settled down "with the pretext that he had rid himself of all obedience and subordination to the laws of the United States."[14] In an attempt to defend his decision to take no part in suppressing the expedition, Mathews argued that the entire project would soon collapse provided Clark was not molested and was denied access to supplies, since both he and his men would soon fall "victims to Indian knives."[15]

Quesada forwarded this news from Atkinson to the governor general in Havana, together with a copy of a letter from Mathews which accompanied a dispatch from the secretary of war, offering federal aid in suppressing the latest move of Clark against the Indians.[16] The governor of East Florida expressed his appreciation to Mathews for sending Knox's letter. At the same time, he complimented Mathews on all that was being done to protect the peace of the frontier.[17] Without doubt Quesada was writing with his tongue in his cheek, for the general trend of his remarks to Las Casas did not indicate that he had any such trust in Mathews as the guardian of the frontier. Quesada did give the impression, however, that there would be no immediate danger to East Florida, even if the rumors of Clark's renewed activity were true.

Nevertheless, Quesada was determined to ensure the continued friendship of the Creek Indians, since their support might be needed in the future. In carrying out this policy of close association with the Indians, he was following suggestions made by the governor of Louisiana. Carondelet urged Quesada to make every effort to convince the Creeks of the need to adhere to their Spanish treaties, in order to maintain a static force between the United States and the approaches to the Mississippi River. John Hambly, who had served the governor so well earlier in the year, was selected late in June to convey a message to the Creeks. In this "talk," Quesada complained bitterly about the continued activities of the "pestiferous number of French" who still haunted the border regions and the Indian country. He pointed out that the French were being given assistance by their friends in South Carolina and Georgia, in spite of the neutrality proclamation of the president. The chiefs were urged to abide by the treaty of 1784, and thus together they could thwart these Franco-American plans.[18] Writing to Las Casas, Quesada outlined the plan of defense that he was following, one that would draw the Indians away from any alliance with the United States. He urged the governor general to lend his assistance by forwarding a steady stream of gifts to accompany each new "talk" sent to the Creek chiefs.[19]

In keeping with his policy of watchful waiting, Quesada ordered his agents to continue to observe the coming and going of Americans along the southern borders of Georgia. In the middle of July, news reached St. Augustine from one of these agents that a few of the Americans who had assembled along the St. Mary's River in April had now decided to leave Temple and Coleraine and join Clark in his proposed attack on the Indians in the area to the west of the Oconee River. A magistrate in Camden County confirmed this report when he wrote to a friend in East Florida, "Yesterday we learned that Mr. Samuel Hammond had gone to unite with General Clarke, and that all, or rather the rest of the people of Temple, had broken camp the day before yesterday."[20] This information about Samuel Hammond is questionable, since other evidence indicates that after the failure of his plans in April he returned to Savannah where he settled down quietly.[21] A citizen of East Florida, one Leven Gumby, reported to Quesada on his return from Baltimore that the newspapers in that city were filled with accounts of preparations for an attack to be directed at Louisiana, Pensacola, and East Florida. According to him there were 20,000 men involved under the leadership of General Clark. However, when Quesada read the articles in question both in the Baltimore newspapers given him by Gumby and in Philadelphia newspapers received from another source, he realized that the man had been confused by the similarity of the names of General Elijah Clark and General George Rogers Clark. The second General Clark, and the one mentioned in the newspapers, was the leader of a proposed invasion from the Kentucky region.[22]

Quesada hastened to transmit this information to Havana with some of his own views on the subject and some additional reports lately received from the British consul in Savannah. Wallace had reported that all frontier communities felt that Washington and the Congress would not dare take active measures against George Rogers Clark, since both feared that the restless border citizenry might band together and join those already under arms in western Pennsylvania. Quesada associated these schemes with a vast French plan to recultivate French interests in the New World, particularly in the lower Mississippi Valley and along the Gulf of Mexico. He was convinced that the difficulties in Georgia were closely allied to the troubled situation on the European continent and would continue until peace was achieved between the warring nations. George Rogers Clark was receiving support in higher governmental circles. The governor feared that this might lead to another attempt to attack East Florida. To prevent this, he intended to keep the province in a state of perpetual alert against any move from the north. He hoped that Las Casas would concur with his decision and would express approval of his suggestions for the defense of East Florida.[23] The approval of the governor general was received in September.[24]

The first report of the Trans-Oconee scheme to come directly from the Upper Creek region was contained in a letter from an Indian agent at Hillabee to William Panton.[25] This letter gave an account only of the continued presence of a band of armed men in the Oconee area, but did not mention their avowed purpose or name the leader of the group.[26] A few days later, Panton decided to send this information to Enrique White, governor of West Florida,[27] with an additional report that the "French-American" force had now moved across the Oconee River.[28] White had been ordered to be on the alert for any such move and, in consequence, sent a report to New Orleans, informing Governor Carondelet of Panton's letter and of the reaction of some of the Creek chiefs to the presence of Americans in their hunting grounds. The Indians as a whole were very angry with the Georgians, principally because of the stubborn attitude of Governor Mathews. White believed that the Indians were excited enough to contemplate an attack on the Americans, provided the Spanish authorities would help them.[29]

The governor of Louisiana in turn laid the whole matter before Las Casas. His dispatch of October 30, however, left New Orleans more than a month after the final destruction of the Oconee settlement by the Georgia militia.[30] It was not the first information that Carondelet had sent on the subject of this settlement, for he had mentioned Clark briefly in a letter written September 17.[31] Carondelet was particularly worried because of the miserable state of the forts in East and West Florida. White had informed him that an attack by a small number of well-armed men would mean the loss of the fort at St. Mark's and perhaps the one at Pensacola.[32]

Panton also was interested in keeping a close watch on the activities of all Americans in the Creek lands lest they interfere with his trade monopoly among the various Indian tribes. He wrote to Carondelet in mid-September that there had been no serious change along the Oconee River, although Clark was still there with his band of settlers. He declared that the American leader "was busily employed in securing possession of that country by establishing temporary forts and block houses."[33] Writing two weeks later, Panton reported that the Indians were eager to help in any move to drive the Americans back across the Oconee River and destroy the forts. He proposed that an armed force be collected at Pensacola to ascend the Apalachicola and Chattahoochee rivers in flatboats. An attack of this sort would have the element of surprise, as Clark would not expect such a move across the swampy region lying between the Oconee River and the falls of the Chattahoochee River. Light artillery could be dragged through the swamps, provided sufficient horses were made available at Pensacola.[34]

When Las Casas received Carondelet's dispatch of September 17, he deemed it wise to send a long report to Quesada to warn him of the possible threat to St. Augustine from the Upper Creek region, and to confirm Quesada's earlier report of Clark's rumored reappearance there. According to Las Casas, Clark was reported to have but 19 men in his party, quite a different figure from the 1,000 reported by Mathews. In spite of this pitiful number, the governor general expressed some alarm at Clark's plans to occupy the territory between the Oconee and Okmulgee rivers. Carondelet's letter, wrote Las Casas, confirmed Quesada's suspicion that Clark had decided to settle down and erect towns and forts. He, too, shared the governor's fears that Mathews had no intention of opposing Clark's permanent settlement in that area. He declared that the actions of the governor of Georgia "did not then live up to his pronouncement." Quesada was urged to make the best of the situation, since no help could be sent at that time from either Mexico or Cuba.[35] This dispatch did not reach St. Augustine until the middle of November, long after the Oconee settlements had been dispersed. Fortunately for Quesada, there had been no need for additional troops.

The earliest news of Clark's move across the Oconee to reach Quesada directly from the Upper Creek country was presumably contained in the reports of his Indian agent, John Hambly. It will be recalled that Hambly left St. Augustine in June with a packet of letters for some of the Creek chiefs, at a time when the threat to the province was still imminent. At the end of August he reported to the governor that at one of his many conferences certain Indians had told him of Clark's new settlements. This meeting had been held on June 26, at which time Kinnard and other Creek chiefs gave him several letters to present to Quesada.[36] Kinnard told Hambly that Clark had at first attempted to be friendly with the Creeks, but later had threatened to "throw Canard out of his house" if he attempted to interfere or aid the hostile Indians.[37] Another Creek chief reported that a letter had been sent to Governor Mathews protesting the encroachment of so many Georgians on the Indians' hunting grounds. Kinnard mentioned Mathew's reply to an earlier Indian protest. He declared that the governor of Georgia had made it clear that he would take no action without direct orders from the Congress or the President.[38] In addition to this information, Hambly gave Quesada a fairly complete account of the activities of Clark, piecing together the stories told him by Kinnard. The chief had mentioned at least two forts recently built by Clark where one hundred men were reported to be stationed, but he had been unable to estimate the total number of men in the expedition. Kinnard had further declared that the Indians were divided into two camps, one supporting Clark, and the other equally opposed to him. The latter group had not been misled by Clark's declaration that he and his followers desired to maintain peace and amity with the Creeks. Those opposed to Clark had held a grand council and had agreed to raise five thousand warriors to destroy the American forts and to drive the settlers back across the Oconee

River.[39] But from all accounts, it would appear that the Indians actually made no attempt to carry out this plan of attack. The report of the Indians' reaction to Clark's presence confirmed the information that Panton had sent to Carondelet at a slightly earlier date.

Hambly's information seemed important enough to be sent on to Havana. Quesada sent off a long dispatch on September 11 with a copy of Hambly's personal diary and with copies of all the letters that the agent had brought back with him from the Creek chiefs. In this letter Quesada attributed Clark's success to the assistance given him by "several Frenchmen and their supporters." Apparently he persisted in his belief that the renewed activity on the part of Clark constituted a second phase of the French schemes. It was in this same letter that Quesada sent a copy of Mathews' proclamation of July 28 which discredited but did not outlaw Clark's expedition across the Oconee River.[40]

Shortly after concluding his interviews with Hambly, Quesada decided to inform the two Spanish commissioners in Philadelphia what had happened. He instructed Jaudenes and Viar to lay the entire matter before the Congress, with the request that appropriate steps be taken to bring Clark's activities to an immediate end.[41] This letter was intended to supplement an earlier one of September 3 in which he had mentioned the presence of Clark in the Indian lands. At that time, Quesada had shown ignorance of the purpose of the new settlements.[42] In his second letter the governor told the two commissioners of his doubts that the governor of Georgia intended to follow the recommendations of the President, since Washington appeared to have the interests of the Indians too much at heart to please the Georgians. Washington, according to Quesada, desired to see both the Indians and the Georgians respect the terms of the treaty of 1790. The governor mentioned that he was sending a dispatch to Las Casas with the request that the captain general send the latest available information to Philadelphia. In this letter to Havana, he reported having received a letter stating that Clark's settlements numbered thirteen, one being fairly large. He complained that the inauguration of his plan to shower gifts on the Indians to make sure of their friendship was being delayed by the shortage of supplies from Havana. He expressed dismay at seeing some of the Creek chiefs coming to his "talks" with medallions of Washington and George III around their necks, and suggested that the Spanish government might do well to cast some medals of its own.[43]

In spite of these difficulties Quesada continued his attempts to maintain cordial relations with the Creek chiefs, particularly Kinnard, to whom he wrote on February 20, 1795, "I am very glad to learn that the American General Clark has retired out of your country, especially as that event took place without the necessity of the hostility intended for that purpose by your countrymen."[44] He went on to commend Kinnard and his chiefs for their continued loyalty to their Spanish allies.

Mathews was not so certain that Quesada's cordiality toward the Creeks was motivated solely by the desire to maintain a defensive alliance. He had received a letter late in August from Captain Armstrong containing the news that the Spaniards were arming a party of Indians near St. Augustine and were supplying them with more than one thousand head of cattle. This food supply would enable them to attack Camden County. Mathews urged Armstrong to investigate this rumor further before taking drastic action. The governor recommended that the officer prevent additional sales of American cattle to the East Floridians or to the Indians.[45] Nothing further came of this rumor of Armstrong's, and it is probable that the Spaniards were arming a body of Indians to guard the region between the St. Mary's and St. John's rivers.

The situation at St. Augustine remained comparatively static until the governor received Howard's dispatch of October 22 reporting that the entire Trans-Oconee scheme had come to an end with Clark's surrender and the burning of his forts.[46] On November 10, Quesada forwarded this information to Philadelphia and Havana with the assurance that it marked the conclusion of that phase of the frontier problem.[47]

Thus the Trans-Oconee affair passed from the scene without the necessity of positive action on the part of the Spaniards either in East Florida or in the Gulf region. It is evident that this threat to the colonial possessions of Spain did not create much of a stir in Havana, although it did worry Quesada, White, and Carondelet. It is to be doubted that Las Casas would have authorized an attempt to dislodge Clark even if the general had been allowed to remain in the Indian hunting grounds unmolested by the Georgia militia. But this adventure, or misadventure, of Clark's did have one salutary effect: Quesada was obliged to keep the military forces in East Florida on an emergency footing.

CHAPTER VII

RENEWED ALARMS

IN THE FALL of 1793, the Spanish authorities became aware of a new and even more imminent threat to their established position in East Florida, this time from within the province itself. For some time there had been evidence of discontent among the non-Spanish settlers who had been granted permission to establish themselves in the general area between the St. Mary's and St. John's rivers, and among the small number who had been permitted to live in St. Augustine. Some of these settlers were former Loyalists who had left the Carolinas and Georgia after the Revolution. Others were American frontiersmen who believed that the fertile soil of East Florida might offer an excellent opportunity for agricultural development, even under the burdensome rule of Spain. According to law, all newcomers had to take the official oath of allegiance to the Spanish monarch. Few, however, were actually required to obey the law prescribing submission and conversion to the Catholic faith. A few like John McQueen were converted and quickly found favor with the local authorities.[1] Some of the colonists who refused to be converted did permit the baptism of their younger children in an effort to please the Spanish authorities.[2]

Governor Quesada was in general a lenient man who thought that a steady flow of American settlers into the border region under the auspices of Spain might develop a buffer between St. Augustine and the Georgia frontier. When Colonel Howard reported that the Indians were murdering many Americans on the northern bank of the St. Mary's River and that refugees were fleeing southward into East Florida, the governor adopted a very charitable attitude. He told Howard that it would show a "lack of humanity" to deny shelter and assistance to these people.[3] Later there were unofficial suggestions about opening the province to unrestricted American immigration, in the hope that the new settlers would fight loyally for Spain to protect their new homes and lands. Officially, nothing was done in St. Augustine about forwarding these suggestions to the governor general in Havana. The Spanish officials were not yet ready to make a complete reversal in their colonial policy, which denied foreign immigration to the New World. Unofficially, new settlers were permitted to settle along the St. Mary's River. Obviously the admission of these people was in part an unconscious yielding

---

[1] For notes to chap. vii, see pp. 162–166.

to the almost inevitable westward surge along the American frontier. Their presence was finally recognized officially by the Spanish government, for a royal order of March 14, 1793, declared that any settler who had not lived for more than five years in East Florida was free to return to his native land and need pay taxes only on the goods accumulated during his stay in the province.[4]

Governor Quesada was not misled into placing too much reliance on the loyalty of these new settlers. As early as August, 1793, he complained to Las Casas that many of them were of very bad quality.[5] In replying, the governor general recommended a close watch over them in order to prevent large assemblies. He pointed out, however, that these new arrivals would be useful in controlling future American territorial encroachment. The people of Georgia would be less likely to participate in raids across the St. Mary's River if their friends and relatives would be the ones to suffer.[6]

Some of the more favored settlers had received handsome land grants from the governor. John McIntosh apparently was the recipient of 1,700 acres in grants of various sizes, acquired over a period of several years.[7] A second settler, John Peter Wagnon, was permitted to purchase a two-storied house on St. Hippolyte Street in St. Augustine.[8] A third, William Plowden, was allowed to do the same in June, 1794, his new house being on the Calle de la Marina.[9] The records of St. Augustine in the early 1790's show that many of these settlers were permitted to make business arrangements of one sort or another. In addition, frequent slave sales were carried out between the Spaniards and the settlers. However, in all transactions the new settlers had to be guaranteed by the bond of a reputable Spanish citizen. Thus it would seem that the American settlers were regarded with more than a little toleration. Many able-bodied young men, usually single, were permitted to enroll in the ranks of the rural militia. This body of troops, frequently under American officers, patrolled the frontier region with the regular infantry forces, both under the direct command of Colonel Howard.[10]

Unfortunately for the Spanish authorities, these new arrivals, even after taking the required oaths of allegiance to Spain, showed neither the desired loyalty to their new flag, nor much gratitude for favors granted them by their new rulers. Their lack of coöperation became a constant source of annoyance for the local authorities in St. Augustine. As was to be expected, the settlers were reluctant to accept the slightest show of Spanish authority, and were constantly at the governor's house demanding the lightening of restrictions and the extension of privileges.[11]

On the other hand, if the governor requested the presence of these settlers in St. Augustine, he was often forced to send several invitations before his orders were obeyed. Certain of the more turbulent of them were soon involved in open altercation with the Spaniards over the question of carrying on trade with their American friends north of the St. Mary's River. Much of this trade involved items prohibited by Spanish colonial law. The governor was certain that there never would be any security in East Florida as long as these people carried on illicit trade in open defiance of Spanish regulations.[12] Howard informed the governor that those who did not take an active part in this trade opened their homes to those who did.[13] The situation was often made more difficult by arbitrary decisions taken by Las Casas in Havana. Quesada and his assistants frequently had to carry out orders against their better judgment.

The abortive attempt of the Hammonds and Elijah Clark to invade East Florida had drawn the attention of the governor to the unrest among the American settlers and to their willingness to assist the enemies of Spain. He was now convinced of their lack of loyalty and of the need for a more restrictive immigration policy. The arbitrary arrest and imprisonment of some of the settlers in the spring of 1794, in spite of their pleas of innocence, had made them bitter critics of the Spaniards. Chief among this group were Richard Lang and William Plowden. These two were apparently determined to be avenged for what they considered to have been illegal imprisonment. Lang presumably left East Florida immediately after his brief prison term. He soon appeared in Georgia and settled somewhere in the Coleraine area.[14] His presence was noted, however, from time to time in the region south of the St. Mary's River. A few of Samuel Hammond's former followers were still in Coleraine where they had joined forces with a handful of French agents left behind when the *Las Casas* departed in April, 1794. Lang was soon frequently to be seen with these men at the local Coleraine tavern.

Other disaffected Floridians joined Lang and Plowden. One of these was William Jones, the father-in-law of Abner Hammond. Governor Quesada had been convinced that Jones was in collusion with the Hammonds. Bartolomé Morales,[15] the acting governor, gave Jones permission to go to Georgia, but withheld it from his wife and children.[16] It seemed fairly obvious to Morales that Jones intended to move out of East Florida permanently, possibly to carry on subversive activities with Lang and Plowden. There was very little upon which to base this suspicion, since Jones had returned to his plantation after his period of detention and to all outward appearances was conducting himself in a peaceful and law-abiding manner. Morales reasoned that if the Spanish government were to detain Jones' wife and family there would be no reason to believe that Jones would consider taking part in further border intrigue. The holding of families of suspected individuals as hostages was a practice frequently followed in East Florida. Unfortunately for both the Spaniards and the families involved, this policy did not always deter these men.

Lang, Plowden, and Jones were not the only new colonists to turn against the Spanish government. Many of the small farmers and towns-people, either newly arrived settlers or former British subjects, were ready and willing to turn on their rightful rulers. These people formed by far the largest part of the rural militia under the command of Colonel Howard. He had long been skeptical of the loyalty of these men, much more so than the governor, perhaps because of closer association. Because of the extreme shortage of regular Spanish troops, it had been necessary for Howard to rely on the rural militia to carry the burden of frontier scouting. The geographic features of the region made foot soldiers virtually useless, since mounted troops alone could struggle through the thick palmetto swamps. Constant desertions from the ranks of both the militia and the regular troops made Howard's position even more difficult. Some of these deserters found their way to Coleraine and Temple where they spread rumors among the Georgians about the poor conditions and lack of discipline that existed in the Spanish forces. Such reports exerted considerable influence upon those making plans to attack East Florida, and increased the enthusiasm with which they renewed their efforts to obtain recruits.

Not all the events that had a direct bearing on the attitude of the new settlers took place within East Florida or along its frontier. The action of the state of Georgia in selling vast tracts of western lands to four land companies stirred up an incredible amount of unrest throughout the entire state. By the act of January, 1795, the Georgia legislature prepared to sell huge tracts in the region guaranteed to the Creeks by the federal government in the treaty of New York.[17] In the middle of January, Colonel Howard warned Quesada that he had just received a report that Chief Mad Dog, with four lesser Creek chiefs, was in the Georgia capital to sell the rights to some tribal lands in the Trans-Oconee area.[18] The colonel was certain that such a sale would be illegal, since this area was still claimed by the Spaniards.[19] He also forwarded a report from his friend John Berrien, the inspector of the port of Savannah, who claimed that the sale involved at least 40,000,000 acres in the area once claimed by the Yazoo Land Company.[20] Berrien further reported a rumor that old Elijah Clark was to be the purchaser of all the Oconee lands.[21] The sales were supposed to have already started in Augusta.

Quesada was able to inform Las Casas of the passage of the land act and of the signing of the bill by Mathews. He had received no information, however, about the part that Clark was playing in the purchase of land. Quesada received most of this news in a letter from Wallace, who reported that many of the most prominent citizens of Georgia were involved in the land sales.[22] Las Casas expressed great concern over the news in the governor's letter and ordered him to obtain an official copy of the legislative act.[23] Even though the news of the sale of Georgia's western lands was momentous, the East Florida authorities took no official action by way of protest. Without doubt the internal dissension in Georgia convinced Quesada that the validity of the act was still under debate. As late as May 6, Morales reported to Las Casas that the subject had not been settled, and that the foes of the land sales, led by General James Jackson,[24] were mustering their forces. The acting governor predicted that the stern opposition of the federal government would force Georgia to rescind the act.[25]

It is probable that Lang was in Georgia in the winter and had an opportunity to hear about the land sales, but there is no evidence that he took any part in the dealings. His bitterness over the treatment received from Quesada in 1794 had apparently increased, for he wrote an insulting letter to Quesada in which he gave vent to his feelings.[26] This letter may have been written during one of Lang's several trips to East Florida. Its arrogant tone verged on the abusive, and the governor could not have been expected to view the writer's demands with anything but the greatest disfavor. The letter closed with an implied threat that the governor might expect a revolution in his province. Lang warned that only through the payment of his monetary demands could this catastrophe be avoided. He closed his letter: "The satisfaction of these demands will be the only means of preventing me from exherting [*sic*] myself with all of my power to pull off the yoke of despotism, and spread abroad the liberty, and the freedom that God has bestowed to all mankind."[27]

As Quesada was then suffering from a severe attack of fever, Morales received the letter and forwarded a copy to Las Casas together with the report that Lang was once again near Coleraine where he was supposed to be carrying on discussions with Elijah Clark.[28] As was to be expected, once Quesada recovered from his illness, he made no effort to reply to Lang. The governor was convinced by the contents of Lang's letter that the former settler was the leader of a small band of men who had been involved in border disturbances as early as February.[29]

Shortly after receiving Lang's letter, the governor received one from Susana Plowden[30] which deplored her destitute condition and emphasized the need of financial aid to feed herself and her children. She petitioned the governor to grant her an emergency permit to take her family to Georgia where her parents lived and where her offspring could find a secure home.[31] Morales indicated in a letter to Las Casas that he preferred to keep this woman in St. Augustine as a guarantee for the good behavior of her husband. A *junta de guerra* called by the acting governor and held on June 2, approved this decision and went on to brand Lang and Plowden along with many of the new settlers as "traitorous Floridians." They were blamed for the recent unrest along the St. Mary's and St. John's rivers.[32] A few days later Morales received a brief message from Howard verifying Quesada's earlier contention that Lang was probably the leader of a small force of disaffected Floridians. The commander of the frontier predicted that Lang's previous knowledge of the local militia would enable him to carry out successful attacks on the weakest positions along the Spanish line. He feared that Lang might concentrate his forces against the scattered and practically defenseless plantations along the St. Mary's River.[33]

A short time later, Plowden sent a demanding letter to the governor, although not couched in the same insolent terms as Lang's. Nevertheless, there was an underlying threat of drastic action if his requests were not complied with in short order. The writer stated bluntly that he had no intention of ever returning to Florida and that he hoped that the governor would permit his wife to leave St. Augustine with their children and family possessions.[34] Before the governor had time to act on this request, however, certain events made agreement impossible and the detention of Plowden's wife as hostage the obvious move. It does seem strange that Plowden showed such disregard for the safety and comfort of his family, especially when the Spaniards were so well known for their treatment of hostages.

The authorities in St. Augustine were well aware that some plans were being prepared against the peace of the province, and the letters from Plowden and Lang showed that these two men might be the leaders. The attempts of these men to remove their families and property to Georgia tended to increase the suspicion of Quesada and Morales.

It was fairly obvious that during their relatively short stay under the rule of Spain, these men had become determined to try to overthrow the Spanish government in one way or another. Their willingness to come to East Florida from the United States in the first place may have been prompted by a desire to attain something for nothing. This was the motivating force behind a great deal of the movement to the west, all along the western frontier of America. Once in the new land, these settlers had been quick to discover the relative weakness of the Spanish hold on the area and the apparent vulnerability of the province either to internal revolt or to external attack. There is not sufficient evidence to warrant a statement that Lang and Plowden came to the province with the intention of creating a disturbance. The governor was ready, however, to believe that these people were motivated by a carefully laid plan to overthrow the legitimate government of the province.

The governor recognized that these "discontented and rebellious sub-jects" represented an immediate threat to his province, but he was also convinced that the underlying cause of their disaffection lay in French-inspired plotting. He was certain that Lang, Plowden, and the others were being encouraged by certain French agents in Georgia, no doubt the ones who remained after the conclusion of the 1794 venture. He was not certain that the withdrawal of the *Las Casas* from the St. Mary's River had brought an end to the carefully laid plans of Mangourit and Clark.[35] It is to be remembered that he had maintained that the so-called "republic" of Clark's was nothing but an outgrowth of the earlier French venture.

In January the governor's suspicions appeared to be justified, for a small schooner out of Providence with a cargo of cotton was seized by a French privateer, a short distance off the coast of Anastasia Island.[36] It was reported that the captured vessel had been taken into the St. Mary's estuary, ostensibly to sell the cargo to local merchants. Once there, the crew of the privateer began unloading their armament on the northern end of Amelia Island, where a few scattered French supporters were still hiding.[37] The constant patrol of this privateer with another off the St. Augustine bar added to the governor's worries, for the supply of food in the town was running short, and it was becoming hazardous to send and receive messages by the sea route.

Other French agents, in addition to those already in Georgia and on Amelia Island, were reported to have been landed on the undefended coast south of St. Augustine. Howard sent word that he had heard from a friend in Georgia that five such men had been landed on the coast of

Anastasia Island near the Matanzas battery. His informant said that one of these agents might be an infamous Spanish renegade named Thompson, long sought for his connection with a case of piracy. According to another report from Georgia, this man was in reality a paid agent of the French consul in Savannah. He was said to be the forerunner of several agents who were expected to arrive in the United States aboard a large French war fleet which was being sent to assist in suppressing the civil war in Haiti and in making a new attack on East Florida and Louisiana. A second agent of Howard's, just returned from St. Mary's, reported that the French were preparing to use 2,000 of the 12,000 troops destined for Haiti in the proposed attack on the Spanish colonies.[38]

Quesada was not particularly alarmed by this information from Howard, since the likelihood of an attack from Haiti appeared to be extremely remote. He was determined, however, to keep a watchful eye in that direction, while concentrating his attention on the continued activities of French agents in Georgia and South Carolina. Soon a second letter arrived from Howard, containing an extensive report from John McQueen, who had just returned from a short trip through southern Georgia. The young man had brought back the news that a certain Georgian, using the name of Charles Howard, was aiding the French in a new plan which involved the seizure of Amelia Island. This agent hoped to develop a port where corsairs could be fitted out and repaired. The local Georgia newspapers had carried an announcement that a French agent, M. Colombé, was reported to have landed in St. Mary's with a set of secret orders dealing with the seizure of East Florida.[39] On receiving this news from Howard, Morales reasoned that such an attack could be directed only against the St. Mary's area and not against the rest of East Florida, since the French were reported to be without vessels. It was his belief that the French wanted nothing but a safe haven for their corsairs beyond the jurisdiction of the United States.[40]

Morales informed Las Casas of these rumors, declaring that the little two-gun battery at the northern end of Amelia Island could hardly be expected to withstand an attack from the sea, especially if large armed vessels were involved. The withdrawal of virtually all Spanish troops from the area between the rivers, accomplished by Howard the previous year at the order of Quesada, had left this fort as an isolated outpost.[41] Morales believed that Howard should reoccupy this area, for he claimed that the withdrawal of troops had resulted in the influx of "a considerable number of vagabonds of all nations, without king, without law, and without religion." He appealed to Las Casas for an eighteen-gun ship to drive away the French corsairs which haunted the St. Augustine bar, warning that nearly all necessary supplies were running low in the town.[42]

In order to verify McQueen's information, Morales took a sworn statement from the young man. The questioning revealed that McQueen knew more than he had seen fit to divulge to Howard. He told the acting governor of a report that Genêt was supposed to be in New York with an official order from Paris appointing him ambassador from France. Genêt's orders were to return to Philadelphia to reopen the scheme to attack all Spanish possessions in the New World, supported by a French fleet and a large amount of money.[43] This report of McQueen's appears to have been the only one dealing with Genêt to reach East Florida. As a matter of fact, Genêt had already retired to a small farm on Long Island where he spent several peaceful years before moving to the Hudson Valley.[44]

In the meantime, rumors reached St. Augustine that Elijah Clark was once again involved in French intrigue. This seemed to confirm the suspicions expressed by Quesada in the winter that the old general still cherished an ambition to invade East Florida. A letter from George Fleming, who had just returned from the trading post at Coleraine, was delivered to Morales at the end of May.[45] Fleming reported that some of his friends had told him that Clark had just visited Coleraine. During his short stay there Clark was supposed to have agreed to coöperate with a French corsair which was shortly expected to attack Amelia Island. According to local rumor, he had admitted publicly that this scheme was part of "the plans of Genêt," formulated with the full approval of the French National Convention. The old general had intimated that the Indians now gathered along the Altamaha River, ostensibly to sign a new peace with the state of Georgia, were actually there to help in the planned attack on the St. Mary's region.[46] This was partly confirmed on June 9 when Quesada received a letter from a Spanish agent reporting that the Indians had already signed a peace treaty with Georgia in which they tentatively agreed to cede all rights to certain lands near the Altamaha River. This letter intimated that Clark was preparing to march through these same Indian lands to attack the northern fringe of East Florida.[47] Rumor in Coleraine identified Clark as the American leader who had carried on several conversations with Samuel Hammond on the subject of procuring the supplies for such an expedition. Large contracts had been offered for a supply of lumber, probably for the construction of forts on the south bank of St. Mary's River. Everything seemed to point to the imminent start of operations.[48]

Morales believed that this information was of sufficient importance to warrant calling another *junta de guerra* in order to set up a policy of defense for the whole colony. All members of the junta were agreed that it would be futile to attempt to hold out either on Amelia Island or at any point north of St. John's River. The question of complying with a recent order of Las Casas to return to Havana some of the infantry now in St. Augustine caused a definite split among the members. Finally all agreed to comply with the order of the governor general, though he was to be sent a copy of the proceedings of the junta with the urgent request that the three companies of infantry in question be returned to St. Augustine at the earliest opportunity. The unstable situation along the northern frontier was emphasized. Morales included a copy of Lang's letter to Quesada when he forwarded a transcript of the junta to Havana. He referred to Lang and his friends as "traitorous Floridians," intimating that they were receiving considerable support from the local Georgia population.[49]

Less than a week after the meeting of the junta, Morales received a long letter from Howard setting forth the reasons for his disapproval of further withdrawals of regular troops from his command and his general dissatisfaction with the situation along the St. John's River. He declared that if further reduction of his force was contemplated by the authorities in St. Augustine or Havana, he could no longer guarantee the safety of the frontier. Howard was of the opinion that Lang was the man behind the frequent raids across the river, probably with the full moral support of the local Georgia officials. He further reasoned that Lang's letter of May 18 to Quesada must have been written immediately after a meeting between the Florida fugitive and Clark. Howard laid the success of these minor raids to information that Lang had collected while living in East Florida.[50] Morales sent this information to Las Casas with the additional news that many Americans, who expressed a hatred for monarchy and a love for the republican spirit of France, were trickling into the region along the southern bank of St. Mary's River. He feared that they might arouse the remainder of the population who, though still loyal to Spain, were mostly settlers recently arrived there from the United States.[51]

The very next day, Morales thought it necessary to write again to Las Casas because of more information just received from the frontier. Andrew Atkinson reported that the situation in Camden County was getting out of control, and that a complete report of the recent developments and a request for assistance had been sent to Augusta by one of

the local justices of the peace.[52] Atkinson included a copy of a letter
from a Creek chief who emphatically denied complicity in the sale of
Indian lands by Chief Mad Dog to the four land companies. The Indian
continued that as far as he could tell, the troubles along the Altamaha
River were caused by renegade Spaniards and runaway Negro slaves
and not by adventurous Americans. He threatened immediate Indian
action if the Spanish authorities did not take measures to prevent these
renegades from bothering both the Indians and the Georgians.[53] This
defiant attitude on the part of one of the more powerful Creek chiefs
annoyed and worried the Spanish authorities. Morales blamed the defec-
tion of some of the former Indian allies of Spain on the subversive activities of James Seagrove and Captain John F. Randolph,[54] branding them
as two of Spain's bitterest enemies and as close friends and agents of
Elijah Clark.[55]

In order to keep a close watch on the activities in Camden County,
Morales ordered Howard to maintain a continuous guard along the
southern bank of St. Mary's River. He was to keep in touch at all times
with his trusted agents in Georgia.[56] The frontier commander soon received word from Nathan Atkinson,[57] in reply to an earlier letter, that
Clark was no longer in evidence, and that the plan for attack appeared
to have broken down over the question of the selection of an able leader.
There seemed to be three definite factions involved, each with a different
view of the methods to be employed in and the purpose of an attack on
East Florida. One group favored the use of the French republican flag
with a declaration of allegiance to France; the second preferred to see
the venture develop as an open rebellion against Spanish authority; and
the third advocated, as a middle course, a series of minor border attacks,
with no avowed allegiance to the French cause and certainly with no
declaration of an open break with Spain. The third course would guarantee a safe haven in the United States as a last resort if the plans for
the attack miscarried.[58]

While Andrew Atkinson was on a hurried visit to St. Mary's, he met
some of the leaders of the local "Republican Society." At this meeting,
he learned that the projected land attack on Amelia Island was to take
place within the next ten days. This plan depended on the assistance of
several French corsairs, including the *Mère Mitchele*, the *Delaware* with
forty guns, and at least one other ship of moderate size.[59] Atkinson was
certain that the Georgia officials would do nothing to hinder the plans
of the French as long as the Spaniards ignored the matter of the return
of runaway slaves.[60] Howard forwarded this information to Morales,

with the warning that he could no longer maintain a close watch on the northern bank of the river with his depleted forces.[61] The acting governor called a junta on June 24 to discuss the implications of Howard's letter. By unanimous decision it was decided to send a letter to the governor of Georgia to tell him what was taking place in Coleraine, in case he did not already know. The Spaniards also agreed to begin negotiations to return runaway slaves and stolen property. The members of the junta felt that haste was essential if the projected attack on Florida was to be forestalled.[62]

While tension was growing along the frontier, disaster nearly struck in St. Augustine. An elaborate escape plot involving several French sailors in the dungeon of the fort was discovered just in time. The leader was a sea captain who had been held in the fort since the wreck of his ship on Matanzas Island. The plot involved some of the grenadiers in the garrison, who had agreed to open the cells to allow the French sailors to seize the armory. Then the loyal garrison was to be overwhelmed, and a small vessel in the harbor was to provide the means of escape to the north. The silver plate and other valuables in the fort were to be taken as loot. In this way the little group expected to make its way to Charleston. A loyal member of the garrison revealed the plot a few hours before it was to take place. Morales believed that none of the grenadiers of French extraction could be trusted. All were placed under the closest surveillance to prevent any outbreak. The acting governor decided to attempt the immediate exchange of all French prisoners held in St. Augustine for the Spanish fusiliers who were being held prisoner on board several French corsairs in Charleston harbor.[63] There is no indication that Morales' suggestion received official notice in New Orleans or in Havana, since the Spanish authorities in Madrid had been adamant in refusing to exchange prisoners with the French. As a matter of fact, at a later date, Las Casas forwarded to St. Augustine a copy of the royal order of December 9, 1793, which specifically forbade the exchange of prisoners with France.[64]

Morales lamented that the constant presence of two French corsairs off the mouth of the St. Mary's River, and near the St. Augustine bar, made the citizens of French and American extraction very restless. It also made hazardous the dispatch of news and official documents. This was the gloomy picture of the situation that Morales gave to the sick governor when he visited him on June 27. The next day, at Quesada's request, Morales sent a lengthy dispatch to Las Casas containing the most recent news from the St. Mary's River region.[65]

Although Quesada and Morales frequently consulted with higher Spanish authorities, they did not show the same interest in corresponding with the authorities in Camden County or with the state officials in Augusta. Their fruitless efforts in the spring of 1794 may have discouraged them, or it may have been that they felt capable of handling the situation from St. Augustine. It is certain that they did not want the United States to discover how precarious was the whole system of frontier defense. Only the more flagrant breaches of the frontier had resulted in the exchange of protests by the two governors. One such note was sent to Augusta in the middle of March after a raid on some of the St. Mary's plantations, supposedly the work of Lang and his friends.[66] The Camden County officials took no notice of the protest from Quesada other than to send a report to Mathews. As far as Mathews was concerned, the situation presented certain difficulties since the leaders of the raiding party were obviously still Spanish subjects. According to their story, they had fled from East Florida and were living temporarily within the frontiers of Georgia. Lang frequently made the point of stressing his Spanish citizenship, denying that he was an American and hence not under the jurisdiction of the Georgia courts.[67] Although official opinion in Philadelphia held that these men were still Spaniards, they were regarded as being as dangerous to the peace of the United States as they were to that of East Florida. They were suspected of being responsible for the raids carried out in Camden County, although local rumor attributed these disturbances to small parties of hostile Indians.[68] President Washington's general attitude was that if they desired to remain in the United States they would have to respect its laws.

The *Columbian Centinel* reported in a letter from Savannah that "it now is reduced to a certainty that the late injuries done in the counties of Camden and Glynn were by a few outlawed vagabond Indians from Florida, accompanied by some white men of the same character."[69] It is possible that the "white men" referred to were Lang, Wagnon, Plowden, and others of the same sort, all refugees from the Spanish authorities. Nevertheless, Governor Mathews made it obvious that he did not feel himself bound to apprehend these men in order to return them to their own government for trial. After a careful reading of a copy of Lang's letter to Quesada, the governor of Georgia decided to regard the refugees as "East Florida Revolutionists."[70] Thus it is easy to understand why Lang and his friends believed that they were perfectly safe in Georgia, no matter how they behaved themselves. Quesada's distrust of Mathews is also understandable.

CHAPTER VIII

BORDER REBELLION IN EAST FLORIDA

THE SPANISH AUTHORITIES in St. Augustine were fully aware of the threat of hostilities along the Georgia-Florida border region. As has been shown, frequent reports of these preparations had been coming in from the frontier area, most of them from Colonel Howard. As commander of the frontier, he had solicited this information from agents and friends in Georgia, from loyal members of the militia, and from several residents of the province who had connections of one sort or another in Georgia. In addition, Governor Quesada had received letters directly from some of the participants in the plans, warning him of their intended actions. Some three weeks before the actual attack, Quesada wrote to the Spanish representatives in Philadelphia, informing them of the threatened hostilities and blaming Elijah Clark and his band of refugees. He requested that the entire matter be laid before the secretary of war with the hope that the information would reach the President. Reference was made to the excellent coöperation shown by the Georgia officials during the eventful days in the previous summer.[1] As Quesada had hoped, the matter was laid before the secretary of war, who acknowledged the need for action.[2] Thus it is fairly evident that the governor was aware of the impending threat to the province. It must be remembered, however, that a similar threat the year before had failed to materialize after considerable defensive preparation on the part of the Spaniards. It is quite possible that Quesada believed that the threat in June, 1795, might well resolve itself as quickly and easily as had the one in the previous year.

Unfortunately for the Spanish cause, the governor was subject to frequent and severe attacks of tropical fever. This necessitated the temporary delegation of power to an acting governor at a time when the province was in need of strong leadership. Quesada was ill during most of June and July and his administrative duties were handled by Morales, a man of inferior ability. The chief fault of the acting governor was his hesitation in making necessary decisions without long consultation and procrastination. This hesitation was not due to timidity, but rather to a lack of understanding of administrative procedure. Morales corresponded frequently with Las Casas, attempting either to justify every action taken or to excuse those not taken.[3] Las Casas, quick to

---

[1] For notes to chap. viii, see pp. 166–168.

realize the shortcomings of the acting governor, countermanded several of his orders and accused him of being unnecessarily cautious. In reporting to Madrid, Las Casas declared that some of the decisions of Morales and his junta were utterly "incomprehensible."[4] A month later, Las Casas informed his government that, as he considered Morales incapable of carrying out the duties of the governorship, he had ordered Quesada to resume command immediately or to replace Morales with Colonel Howard. He implied that any administrative failure in East Florida would be due to the inability of Morales to cope with the situation.[5] As matters turned out, Quesada had recovered sufficiently to resume his duties by the time this order reached St. Augustine. Apparently he did not share the governor general's views, since Morales was retained as military commander of the region between the St. Mary's and St. John's rivers.

When the assault on the little post at Juana took place on the night of June 29,[6] the attackers found the Spanish garrison quite unprepared to ward off this sudden blow. The apparent lack of preparation could hardly be held against Howard, since the depletion of his forces left him in no position to strengthen the border guards, even at the vital river crossing. In addition, the attacking party outnumbered by four to one the garrison of the little post.[7] With the greatest care, the attackers crossed the river, advanced through the palmetto swamps, and approached the post under cover of darkness. It was easy to overcome the single sentry and to make prisoners of the sleeping garrison without firing a shot. After taking all arms and ammunition from the armory, the attackers then ransacked the storerooms in search of provisions. When the guardhouse had been thoroughly explored and then partly wrecked, the enemy turned to the barracks building. Nothing of importance was found there and it was set on fire. A large herd of cattle numbering over one hundred head was grazing in the neighborhood of the post, and these were rounded up by a few rebel horsemen.[8] It was decided to retire with the spoils of victory into the swamp area north of the St. John's River. This withdrawal was accomplished with the prisoners being driven along with the cattle.[9] A temporary camp was made somewhere in the region between the two rivers. Permanent headquarters were finally set up at a spot designated as Mills Ford on the St. Mary's River.[10]

The first news of these events to reach St. Augustine was contained in a dispatch from Howard written just a few hours after the attack. The commander of the frontier enclosed a brief summary of events from one of his aides, Peter Carne,[11] whose information came directly from a youth named Burnett,[12] arrested by Carne as a suspicious character. According to Carne's report, Burnett had admitted taking part in the attack and was willing to inform on some of his associates. The youth was able to identify members of the attacking party as former residents of East Florida, and some as citizens of Georgia. According to his story, Lang and Plowden had acted as the leaders, although neither was actually present during the capture of Juana.[13] Two of the Americans were identified as members of the Camden County militia stationed at Coleraine.[14] Howard was anxious to get this information to St. Augustine as soon as possible and did not wait to write a letter of his own. He merely asked for advice on what plan he should follow.[15]

When this information reached Morales, he decided that it was more important to protest to the authorities in Camden County than to address the governor general. He accused the justices of the peace of having failed to inform him of the impending attack. He was certain, so he wrote, that they themselves were not involved in the preparations, but he accused them of having been aware of what was going on in a place as small as Coleraine. He protested against the participation of Americans in this violation of Spanish sovereignty, and he requested that the authorities take immediate action. If they were unable to cope with the situation, he asked that they send the necessary information to the proper authorities. He sent two copies of this letter, one to be forwarded to Governor Mathews.[16]

In his first report to the governor general, Morales expressed fear that further inroads would occur and that the loss of Juana would reflect on his administration of the province. He enclosed a letter from a citizen of East Florida who had just returned from a visit to Savannah. The writer said that the temper of the local population had been aroused against the Spaniards and that many were ready to assist in an attempt at open rebellion. On his way back from Savannah he had passed through Coleraine at the risk of his life in order to discover what was going on. The townspeople had been aroused by Lang and Plowden and were clamoring for Spanish blood.[17]

Some of the older and more conservative of the Anglo-Saxon settlers in the St. John's River region were also apprehensive. One of these, George Fleming, the owner of most of the cattle stolen at Juana, requested that the authorities in St. Augustine take steps to protect him, his family, and his herds. He feared for his life and property if Plowden should get loose in East Florida. His particular anxiety was for the life of his aged father-in-law who was known to be a strong supporter of the Spanish government.[18] Apparently Fleming feared that the rebels held a definite grudge against him for the aid he was supposed to have offered Quesada in 1794, when the previous attack against the province was being planned in Georgia and South Carolina. There had been vague rumors that he and his father-in-law had betrayed certain plans, thereby causing the arrest of Plowden, Lang, Jones, and others.

When a more detailed account of the attack on Juana was sent by Howard to Morales, the acting governor decided to attempt counter-measures to forestall further assaults on the defenses of the province. He called a *junta de guerra* for July 4, in order to learn the opinions of his aides on the best course of action. After the customary prelimi-naries, he read aloud Howard's latest dispatch which included en-closures from some of his scattered agents along the frontier. All stressed the need for utmost caution in taking the field against the rebels, as they were numerous and well armed. In one of these reports, a Captain Hall in the militia declared that he dared not make an attack on the rebels with his small force of militiamen. He informed Howard that Lang had paroled Sergeant Jonathan McCoulloth so that he could deliver a letter from Cornet Wheeler, the commanding officer of Juana, which said that Lang wished to exchange him for some of the French sailors held in the fort at St. Augustine. McCoulloth reported that Lang had between forty and fifty armed men in his camp and was expecting two additional groups, one reported to be under the command of Elijah Clark.[19] The most discouraging news from McCoulloth was the report that nearly all of the garrison of Juana had expressed a desire to join forces with Lang.[20] Howard confirmed most of Hall's information by reports from other agents. One of these agents declared that Abner Hammond with a force of fifty Frenchmen was on the march to join Lang, with another five hundred supporters due to arrive later. Howard made several suggestions for the preparation of a defense line along the St. John's River, including the building of a small fort on the north-ern bank and a battery at the estuary. Armed Negroes and a small num-ber of Indians were requested to be used as scouts. He was emphatic that no offensive action could be taken until the whole military situation was reorganized. He concluded with a report that Lang had announced his desire to harm no one in East Florida, if the whole province would yield to him peacefully.[21]

A long and heated debate followed the reading of these dispatches, the main controversy centering on the advisability of attacking the

rebels before reinforcements could reach them from Georgia. The acting governor was alone in favoring an immediate assault, but he finally
agreed to follow Howard's suggested plan of watching and waiting.
The junta then made six important decisions for the defense of the
province: to collect and arm all free Negroes and mulattoes who had
fled from Georgia to Florida; to solicit all possible aid from the neigh-
boring Indians in return for the promise of supplies and arms; to unite
all available militia groups north of the St. John's River, still loyal and
above suspicion;[22] to send an additional eight men to reinforce the garrison of the battery at the bar of the St. John's River; to request the
governor general to send at least two small armed vessels to aid in the
defense of the province; and to approach the captain of the English
privateer *Conquest,* then in port with a small prize schooner, on the
subject of the purchase of his vessel.[23] With this the junta adjourned
to await further news from Howard.[24]

Morales forwarded a copy of the proceedings to Havana with a short
letter of his own expressing some personal views on the situation. He
pointed out to Las Casas that he alone had stood out for an immediate
attack on the rebels, but that he had yielded upon the insistence of the
other members. Having agreed to abide by the decision of the majority,
he was now recommending the immediate withdrawal of all regular
troops to the south bank of the St. John's River to prevent any from
being cut off from their base of supplies. If the defense line based on
the river were broken, then St. Augustine would be in dire peril. His
total operative strength amounted to some five hundred veteran troops
in addition to ninety thoroughly loyal militiamen. The remaining four
hundred and seventy veteran troops were either sick or incapacitated
for some reason or other, many being of French extraction and therefore under strict surveillance since the discovery of the escape plot two
months earlier.[25]

The last of the six measures decided upon by the junta, the purchase
of the schooner *Micaela,* was carried out immediately, and the small
vessel was soon made ready for sea duty. This little vessel was re-
christened the *Santa Mónica* and was put into service as the official
message boat, a service it performed for several years. The *Santa Mónica*
was put under the command of Captain Sebastian Antonio Verazaluze.[26]

While Morales and the junta were considering what steps to take in
the defense of the province, there was constant activity along the northern frontier. Small parties of mounted militiamen continued to reconnoiter the region between the two rivers. As far as they could tell, Lang's
forces were well entrenched and appeared to be awaiting the arrival

of reinforcements from the north. There were no signs that a second incursion across the St. John's River was being planned. The Spanish authorities were lulled into a false sense of security by the lack of activity at Mills Ford.

Apparently emboldened by their success at Juana, the rebels decided to venture across the St. John's River again, in order to attack one of the main posts in the river line of defense. The point selected for the next attack was the little military post at San Nicolás. According to Columbus Drew:

> The location of Fort St. Nicholas [San Nicolás] was about a mile east of the present South Jacksonville ferry, back from the river 250 to 300 yards. Around the fort was a moat, or excavation, 100 feet square, and surrounding this was a cantonment or settlement, together with offices, quarters, and barracks for the men. Toward the end of the Spanish rule, Fort St. Nicholas was maintained principally as a port to prevent smuggling.[27]

In spite of the observance of Quesada's standing order for night and day patrols along the St. John's River, Lang's men managed to filter through the outer Spanish lines and to make a second attack, this time on the evening of July 9. They succeeded in crossing the river in several small boats belonging to John McIntosh, at a point a league or so below the two-gun battery at San Nicolás. They paddled along the shore to a small gunboat, the *San Simeon*, swinging at anchor off the fort, and took it without firing a shot. After landing, the rebel force approached the battery with no attempt at a concealment, passing themselves off as a Spanish relief force from St. Augustine. By speaking Spanish, they completely fooled the sentries, and it was not until the rebels were inside the fortifications that the ruse was discovered. In the ensuing scuffle, three of the garrison were killed and several received wounds. The commander of the small artillery force, Lieutenant José Alforeso, was killed as he attempted to jump through an open window in the barracks building. The remainder of the garrison including the commander of the post, Lieutenant Ygnacio López, were taken prisoner. In all, some twenty-eight members of the Catalan Light Infantry Company were seized.[28]

The news of the attack reached the next outpost at Santa Ysabel, six miles downstream from San Nicolás, in a matter of a few hours. The commander of the garrison, Sergeant José Pellicier,[29] fearing lest he and his fourteen men be cut off and overwhelmed by the rebel force, decided to abandon his post and retreat toward Howard's headquarters at San Vicente Ferrer. Before leaving his post, he ordered his men to spike the single cannon.[30] With the loss of this post, the Spaniards held no fortifications along the lower St. John's River except San Vicente Ferrer and the little battery at the bar of the river.

It appeared for the moment as though the entire defense line along the St. John's River were on the verge of complete collapse. At this point, however, Howard took a hand and put into motion the plans already drawn up for just such an emergency. He ordered all regular patrols scattered along the southern bank of the river to report at once to his headquarters at San Vicente Ferrer. In addition, he gathered all available militiamen who could be trusted, and their spare mounts. A small gunboat, the *Santo Tomás,* lying off the battery, was ordered made ready for action. While this concentration of forces was being prepared, Howard sent out several reconnoitering parties, including one small group led by Luis Maas[31] who knew English. Maas was able to penetrate the rebel lines and to creep into the post at San Nicolás where he found John McIntosh in a highly intoxicated condition,[32] celebrating the rebel victory and bragging noisily about his recent exploits in the attack on the little fort.[33] Another group, led by Captain José de Córdoba, was sent out in canoes to scour the river for signs of additional forces coming from the north.[34] He sighted the garrison from Santa Ysabel struggling along the bank of the river on the way to Howard's headquarters. When Córdoba returned with Pellicier and his men, he, Howard, and McQueen held a council of war to determine what course of action to follow. The reports of Maas, Pellicier, Córdoba, and others showed that the situation was very grave indeed. It was decided that the small battery at Dos Hermanos, which defended the crossing over the Nassau River near its mouth, was too remote to warrant an attempt to hold it, and orders were sent to the commanding officer, Lieutenant Benito Panqua,[35] to abandon his post. The guns were to be spiked and the men embarked on the launch *San Augustín de Patrón,* in order to proceed to San Vicente Ferrer through Nassau Sound. Finally, Howard decided to withdraw to St. Augustine with his ranking officers where a complete reorganization of defense plans could be undertaken. According to this scheme, the main force would be concentrated at Howard's headquarters.[36] He felt that this move would not be unduly dangerous, since there were no indications that the rebels intended to drive directly toward the populated region south of the St. John's River.

At this crucial moment, Morales was able to send much-needed naval support in the form of the small schooner recently brought into St. Augustine as a prize by the English privateer *Conquest.* In addition, the captain of the *Conquest,* John McCockburn, offered his services to the governor, in conformity with the spirit of the Anglo-Spanish alliance. The acting governor was able to send quite a sizable force of veteran troops drawn from the Cuban Regiment which formed part of the garrison of the town. This force was under the command of Captain José de los Remedios of the Royal Artillery.[37] A small force of urban militia was also sent under the command of Andrew Atkinson, who insisted on going in spite of his age and ailing health. The two vessels crossed the bar and sailed up the St. John's River, reaching San Vicente Ferrer on the afternoon of July 11. The *Conquest* sailed on up as far as the rebel stronghold at San Nicolás and reported that it would be a fairly simple matter to drive the rebels off and to reoccupy the fort. Apparently the rebels had made no attempt to seize the abandoned post of Santa Ysabel, and there were no signs that they realized that the Spanish garrison had been withdrawn.

In view of these favorable reports and of the large reinforcements from St. Augustine, Howard decided that the time was propitious for a direct assault by a water-borne force. He carefully organized the little armada before sailing up the river from San Vicente Ferrer. The brig *Conquest,* under Captain McCockburn, carried Howard, most of his staff, forty veteran soldiers of the Cuban Infantry Company and their commander, Lieutenant Manuel Rodríguez, forty-two free mulattoes, and thirteen members of the urban militia. The last group was supposedly under the command of Andrew Atkinson, but at the last minute illness forced him to relinquish his command to Santos Rodríguez, the arsenal guard. The schooner *Santa Mónica,* under the temporary command of Lieutenant Sebastian Verazaluze, carried John McQueen and thirty soldiers. The gunboat *Santo Tomás* carried Captain Remedios, the commander of the reinforcements from St. Augustine, and Subaltern Pablo Catafal,[38] with twenty men from the Catalan Company. Finally, the launch *St. Augustín de Patrón* carried all the supplies and ammunition.[39]

When the vessels arrived off San Nicolás, Howard ordered the firing of a couple of cannon balls and a round of small arms. The rebels were seen to leap into their canoes and make off into the thick marshes that lined the river, without making an attempt to defend the position. Small boats were put out which scouted the area and reported that the enemy had disappeared. The Spanish personnel then landed in small boats and immediately reoccupied the fort. Scattered supplies, forty grazing horses, and a pile of discarded saddles testified to the haste with which the rebels had departed. The short rebel occupancy of the post had done no apparent damage. The gunboat *San Simeon,* captured earlier by the rebels, was found undamaged, although hard and fast on a sandbank in the river. Two small boats, evidently the ones used by the rebels to cross the river, were found on the shore near the fort. They were identified as the property of John McIntosh. Further investigation by scouts showed that there were now no rebels south of the St. John's River.[40]

Once the post had been put in order again, Howard dispatched a small mounted party of militia and free Negroes across the river to see if the rebels were contemplating a stand anywhere in the region to the north. The shortage of sound mounts prevented him from sending a larger force. As this situation had hindered his efforts for some time, he wrote to Quesada requesting additional mounts, if day and night patrols were to be maintained.[41] The scouting party could find no trace of the rebel force, but did discover a hastily constructed fort near Mills Ford, perhaps the site of Lang's headquarters. After burning this building, the scouts returned to San Vicente Ferrer to report to Howard. The *Conquest* set sail for St. Augustine to return the members of the garrison employed in the attack on the post at San Nicolás. After a visit with the governor to tell him the latest news from Howard, Captain McCockburn sailed for Providence.

In reporting the whole matter to Havana, Quesada pointed out that the efforts of Howard were largely responsible for the successful recovery of the two posts. He recommended that Las Casas promote Howard to full colonel. The governor also expressed great pleasure at the way in which Andrew Atkinson and John McQueen had carried out their parts in suppressing the rebellion. He recommended royal acknowledgment of their loyalty. Finally, he recommended that the governor general inform the British government of the coöperation and assistance offered by Captain McCockburn of the *Conquest.*[42] A similar note was sent to the British consul in Charleston, with the request that he inform his government of the fine work of the British sea captain.[43]

Thus, without the loss of a single Spanish soldier, Howard was able to drive the rebels back over the St. John's River and regain control of the fords across the river. The two small forts were reoccupied and most of the garrison released from imprisonment. In addition, forty serviceable horses were added to the meager supply available to the militia. The action taken by Quesada in 1794, in setting up a loose defense line along the river, had once more borne fruit, since the Spaniards had again been able to repel an invading force without having to fight a pitched battle.

CHAPTER IX

AMELIA ISLAND AFFAIR

WHILE THE SPANISH forces along the St. John's River were struggling to maintain their positions in the face of rebel attacks, important events were taking place fifty or more miles to the northeast. Here lay the long, narrow island called Amelia, the object of many assaults throughout the colonial period of Florida history. As early as January, 1795, Quesada had received reports from Georgia that there were plans afoot in South Carolina for an expedition to move on Amelia Island to set up a deep-water port for French privateers.[1] Several months later Morales reported having received news of a French attempt to seize the estuary of the St. Mary's River and the northern end of Amelia Island for a base of operations against shipping in the Bahama Straits. This would enable French vessels to rendezvous at a point outside the boundaries of the United States. The acting governor pointed out that the little two-gun battery at the northern end of the island could hardly be expected to hold off the French fleet that was reported to be outfitting in Charleston harbor.[2] To forestall any possibility of the garrison being cut off by the arrival of a hostile naval force, he recommended immediate withdrawal of the garrison from this post and its incorporation in Howard's forces along the St. John's River.[3]

At the junta held on June 2, the question of the advisability of attempting to defend the island was one of the main issues discussed. This was because recent dispatches from Charleston and Savannah alluded to the outfitting of several large French privateers and implied that they were to be employed in an attack on Amelia Island. It was rumored that this assault was to be carried out in conjunction with a land attack from southern Georgia.[4] Morales asked Captain Pedro Diaz Berrio of the Royal Engineers[5] to make a report on the wisdom of maintaining a sizable force on the island. This officer stressed the disadvantages of such a plan and closed his report by referring to an earlier survey made by him at Quesada's request at the close of the previous year. In this document, Berrio had emphasized the need to maintain the defense line along the St. John's River, even at the expense of abandoning everything to the north.[6] When the acting governor called upon Captain Juan de los Remedios of the Royal Artillery for his opinion, this officer agreed in principle with Berrio. After further discussion, the members of the

[1] For notes to chap. ix, see pp. 168–171.

[93]

junta agreed unanimously that Amelia Island should be abandoned at once, and that all artillery and personnel there should be withdrawn to augment Howard's forces.[7] In forwarding the recommendations of the junta to Las Casas, Morales said that the order for abandonment of the island had been issued, and that no attempt would be made to reoccupy the place until at least two well-armed vessels could be obtained to guard the seaward approach to the island.[8]

Apparently the order to abandon the island was carried into effect almost at once, for less than a week later Howard reported that he had assigned a force of fourteen men to hold Talbot Island,[9] with the added duty of patrolling Amelia Island at regular intervals.[10] He requested that the governor send him an officer to take charge of this force. An additional force of nine men was assigned to patrol the small islands at the northern end of Amelia Island near the estuary of the St. Mary's River. These men were to keep close watch on the various channels that might be used by ships entering the river. All these patrols were supplied with mounts, since the distance to be covered was considerable. They were ordered to send frequent reports to Howard at San Vicente Ferrer.[11]

The Spanish authorities were worried by the continued presence on Amelia Island of several members of the crew of the *Las Casas* who had been left behind when the vessel left the St. Mary's in April, 1794. These French agents led a nomadic existence, turning up at frequent intervals in Georgia, on the East Florida mainland, and on the small islands lying off the coast. Quesada was unable to uncover the hiding place of these men and their caches of arms and supplies. Howard made an unsuccessful effort to intercept the small boats plying between St. Mary's and Amelia Island.

In June, Andrew Atkinson made a short visit to friends in Coleraine in an effort to obtain information about the reported movements of suspicious characters in the border area. He collected additional information about the French fleet previously reported to be lying off Charleston. He wrote Howard that the owner of one of the French privateers boasted in his presence that French forces would be in full possession of Amelia Island within ten to fourteen days.[12] On receiving this news, Morales once again wrote a hasty note to Las Casas saying that the information from Atkinson made the defense of Amelia Island unthinkable. The acting governor went to great lengths to defend his actions, claiming that the joining of land and naval forces would give the French great numerical and strategic advantage.[13]

Once the attack on the outpost at Juana had taken place, the question of Amelia Island ceased to be of paramount interest to Morales. At the important junta of July 4 no mention was made of the defense of this strategic point, although the assembled officers discussed many of the more important questions dealing with the protection of the province. As had been predicted by Las Casas, the rebels soon took advantage of this situation and sent a small force of armed men to join the French agents and to occupy the northern tip of the island. A few days after the junta, it was reported to St. Augustine that a number of men had landed at a point on the northwest corner of the island where they were constructing some sort of fortification. According to one witness, these men had been seen to raise the flag of the French Republic above the ramparts of their little fort.[14] When this information reached Howard, he hesitated to believe that this small force actually constituted a full-fledged attack upon the northern frontier, or was even a serious attempt to occupy the whole of Amelia Island. The attack on San Nicolás strengthened his belief that the occupation of a part of the island was merely a ruse to induce him to split his forces in such a way as to make the whole frontier vulnerable to attack.[15] After the recapture of San Nicolás, some of the rebels were seen to paddle off in the general direction of Talbot Island and probably toward Amelia Island. Howard presumed that they were on their way to join those already at the northern tip of the island.[16]

The occupation of Amelia Island by French agents was confirmed by Pierre Auguste Adet,[17] the new French minister, in a letter to Paris. According to him, his predecessor, Fauchet, had tried to prepare the way for the rebellion in East Florida and the occupation of Amelia Island. Writing some time after Fauchet's recall and the collapse of the Amelia Island affair, Adet declared, "The American citizens who comprised the army and the Florida patriots who had abandoned their homes to range themselves under the tricolor, all met reverse with him [Fauchet]."[18] He went on to describe in some detail how the rebellion broke out late in June, when these agents, aided by a few wandering Indians, raised the French flag over their fort on the island. He reported that he had received a petition, drawn up on July 18 after a lengthy meeting of the rebel leaders and purporting to bear the signatures of a large number of local Floridians, which requested French naval aid in throwing off the yoke of Spain. Adet sent an agent, Colonel Samuel Fulton,[19] to Amelia Island to discover whether or not this was in reality an open rebellion. Adet then advised the French consul in

Charleston to give all possible assistance to the Amelia Island expedition if it was indeed a rebellion with a fair chance of success, but not if it turned out to be an invasion from the United States.[20] Apparently the consul decided that the expedition was a rebellion, for he prepared to send a large supply of arms and ammunition collected in Charleston by a group of French sympathizers. These were later identified by the consul as members of the Popular Society of Charleston which was composed of captains of several privateers, then in port, who desired a safe haven for their ships in a region beyond the bounds of the United States. This confirmed the theory advanced by both Quesada and Howard as to the reason for the appearance of French agents on Amelia Island. But as Adet explained to his superiors, the arrival of the news of peace negotiations between France and Spain caused him to rush orders to Charleston to stop all assistance to the rebels. He further ordered the consul to purchase all the supplies prepared for Amelia Island so that they might be sent to Haiti to assist the French in the struggle there against the English and the Negroes. According to Consul Dupont's report, he was able to purchase 450 pounds of powder, 200 sabres, 20 rifles, 5,000 rifle balls, and 500 cartridges.[21] Thus ended the short period of active French interest in the Amelia Island affair.

In the meantime, the news of the decision of the junta of June 2 to abandon Amelia Island and to withdraw all regular forces to a line behind the St. John's River reached Havana early in the next month, together with Morales' account of his partial abandonment of the island.[22] The governor general was more than startled by the decisions of the acting governor and the junta. He hastened to reply to Morales, making no effort to hide his displeasure at the turn of events in St. Augustine. He denounced the actions of the junta of June 2 in blunt terms and generally disapproved its findings. After pointing out the extreme danger to the whole province if a point as strategic as Amelia Island were unguarded, Las Casas proceeded to issue several orders concerning the defense of the island. Morales was to send a sizable force of veteran troops to reoccupy the island as soon as such a force could be readied. A number of engineer troops were to accompany this force with instructions to construct a small but adequate fort. The governor general forwarded specific instructions for the laying out of the fort and for the materials to be used in its construction.[23] He agreed that more troops were needed in the province and promised to send all available forces in a few days.[24] These soldiers were to be transported to East Florida in two small armed vessels at present at anchor in Havana harbor. These were

the brigs *Flecha* and *San Antonio,* both under the command of Captain
Pedro Saenz de la Guardia. Las Casas hoped that the two vessels would
drive off the privateers that had haunted the St. Augustine bar. The
officer in command of the two warships was ordered to return to Havana
without delay as soon as his orders had been carried out.[25] The governor
general concluded his dispatch to Morales by urging him to follow a
more stringent policy in arresting suspicious characters within the province. He expressed great disapproval of the lengthy correspondence
carried on between both Quesada and Morales and those suspected of
being rebels. The governor was ordered to seize and hold all possible
hostages, including Mrs. Plowden and other relatives of known rebels.[26]
Las Casas hoped that Morales would be able to return the province to
its former peaceful state.

At the same time, Las Casas sent a dispatch to Madrid expressing his
lack of faith in the ability of Morales to carry out the duties of acting
governor of East Florida. In addition, he voiced his utter amazement
at the unanimous agreement of the other members of the junta in dealing with the Amelia Island affair. He did not approve of Quesada's withdrawal of all front-line forces to the south bank of the St. John's River.
Neither did he approve of using settlers recently from the United States
in the local militia. As far as he could determine from reports from East
Florida, the entire population along the south bank of St. John's River
and in the region extending northward to the St. Mary's River were a
low grade of people, mostly refugees from the Georgia courts and all
a thoroughly bad lot. Therefore, the withdrawal of Spanish forces
toward the south would leave these people in full possession of the abandoned region and greatly encourage them to carry on further hostile
acts.[27]

As has been mentioned, further consideration of the situation convinced Las Casas that the retention of Morales as acting governor might
seriously prejudice the entire province. His letter of July 13 to the
ailing governor ordered him to resume his position or to replace Morales
by Colonel Howard.[28] The receipt of additional dispatches from East
Florida giving accounts of the attack on Juana increased Las Casas'
belief that the military affairs of the province were badly mismanaged.
He wrote to Madrid that he hoped sincerely that the two armed vessels
sent by him on July 20 with food, arms, and reinforcements had arrived
before the situation became too desperate. The loss of Juana to Lang's
force of sixty-two men and the ensuing indecision exhibited by Morales
thoroughly exasperated the governor general. He expressed the opinion

that the success of such a small force of ill-armed men, at a time when Spanish forces in the province numbered well over nine hundred, was a direct reflection on the honor of Spanish arms.[29]

In order to make certain of the support of his council of officers, Las Casas called a *junta de guerra* on August 14, at which official sanction was given his orders sent earlier to St. Augustine. After studying all recent dispatches from Florida, the members of the junta came to the conclusion that, since Lang's small force had been concentrated on one specific objective and not on the entire frontier, the attack must be regarded as an isolated hostile act and not as a general assault on the whole province. As far as the junta could see, revenge was the only motive for the attack. They suggested that the rebels' desire for revenge against the Spanish authorities might be satisfied by the seizure of the herd of cattle belonging to George Fleming. On the other hand, it was suggested that after disposing of the cattle the rebels might join forces with the French agents already on Amelia Island preparing a safe haven for French privateers. Thus, if the Spanish forces had actually been withdrawn from the island as Morales indicated, and if the rebels were able to take complete control, then, the junta pointed out, a large Spanish force would be needed to clear the island.[30] With this in mind, Las Casas sent a letter to the governor of Georgia, expressing the hope that Mathews would prevent the departure of further forces going to assist those already on Amelia Island. Mathews was urged to seize any of those responsible for the attack on Juana, if they should return to American soil. The governor general indirectly suggested that Mathews might offer to coöperate with Howard's forces in clearing the frontier region of the French agents and their American supporters.[31] This letter was given to Colonel Kindelan to deliver to Mathews since the colonel was known to the Georgia executive, having visited him the previous fall.

Las Casas' fear that the rebels involved in the attacks on East Florida might be gathered eventually in Amelia Island under French auspices appeared to be well founded. A dispatch from Quesada which arrived in Havana in the middle of August reported that the number of rebels reaching the island was steadily increasing.[32] The governor informed Las Casas of the complete success of Howard's undertaking to recapture the post at San Nicolás, achieved without the loss of a single man. He expressed great dissatisfaction, however, over the escape of all the rebels, saying that most of them had gone off in the general direction of Amelia Island. He expressed the opinion that Howard should be able to dislodge the enemy from the island if no heavy artillery had been landed from French privateers. According to Quesada, the rebels had combined forces with the French agents and had raised the flag of the French Republic over the ramparts.[33] Because of the recurrent illness of the governor and the overcautious policy of Morales, relatively few dispatches were sent to Las Casas at this crucial time. The governor general was forced to wait several weeks for much-desired news.

After the recapture of San Nicolás and the disappearance of the rebel force, the situation along the St. John's River appeared to be fairly well stabilized. When Quesada resumed his duties, there seemed to be no reason to countermand Morales' orders to withdraw all forces from Amelia Island. The rebels were reported to be there in sufficient strength to require the postponing of offensive action until the fresh troops and naval support just received from Havana could be readied for action.[34] It was necessary to unload the supplies for St. Augustine from the two vessels and to reload them with troops to be transported to Howard's headquarters at San Vicente Ferrer. Once there, the new troops had to be landed and integrated with Howard's regular force.

While this was being done, the *Flecha* and *San Antonio* were sent up the St. John's and St. Mary's rivers to see if any rebels were lurking in that region. Upon returning to St. Augustine, Captain Saenz reported that with the exception of a few canoes seen at some distance, there were no signs of hostile forces in that part of the province. This report, however, did not cover Amelia Island since it was an accepted fact that there was a concentration of rebel forces in that region. In an effort to keep close watch on these rebels, Howard requested Andrew Atkinson, then at Fort George,[35] to send out a mounted patrol with orders to observe the activity at the northern end of the island. Atkinson hastened to comply with these orders and was able to send several interesting reports to his superior officer. In this manner the commander of the frontier was able to keep Quesada well informed on the progress made by the rebel force. As a matter of fact, Atkinson arrived on Talbot Island none too soon, for on the first day there he was able to seize a small boat loaded with supplies for the forces on Amelia Island. Unfortunately, the crew of the little vessel managed to escape seizure.[36] In one of his dispatches to Howard, he reported that there were several small boats at the site of the rebel camp which were being used to ferry supplies from the north bank of the St. Mary's River. At times these boats were seen to come directly from the wharf at St. Mary's, showing that the rebels were drawing supplies from their friends in Georgia. Atkinson was certain that he could disperse the entire rebel force with a small body of heavily armed troops assisted by a gunboat or two. He suggested that the ten militiamen under his command on Talbot Island be used as the nucleus of an attacking party. He tended, in general, to make light of the offensive strength of the enemy, but he warned that over a period of time their strength would increase, and the fortifications at the northern end of the island would be completed. If this were allowed to happen, it would require a large naval force to attack and remove the enemy.[37] His reasoning was in perfect agreement with that expressed by Las Casas in his various letters to St. Augustine.

The arrival of the *Flecha* and the *San Antonio* with supplies and reinforcements gave Howard the support needed for a large-scale drive on the rebel forces on Amelia Island. He held a conference with his assistants and Captain Saenz, the naval officer in charge of the two vessels, and a man well suited for the task of sailing his vessels in and out of the narrow waterways between the low-lying sandy islands. Howard explained his plan of attack, indicating that the two vessels were to figure heavily in the scheme. Although the captain was under direct orders to return to Havana within two weeks after landing the reinforcements and supplies and breaking the privateer blockade, he nevertheless agreed to give his support to Howard's plans, when it was pointed out that Amelia Island could not be attacked without naval support. Further meetings were held so that Howard could acquaint each officer with his particular part in the scheme of attack.

Early on the morning of August 2, Captain Saenz led the way across the bar of the St. Mary's River on the *Flecha*, closely followed by the *San Antonio* and the *Santa Mónica*, in addition to two small gunboats, each carrying fifteen regular troops. Howard was on one gunboat and John McQueen on the other. About two hundred soldiers were involved in this attack. After firing a few rounds at the half-constructed rebel breastwork, the *Santa Mónica* and the two gunboats moved in toward the beach. It was Howard's plan to land his forces from these vessels to protect the landing of the larger body from the two warships. First the schooner and then the gunboats ran firmly aground in shallow water, much to Howard's disappointment. It was finally decided to paddle the troops ashore in small canoes, and after much delay, the advance was begun on the rebel stronghold. In the meantime, the defenders, realizing that they were in no position to put up a fight and seeing that the Spanish vessels were busy attempting to extricate themselves from the shallows, scattered out along the shore where they had hidden their canoes. In short order all were seen paddling in the direction of the

Georgia shore. Either because of excitement or lack of foresight, the two warships had not been so anchored that they could fire on the fleeing rebels, and the latter managed to slip away safely.

Upon entering the little fort, Howard was met by the twenty-two Spanish soldiers who had been made prisoner at San Nicolás and who had been brought to Amelia Island before the rebels' retreat from San Nicolás. Apparently there had been some discussion about using these soldiers as hostages to prevent the Spaniards from attacking the island, but the suddenness of Howard's approach had prevented such a plan from being carried out. It was discovered that the rebels had received a few light field pieces which were being entrenched when the attack began. Howard was able to report to the governor that as far as he knew every rebel had fled across the river into Georgia.[38] Once again it appeared that Quesada's plan of falling back at the first onslaught, and then attacking suddenly with concentrated land and sea forces, had succeeded in ridding the frontier of the rebel bands. Except for the three Spaniards killed in the attack on San Nicolás, no other casualties had occurred among the Spanish forces. Unfortunately, the same was true of the rebel forces, and Quesada's desire to seize some of the French agents for identification purposes had been thwarted.

No sooner had the rebels been driven off Amelia Island than the Spanish force made preparations to return to San Vicente Ferrer and St. Augustine. Receiving no orders to the contrary, Howard prepared to abandon the island for the second time. This action which violated the orders of the governor general was taken partly because of the generally accepted opinion among the local military officials that the island could not be held, and partly because of Saenz's anxiety over news just received from Charleston. According to the Spanish consul in South Carolina there were two French frigates in the harbor with a large military force. It was rumored that these vessels were about to depart for Amelia Island to give support to the French agents. The captain did not want to risk having his two small vessels trapped in the St. Mary's River. His plan was to return to the safety of the Matanzas River and St. Augustine harbor.[39] Agreeing with his colleague, Howard informed Quesada on August 11 that, as the island could not be held by his small force without the assistance of a naval force, he had abandoned the half-completed breastwork and had returned to his headquarters at San Vicente Ferrer. He had left four mounted dragoons with provisions for several weeks, with orders to keep a patrol along the seaward side of the island and to report regularly to the Spanish forces under Andrew Atkinson on Talbot Island.[40]

Howard's explanation of the reasons for abandoning the island for a second time appeared to satisfy the governor. He had already made a careful study of the possibilities of fortifying the island. This study had been completed just before the receipt of Las Casas' letter of July 8 ordering the immediate fortification of the northern end of the island. Quesada had requested Berrio to make a thorough study of the situation and to give his opinion on the advisability of taking such a step. When the order from the governor general arrived, the governor turned a copy of it over to Berrio for his consideration. On July 24, the engineering officer gave the governor a long report which emphatically denied the feasibility of Las Casas' plans. He pointed out that the island was over sixteen miles in length, and that a fort, even a large one, at the northern extremity would not be sufficient to prevent a landing on the seaward side. He asserted that stationing nine hundred men on the island—the total number then available in East Florida—would not guarantee its retention by the Spaniards. In conclusion, he informed the governor that the orders of Las Casas could not be carried out under present conditions, as materials were not available with which to build the required fort, nor was there heavy artillery with which to defend it. As an afterthought he emphasized the complete absence of a force of laborers to build the fortifications.[41]

The report of Berrio was read and approved by the junta held on August 25. All the members agreed that it would be out of the question to try to garrison the island adequately and still hold the St. John's River posts and the castle at St. Augustine.[42] Morales, who was in command once again during a recurrence of the governor's illness, agreed with the junta. In the light of Las Casas' orders of July 8, the convalescent governor sent both Morales and Captain Saenz to Amelia Island to make a more thorough report.[43] After a complete survey of the situation, Morales wrote to Quesada from Amelia Island that he and the captain were agreed that successful defense of the northern end of the island would require a large fort and a sizable garrison with sufficient supplies and ammunition for at least three months, the period needed to build the fortifications. The captain added that as a frigate of forty-four guns could cross the bar of the St. Mary's River at high water, it would require several ships-of-the-line to defend the river mouth. He pointed out that the small armed brigs and schooners then available for that purpose were utterly inadequate. The two officers concluded that it would require most of the nine hundred men then in the province to hold the island, since the enemy could make landings not only along the sixteen miles of open seacoast, but also along the dozens of little water-courses on the landward side, where no armed vessel of any size could go."

Quesada had another reason for sending Morales to investigate conditions on Amelia Island, for it had been brought to his attention that the United States government was preparing to place buoys in the St. Mary's River in order to locate the more dangerous shoals and bars. A similar rumor had reached St. Augustine a year earlier, but later events proved it to be false.[45] At that time the governor general had ordered Quesada to oppose such a plan with all possible tact, since it violated the agreement of 1784 with the United States that either nation would take such action only with the knowledge and consent of the other. Thus, when Quesada sent Morales to Amelia Island, he had given him the additional duty of visiting Georgia to investigate these rumors. After talking with the commander of the fort at St. Mary's, Morales reported that the United States was planning to erect a fort on Cumberland Island and to mark the channel in the river so that vessels carrying building materials could reach port safely. He pointed out that marking the channel over the bar would assist Spanish vessels as well, if Spain would agree to the step.[46] When the governor general finally heard this news, he commended Quesada for his foresight in sending Morales to Georgia. He ordered the governor, however, to use every method short of force to prevent the survey of the channel, until such a step should receive the approval of the government in Madrid.[47] Here the matter was to rest for nearly a year, until an amicable settlement was finally reached between the two nations.

When forwarding these reports about Amelia Island to Havana, Quesada attempted an elaborate defense of his stand against fortifying the island. He hoped that Las Casas would change his views and accept the St. John's River as the best natural defense line for the province.[48] In reporting to the government in Spain that these important dispatches had arrived from Florida, Las Casas stated that he was still convinced of the need for a fort on the northern extremity of Amelia Island. He referred to a new set of instructions sent to Quesada to carry out the orders of July 8. He did admit, however, that he had made certain modifications in his plans for the size of the fort and for the number of men necessary to defend it.[49] These modifications, as he admitted, were a direct result of news that Spain and France were in the process of drawing up peace terms.[50] He emphasized, however, that the Florida officials had not only neglected to obey his direct orders, but also had had the temerity to argue the matter with him.[51] A change of attitude later became evident, for in a letter sent to Madrid in November the governor general reported that as he had received no recent news from Florida, it was safe to assume that the governor had managed to keep the province in a state of "pacific tranquility."[52] A little later he completely reversed his earlier stand by praising the policy of Quesada as a successful and logical one.[53] This, however, was some time after the concluding of the Franco-Spanish treaty of peace had become known in Havana and St. Augustine. Las Casas could no longer logically base his arguments for fortifying the island on the expectation that French agents might make another attack. Nearly twenty years later, when two attempts were made to seize Amelia Island in order to "cede" it to the United States, it seemed that Las Casas' warning was about to come true. Only the cession of both the Floridas to the United States brought an end to attempts to seize this key island.[54]

It is of interest to note that upon receiving the news of Howard's success in driving the rebels back to Georgia, Las Casas made certain recommendations to the Spanish government. He based his suggestions partly upon Quesada's requests that some recognition be given to the work done by the lesser military figures in East Florida. Notably the governor general urged that Howard be promoted to the rank of full colonel, that both Andrew Atkinson and John McQueen be accorded recognition for their outstanding work, and that Captain Saenz be suitably rewarded, even though he had violated Las Casas' orders about returning at once to Havana.[55] There were several other lesser military and political figures mentioned as having shown particular enterprise in carrying out their special assignments. Notable, however, for its absence from the list of the deserving was the name of Bartolomé Morales, the acting governor. Even his friend, Governor Quesada, failed to mention him as meriting a reward.

CHAPTER X

PUNISHMENT OF THE REBELS

WHEN HE RECEIVED the news of the attacks on Juana and San Nicolás and of the successful seizure of Amelia Island, Quesada found himself confronted with a difficult problem, one not directly connected with the military defense of the province. It was evident that a number of citizens of East Florida had been involved directly or indirectly in these ventures. Evidence in the possession of the governor made the identification of Lang, Plowden, Wagnon, and their friends certain beyond a doubt. Lang had admitted in writing that he was acting as the commander of all rebel forces along the St. Mary's River. McIntosh was known to have permitted the rebels to use his boats to cross the St. John's River. Later, he had taken an active part in the capture of San Nicolás. He had been seen in the rebel camp by Maas when the latter successfully penetrated the rebel defenses. Plowden and Wagnon had both fled to Georgia and refused to return to East Florida to answer the charges against them. All these men had left families and property behind in the province. Quesada could find no excuse for their conduct and his duty seemed clear. He was determined to seize their property and make an example of them for the rest of the American settlers in the province.

On July 16 Quesada issued a decree in which he declared that a group of "Anglo-Americans" under the protection of France and associated with a band of wandering French agents had joined forces with a certain number of vassals of Spain.[1] He went on to name two of these vassals, Daniel William Lane and his son William, who had already been apprehended by Howard when they tried to join the rebels at San Nicolás. He than named Lang, Plowden, Jones, and McIntosh as others already under arms against Spain. Howard was ordered to find and arrest these men. In addition, he was ordered to collect their belongings and send them under guard to St. Augustine, where the governor and his council would decide how to dispose of them. Bernardo Joseph Segui, a captain in the urban militia, then at San Nicolás, was detailed to begin an extensive inventory of all nonmovable goods belonging to the rebels named in the decree. On the presumption that the families of the rebels could speak no Spanish, Dimas Cortés was assigned as interpreter to aid Segui in his duties. The governor stressed the need for speed and discretion in drawing up these inventories.[2]

[1] For notes to chap. x, see pp. 171–172.

A copy of the decree was sent to Howard to inform him what he was to do about the rebels.[3] Acting on these orders, the colonel sent several scouts to visit the homes of those named to find out if any of them were still in the province. Although no trace of them was found, Howard determined to keep a number of the militia on constant watch, for he felt certain that the rebels would attempt to communicate with their families along the St. John's River. As for seizing their property, he pointed out that neither Plowden nor Wagnon owned anything outside the bounds of St. Augustine. After some investigation, Howard recommended that the governor add the names of George Fillet and Joseph Mills, both sons-in-law of William Lane, to his list of suspected rebels. He was not able to lay his hands on either of them or on any of their belongings.[4]

A second copy of the decree and full instructions were sent to Segui at San Nicolás. He acknowledged the receipt of Quesada's orders on July 22, at which time he appointed a second interpreter and assistant, one Juan Machogui, a sailor on the gunboat *San Pablo*.[5] According to Segui's interpretation of his orders, he was to collect all available supplies of grain and livestock on the rebels' plantations, as well as all slaves. These were to be sent to the governor at St. Augustine pending public sale. He therefore made arrangements to store these perishable foodstuffs at San Nicolás to await water transportation south. The only vessel then available was the *Santa Mónica* under the command of Captain Verazaluze, who agreed to undertake the necessary voyages between San Nicolás and St. Augustine.

The first plantation visited by Segui and his assistants was that of Jones, which was approximately half a mile from San Nicolás. A careful check was made of the contents of the barnyard and grain fields before the inventory of the house was undertaken. A full day was needed for Segui and his men to make a thorough job of the checking. When the inventory was completed, Segui ordered Nathaniel Hall, a captain in the rural militia, to look after the plantation and to keep watch for Jones' possible return.[6] Two days later, he visited "Egan" plantation, the home of the two Lanes, some three miles from San Nicolás, and on the next day he was at the Lee plantation. A few days later, he went a little farther afield to visit "Spring Hill,"[7] the home of the McIntosh family. Each time, after the inventory was completed, Segui followed the plan he had adopted at the Jones house and left the plantation in the care of a reliable person who assumed full responsibility for everything enumerated in the official list. Sometimes, the person left in charge was a member of the family of the suspected rebel. In this way Lee's home was left in the charge of his wife, Jane Clementina, and the home of Lane in the care of his brother, Peers. Segui wanted to leave the McIntosh plantation in the charge of Mrs. McIntosh, but he discovered that she had fled the day before to St. Mary's, taking all the family valuables with her.[8]

A second set of orders came from St. Augustine to supplement the earlier list of rebels. Several well-known citizens of the province, including George Knolls, John Dudley, William Ashley, James Leslie, and Francis Goodwin, all former members of the rural or the urban militia, appeared on the new list. These men were suspected either of direct participation in the rebel attacks on Juana and San Nicolás or of having given moral support to those actually involved. As a result, Segui was ordered to seize and inventory their property, and Howard was requested to apprehend the suspects. Since their plantations lay within six miles of San Nicolás, the task was a fairly simple one for Segui. The governor's instructions to seize the men did not remain secret, for all managed to elude Howard's forces and to slip across the St. John's River. When Segui reached the houses of Knolls and Leslie, he found that the former had succeeded in escaping with his slaves and livestock, and that the latter had attempted to remove some of his blacksmith equipment.[9] In only one home did Sequi find any truly suspicious material. While searching Goodwin's plantation at "Travers," a pair of United States captain's epaulets, a selection of books printed in English, and a packet of letters and papers in English were discovered. Segui sent all these items to St. Augustine with his latest report on the progress of the inventories.[10]

In the meantime, Howard had begun to inventory the items left behind by the rebels when they fled from San Nicolás. This was completed on July 31, with the help of several of his assistants. Eighteen of the forty or more horses seized at the fort were found to carry distinguishable brands. These were auctioned off to the nine loyal members of the militia then at the fort, each of whom bought two animals. Apparently this policy of auctioning off the property of rebels was one that pleased Quesada, for he adopted it later when disposing of other items of seized property.

When these reports and inventories reached St. Augustine, the governor and his council held a lengthy meeting in order to read each carefully. After some discussion, it was decided that the work of Segui should be continued and that he should be sent a list of the names of all

American settlers under the slightest suspicion of having sympathies with the rebels. He was ordered to arrest them, impound their goods, and forward copies of the inventories to St. Augustine.[11] The governor was worried over the difficulty of determining the innocence or guilt of the American settlers. He hesitated to accept as truth all the rumors about the complicity of certain of the citizens of the province. He wrote Las Casas that it was virtually impossible to determine with accuracy the number of those who were guilty of having given moral support to the rebellion. As he pointed out, many of the settlers tried to settle ancient grudges against their neighbors by spreading false and malicious rumors about their lack of loyalty. Some used this method to try to get possession of valuable lands belonging to their neighbors. The care and secrecy with which the rebels had developed their plan of attack made it most difficult to determine who was really involved. What gave Quesada the greatest concern was the report that several citizens of Spanish descent were guilty of conniving with the American settlers. He stressed the need to progress slowly and carefully in arresting suspects, lest others of greater guilt become alarmed and flee the province with valuable evidence. The arrest of Lane and Lee was mentioned as well as the detention of the wives of Plowden and Wagnon and the seizure of the movable goods of those definitely linked with the attacks on Juana and San Nicolás. The governor emphasized the need for additional troops to overawe the local populace and thus convince those of wavering loyalty of the rashness of aiding the rebels. He wrote, "The presence of soldiers will make loyal subjects of tepid rebels."[12] As a final argument against arbitrary arrests, he pointed out that the jail in St. Augustine was too small for such a policy, and that he did not have sufficient troops to guard an outdoor camp housing a large number of prisoners.[13]

The governor's council recommended that he issue orders to send a reliable member of the militia, preferably Andrew Atkinson, to round up all Negro slaves then in the St. John's River region who were supposedly the property of the rebels. A careful investigation was to be made to determine their true owners, to discover if any were in reality runaways from Georgia.[14] Quesada agreed to this suggestion and wrote to Atkinson, who was to go to Georgia to confer with the local authorities in Camden County in an effort to obtain a complete list and full description of all recent runaway slaves. In this way it was hoped that the ownership of some of the slaves in East Florida could be established. Quesada hoped that this attempt to return runaway slaves to their rightful owners might convince the local authorities in Georgia of the advantages of a more conciliatory attitude toward East Florida problems. Acting on these orders, Atkinson made the trip to St. Mary's where he held a series of conversations with the local, state, and federal officials, but all to no avail. His visit began under difficult circumstances, for he was set upon, beaten, and robbed by a band of brigands on the outskirts of the town.[15]

After further study of the problem of the rebels, Quesada and his council issued a lengthy decree in which all those previously mentioned as rebels were now declared to be guilty of treason and to be proscribed. An additional list of twenty-two names was included, all suspected of aiding the rebel cause.[16] Those named were of American origin and were residents of the St. John's River region. Segui was ordered to seize their property, make further inventories, and send certain of the movable goods to St. Augustine at the earliest possible opportunity. He was urged, however, to be careful to keep these goods separated from the property of those identified earlier as rebels. Both he and Howard were to make every effort to apprehend all those on the new list.[17] An attempt was made to keep the contents of this decree secret in order to catch some of these people red-handed. When Segui received his copy, he made haste to visit the homes of those named, and he was successful in finding and arresting four suspects.[18] These men were taken to San Nicolás where they were placed in a small cell pending the receipt of further orders from the governor.

As the days passed, additional information was received in St. Augustine which enabled Quesada to determine the guilt or innocence of certain other settlers under suspicion. As soon as each case was settled, orders were sent to Segui to seize and inventory the property and to Howard to try to apprehend the individual. The governor made frequent requests for grain and food products to be sent to St. Augustine. The brig *Manolita,* commanded by Captain Manuel Marixal, left San Nicolás on August 16 with a cargo of grain, livestock, chickens, and household goods taken from the plantations of several of the rebels. Additional cargoes of foodstuffs, mostly from the McIntosh plantation, were sent to St. Augustine on September 1 and 6, each with a carefully drawn inventory. These supplies were received at a time when the need for them was great, and the governor expressed gratification at Segui's conduct.[19]

When the strain of long working hours began to tell on Segui, the governor sent instructions that Timothy Hollingsworth, Robert Pritchard, and Isaac Wheeler were to assist him in carrying out the inventory of rebel property.[20] Unfortunately, Hollingsworth, the most energetic of the three, was unable to read or write, and this added to Segui's difficulties. He was extremely methodical and increased his own labors by attempting to keep an accurate tally of all supplies consumed by himself, his assistants, and the crew of the gunboat *Santo Tomás* which was under his supervision. He kept careful count of each animal slaughtered, of each pound of corn consumed, and of the number of men fed at each meal. He went as far as to give the exact weight of meat consumed each week.

A list of eight new suspects was sent to Segui on October 2, with instructions to seize and inventory their goods. All had been seized earlier at the order of the governor, and two were reported to have admitted taking part in the attack on Fort San Nicolás. Their confessions were supposed to implicate the other six.[21] The work of inventorying the goods of these men continued until October 15, when Segui informed the governor that he had exhausted the list of names. A lengthy report was prepared by Segui and Howard in order to present all the information collected in the three months since the first executive decree. When this document was received in St. Augustine, the governor met with his council to discuss the new developments. According to Howard, at least six members of his militia, not named in the governor's order of August 3, were known to have taken part in the attacks on Juana and San Nicolás and were now living in Georgia. Howard's information implicated an additional twelve men, some members of the militia and some of the regular army. Among those listed was Captain Timothy Hollingsworth, long held in great esteem by Quesada. It was quite a shock to the governor to learn how many persons had been involved in the rebellion and how many more had expressed sympathy for those actually involved. The council decided that Segui should go to the houses of the men named by Howard in order to impound and inventory their personal effects.[22] The evidence against Hollingsworth seemed sufficient to warrant the seizure of his property.[23] It required nearly a month for Segui to complete these additional inventories, the last one, completed on December 11, being that of the property of Captain Hollingsworth on his plantation, "Newly United."

In compliance with the governor's orders, Howard made haste to visit the homes of the twelve new suspects, in an effort to seize them before they could flee to Georgia. The rapidity with which this action was carried out and the secrecy surrounding the governor's order resulted in the capture of all twelve. They were sent to St. Augustine where they were imprisoned on the charge of complicity in the rebellion and intelligence with the enemy.

While Howard was attempting to apprehend various suspected citizens and Segui was busy inventorying their personal effects, the governor was handling the problem of the disposal of rebel property in and around St. Augustine. He ordered the attachment of the property of Plowden and Wagnon in addition to Plowden's house, which served as a home for both families. José de Ortega, councilor for the assessor general, was appointed to draw up an inventory of the contents of Plowden's house. This assignment was completed under difficulties, since the two wives refused to coöperate with the officer, claiming that the slaves and most of the household goods belonged to them and not to their husbands.[24] Some time later, the governor ordered a public sale of the belongings of the Wagnon family.[25]

Another problem facing Quesada was the future disposal of the rebels' property being sent to St. Augustine by both Howard and Segui. The governor discussed the matter with his council, who recommended that public auctions be held. The proceeds of these sales were to be placed in the royal treasury and then drawn upon to help defray the expenses of the investigations, inventories, and public sales. The governor agreed to these recommendations and ordered the first auction held on August 22, when a large collection of livestock and poultry was sold for the sum of 178 pesos.[26] A second public sale of livestock and poultry was held a month later. It became apparent, however, that some better system was needed for an equitable distribution of the rebels' property. The governor was informed that nearly all the goods on sale had been sold to a handful of wealthy buyers who could afford to offer high prices. In this way the public did not benefit in the slightest from the sales, and if an attempt was made to purchase the rebels' property from the new owners, the prices demanded were extremely high. To prevent this practice, a decree was made public which established certain regulations under which sales were to be conducted. Several appraisers and auctioneers were named who were to set a rigid price scale for all rebel property then in the local warehouses. When later sales were held, the auctioneers were to limit the quantity purchased by each customer, and in this way it was hoped that the distribution of goods would be more equitable.[27] Three days later, a price list of goods for sale was posted in the town. In spite of these rules, nearly all the harvested grain sold at the November sales was purchased by Francisco Felipe Fatio, one of the wealthiest landowners in the province. He agreed, however, to store the grain in his granaries and then release it from time to time for public sale at current prices. In this way he hoped both to stabilize the grain market and to prevent periods of want.

An all-day auction of horses, saddles, farm equipment, foodstuffs, and household goods was held on November 25 under the new regulations, and this sale netted 1,960 pesos.[28] In general, when a large herd of horses reached St. Augustine, the better mounts were withheld from public sale, since it was the wish of the governor that the militia should have the first selection. The animals thus withheld were usually branded and then sent to San Vicente Ferrer for distribution among the loyal militiamen. The last major sale of the year was held on December 24, when a large number of pigs were put up for disposal.

The disposition of the slaves found on the rebels' plantations was difficult, since it frequently took time to establish legal ownership. Relatives of several of the rebels attempted to prove ownership of the slaves on the basis of bills of sale made out in the United States at some earlier time. It was necessary for the governor to settle each case individually. As a result of these delays, the slave sales were not held until the next year, and many of the transfers of ownership were not made final for several years.[29]

Some wives and mothers of rebels attempted to obtain the return of part of the seized property on the ground that these items were their property and had been brought by them to East Florida at an earlier date. Decisions in some of these cases were still pending at the turn of the century. Another series of protracted arguments arose over the question of the debts incurred by those involved in assisting in inventorying the rebels' property. The captain of the *Manolita* attempted to collect back payments for the time and labor he had expended in carrying cargoes of goods to St. Augustine.[30] Even the accounts of Segui were carefully investigated when Enrique White replaced Quesada as governor, and the captain had to go to great lengths to defend his activities successfully.[31] An executive investigation revealed several gross irregularities in the treatment accorded the slaves confiscated from the rebels. It was discovered that some of those in charge of the slaves had made use of their labor on their own plantations.

The final and in some ways the most perplexing problem arising from the rebellion was the question of the disposition of the rebels captured at various times either along the frontier or in St. Augustine itself. Quesada and his successor, Enrique White,[32] both men of considerable circumspection, realized that the evidence against some of the prisoners was purely circumstantial and of little weight. As a result, some suspects were released immediately, while others were detained for a period of weeks or even months. Apparently each case was heard by the governor individually, and the verdict was rendered at the conclusion of the hearing. Those who were found guilty of giving comfort to the rebels were fined various sums and usually had all their property confiscated. All were permitted to remain in the province, although some decided to return to the United States. A few suffered the revocation of their land grants and were ordered to leave the province. Men such as Lang, Plowden, Wagnon, McIntosh, and Jones, who had fled the province earlier and who had taken an active part in the attacks on Juana and San Nicolás, were declared to have forfeited all goods, lands, and crops to the government.

It appears that the so-called "crimes" of some of these men were soon forgotten, for by the end of the century, they were once again living in the province and holding positions of respect. Both Lang and Hollingsworth received pardons from White or from Kindelan. According to certain official documents in the first decade of the new century, these two men were residents of St. Augustine and owned large tracts of land as well as prosperous farms. Lang was allowed to return to his plantation, "White House," on the St. Mary's River, which was finally sold for $5,000 in 1817.[33] Apparently none of the prisoners suffered bodily punishment for their participation in the rebellion of 1795, partly because of the relative ease with which the uprising was suppressed and partly because of the conclusion of a permanent peace agreement between Spain and France.

CHAPTER XI

REAPPEARANCE OF ELIJAH CLARK

WHILE THE REBEL attacks were taking place along the St. John's River and the struggle for Amelia Island was developing, the Spanish authorities became aware that their old enemy, General Elijah Clark, had again begun to interest himself in a scheme hostile to their interests. Evidence had reached Quesada purporting to prove that the schemes of the rebellious Floridians were either inspired by French agents, or were being so identified in order to cloak them with a show of legality under the laws of war. It had been known for at least two years that Clark was sympathetic to the French republican cause and that he had received a commission from Mangourit. The Spaniards were unable, however, definitely to associate Clark either with the plans of Lang and Plowden or with the landings on Amelia Island. A lengthy report made late in May by Morales did not mention Clark in connection with the reported plans of the French.[1]

A second report, little more than a week later, indicated that Clark might be deeply involved in a scheme to attack East Florida by way of the Indian lands across the Altamaha River, in conjunction with a French naval force. Morales wrote that he had been informed of frequent meetings between Clark and Lang in the vicinity of Coleraine and Temple, but that he was uncertain whether the two men had decided upon mutual coöperation. Furthermore, he was unable to determine just what were the immediate plans of each.[2] The acting governor was certain, however, that Clark had associated himself with the French cause. The old general was reported to have stated publicly that he was planning to coöperate with a fleet of French privateers and warships in carrying out the original plans of Genêt, this time with the active support of the National Convention. Clark was supposed to have agreed to raise and arm a large force of Indians beyond the Altamaha River in order to attack St. Augustine from the headwaters of St. Mary's River.[3] In this way he could cross St. John's River somewhere to the southwest of the line of Spanish forts. It was rumored also that he had met with Abner Hammond to secure promises of certain necessary provisions and stores from Hammond's warehouse at St. Mary's. According to Morales' information, Clark hoped to use these goods in supplying the needs of his Indian allies and in erecting small forts south of St. Mary's River.[4]

---

[1] For notes to chap. xi, see pp. 172–174.

While Morales was attempting to solve the mystery of Clark's rumored activities, a dispatch arrived from Howard with unpleasant news. Bands of roving Indians, possibly supporters of either Clark or Lang, were on the loose between the St. Mary's and St. John's rivers where they were robbing and generally terrorizing travelers using the road from San Vicente Ferrer to the north. They were reported to have robbed several citizens of East Florida, stolen several horses, and killed a few head of cattle for food. Small bands of Indians were reported to have raided the barns and granaries on some of the plantations in this region.[5] Coincidentally, a group of French agents, possibly associated with Clark's schemes, were reported to be active farther west among the Creeks. Rumors reached Governor White in Pensacola that an assault might be made on his post early in November, if the attack on East Florida were successful. His report to Carondelet expressed apprehension lest this attack occur before he had time to make needed repairs.[6] A short time later, word was received from the fort at St. Mark's that many of the Lower Creek chiefs were pleading with the Spanish commander for arms, supplies, and food to enable them to drive all Americans including Clark from their lands west of the Altamaha and Oconee rivers.[7] Such information was highly pleasing to Carondelet who was always on the lookout for some way to stir up the Creeks against the United States.

This situation in 1795 was like that of the summer and fall of 1794, when the Indians had offered to help the Spaniards drive Clark back across the Oconee River. In neither case, however, did they actually take up arms against the old general. Nevertheless, Howard felt that Clark's very presence on the St. Mary's River encouraged the Indians to indulge in looting and theft in American as well as Spanish territory.[8] Thus Clark remained a threat to the peace of East Florida, even if he did not actually join forces with the refugees from that province. If the followers of Clark and Lang were to combine, Howard feared that the situation might take a turn for the worse. A well-directed and concentrated attack along the frontier might encourage many of the lukewarm patriots to join the enemy, and then the initiative would pass to the opposition. This possibility had worried both Howard and Quesada during the past two years.

Morales, as acting governor, appeared to agree with Howard, although he seemed convinced that the French element would cease to play an important part in frontier affairs. Genêt's successor, Fauchet, had announced his intention to observe strictly every phase of American neutrality. There had been much speculation, however, among those interested in the French schemes of 1794 whether Fauchet had actually replaced Genêt as minister plenipotentiary. In the spring of 1795 it was rumored that Genêt was once more the official French representative in Philadelphia, and that he had been authorized by his government to reopen the Florida and Louisiana affairs.[9] As has been pointed out, little attention had been paid to Fauchet's proclamation of March 6, 1794, prohibiting further activity of French agents within the bounds of the United States.[10] When it was reported to Quesada that the French agents were attempting to raise forces among the French emigrés from Haiti and Martinique, then living in Georgia,[11] he wrote to the Spanish representatives in Philadelphia requesting them to report this breach of American neutrality to the Congress and to the President.[12]

Jaudenes, complying with Quesada's suggestion, handed a copy of the governor's dispatch to Randolph with a request for the earliest possible action by the federal government. The secretary of state replied a few days later that he had already sent an express to Augusta demanding a complete report on the Clark expedition. He did not, however, give assurances that the United States would take direct action against French agents.[13] Later, the Spanish representatives reported to the governor that they had received little but verbal assurances from Randolph. They doubted that the federal forces then in the south were of sufficient strength to take the field against Clark and his numerous friends.[14] The popularity of the old general in Georgia and South Carolina was far too great for reliance to be placed on the loyalty of the state militias in the event of an open break.[15]

It is significant that the presence of Clark during the Juana incident was not mentioned. There was at least one report that he was in the hinterland trying to raise supporters for his schemes. According to this evidence, he could not have been with Lang during the assault upon the Spanish outpost.[16] As a matter of fact, as has been mentioned previously, Sergeant Jonathan McCoulloth, one of the prisoners taken at Juana and later paroled by Lang, reported having heard some of his captors discuss the possibility that Clark might join them at a later date with a large force recruited in the lower Oconee region. According to the same informant, Lang himself had mentioned a force of fifty Frenchmen supposedly under the command of Abner Hammond and coming from Camden County.[17] This may have been the same force that Clark was reported to be raising, since he and Abner Hammond were rumored to be closely associated in some scheme to attack East Florida, making use of the arms and materials collected during the previous year near the St. Mary's River. The other group of 500 French soldiers mentioned by Lang in the presence of his prisoners probably referred to the sizable force of veterans which the French commander on Haiti was rumored to be sending to assist in the projected attacks on Florida and Louisiana.

When Quesada was well enough to resume his duties, he sent an account of the attack on San Nicolás to Jaudenes and Viar. He mentioned the possibility that Clark might be the actual leader of the expedition, even though he was not in East Florida at the time of the assault. Quesada seemed convinced that the rebels hoped to draw the attention of the French government to their venture by hiding under the protection of Clark's French commission of the previous year. According to information reaching St. Augustine, the rebel force scattered by Howard was being reassembled by Clark for a new attack on the frontier. Quesada urged that this information be passed along to the secretary of state.[18] Yet a short time later, when writing to Las Casas about the Amelia Island affair, Quesada failed to mention Clark at all, identifying the participants as "French Republicans."[19] A second report written a few days later again omitted any mention of Clark or of his supposed support of these French schemes.[20] It should be noted, however, that the Spanish officials were very apt to brand anyone opposed to the theory of absolute monarchy as "republicans" and to associate everyone considered a rebel with the new government of France. In general, Quesada appeared to be as uncertain about the activities of Clark as was Morales.

Some time after Howard's successful venture against the rebel position on Amelia Island, Clark again made his presence known along the frontier. According to Morales, then inspecting the frontier fortifications at the request of the governor, the old general had just completed a march of "more than 400 miles" to reach St. Mary's River.[21] Morales questioned the validity of any commission under which Clark might claim to be acting. He had just received the news of peace negotiations between France and Spain from the French consul in Savannah.[22] Once hostilities were ended, Clark's commission from Genêt would be worthless. In the second place, Morales questioned the sincerity of Clark's claim to be inspired by the humanitarian ideals of the French Revolution and by the desire to free the Floridians from the yoke of Spain. On the contrary, he asserted that the general and his men were activated by a desire to despoil East Florida. It was rumored that there was a large supply of silver in the chests of the royal treasury in St. Augustine.[23] Obviously whoever had started this rumor was not in the position to know about the frequent dispatches from St. Augustine to Havana and Mexico, pleading for additional funds with which to pay the back salaries due the soldiers in the various regiments.

As in the past, the reported reappearance of Clark in the frontier region caused consternation in official circles, since it came immediately after the successful campaign against the rebels. It seemed as though the labors of Howard and his companions might be undone if fresh hostile forces should succeed in penetrating the Spanish lines. The situation appeared critical when it was definitely established that Clark was on the march with a force of unknown size. Morales, as acting commander of the forces along the St. Mary's River and on Amelia Island, was the first to receive this news. He recognized the need of some sort of naval support if the enemy should make an attempt to cross the river below Coleraine. An appeal was sent to Captain Saenz, who was still in Florida waters with the *Flecha* and *San Antonio,* requesting his support in defending the lower river crossings. He was warned, however, that once his ships entered over the bar, they would run the risk of being trapped if a French fleet arrived.[24]

Although Captain Saenz was willing to comply with this request, he was alarmed at the possibility of the arrival of enemy ships. He asked Morales for supplementary information on the size and type of Clark's forces, the direction from which the attack was expected, and the number of French warships rumored to be in Charleston harbor. He included information contained in a late dispatch from the north that one of these vessels was preparing to sail for the Florida coast.[25] Morales' reply was neither adequate nor informative. He was unable to give the direction of Clark's attack or the forces involved. As a matter of fact, he could not say for certain if there would be any attack at all. He asked Saenz to send on any information that he might receive from agents in South Carolina.[26] The captain complied by forwarding a copy of the letter mentioned in his earlier note to Morales. This turned out to be a dispatch from the British consul in Charleston to Quesada which had passed through Saenz's hands. In it the consul gave a complete account of information dealing with Clark and his activities. According to this letter, the general was experiencing the greatest difficulty in raising new recruits, probably because of the discouraging outcome of the "republican" attempt to seize and hold Amelia Island. The consul indicated that there was no need to fear further activity on the part of Clark and his French friends.[27]

Saenz was not certain that these encouraging reports about Clark's personnel difficulties necessarily meant the end of the threat of a French fleet from the north or from the islands to the south. After deciding that this potential danger did exist, he informed Morales that he would be unable to offer him support along the St. Mary's River. He intended to obey the orders of Las Casas and return to Havana as soon as possible.[28] This decision to return to Havana was apparently carried out, since no further mention was made of his presence in St. Augustine. A large packet of dispatches from East Florida, including copies of these letters between Saenz and Morales, reached Las Casas shortly before October 20. It seems likely that Saenz brought these letters to Havana on the *Flecha.*[29]

Some time in September, Clark moved his forces from the lower reaches of the Altamaha River and crossed the Satilla River. Once across this river, he penetrated the region west of Coleraine and apparently established headquarters in an area which he claimed belonged neither to the United States nor to Spain.[30] This was west of the line drawn in the treaty of 1790 separating the state of Georgia from the lands of the Creek Indians. That the Indians believed he was actually encroaching on their lands is shown by their immediate appeal to the Spanish commander in St. Mark's for a supply of arms and ammunition with which to drive the Americans out of their hunting grounds.[31] Clark's claim that these Indian lands were possessed by neither of the powers was similar to that made by him a year earlier when he attempted to establish his Trans-Oconee settlement. However, as he was now much closer to East Florida, the Spanish officials took a livelier interest in his activities.

Quesada, now fully recovered from his recurrent attacks of fever, told his council that Clark's renewed activity was the result of the incorporation of the remnants of Lang's rebel band with the forces from Georgia. He had been informed by an agent in Georgia that Clark, Abner Hammond, Lang, and several other rebels had met on September 2 near Coleraine in the home of Major Thomas Skrine.[32] After a hearty dinner attended by the local magistrates and militia officers of Camden County, a secret meeting was held at which Clark donned the liberty cap and took official command of the joint venture. The leaders of the various groups agreed to follow him in an assault upon East Florida. They would adopt the French cause and seek the protection of the French flag.[33] With such evidence available, the governor was convinced that he had sufficient proof to warrant sending a letter to Georgia requesting the local officials to take steps to prevent further recruiting among the Georgians and to attempt to restrain the forces already raised.[34]

A similar letter was sent to Jaudenes, expressing great concern over the latest developments, since it was feared that Governor Mathews would do little more now than he had done in 1794. Quesada declared that the governor of Georgia was far too friendly with Clark to take drastic action without federal intervention. It was left to Jaudenes to persuade the secretary of state that he should use his authority to see that Mathews blocked further assistance to Clark.[35] It was hoped that Mathews could be coerced into action by the forces of the federal government. As early as 1793, at the insistence of Washington and Knox, Mathews had taken cognizance of the activities of French agents within Georgia. A year later, during the development of the Trans-Oconee scheme, federal insistence had forced Mathews to take drastic action. To a lesser degree, the same had been true during the rebel activities against Juana, San Nicolás, and Amelia Island. Thus Quesada had good reason to believe that the federal government might force Mathews to take the steps necessary to check Clark's newest activities.

The governor urged the Spanish representatives to keep in constant communication with Washington and his Cabinet, promising to forward all available information. As a result, a steady stream of dispatches flowed back and forth between Philadelphia and St. Augustine. In his letters Quesada gave more details than he did in his reports to Las Casas. He expressed particular annoyance at the treatment accorded his émissaries sent to deliver protests to the local authorities in southern Georgia. Here they received frequent snubs, were often delayed, sometimes insulted and roughly handled, and even threatened with grave bodily harm. Quesada was convinced that many local officials, appointed or elected, either were actually assisting the troublemakers or were entirely in sympathy with their cause. He was certain that one of the chief offenders was the commanding officer of the Camden County militia, Captain Randolph, who had often been accused of acts of hostility against the Spaniards.[36] At least two of the captain's militiamen had been identified as members of the attacking party at Juana on June 29.[37] The governor went even further in his accusations, for he declared that both the commander of the federal troops in St. Mary's, Captain Abimael Nicholl, and the judge of the inferior court of Camden County, George Pendleton, were completely prejudiced in their attitude toward the East Florida rebels. He asserted that appeals of Spain for justice met with little sympathy in the chambers of Judge Pendleton.[38] The refugee rebels were permitted to walk freely about the streets of St. Mary's, even though the stories of their robberies and murders in East Florida were public knowledge.[39]

Like Morales, Quesada could find no legal basis for the claims of Clark and the rebel leaders that their men were in reality French soldiers. If they had actually expatriated themselves by swearing allegiance to the French Republic, then upon their return to the territory of the United States, a neutral in the European conflict, they should have been interned as armed foreign soldiers. As this had not been done, he assumed that the United States did not recognize them as French soldiers.

He urged Jaudenes to stress this point in his communications with the secretary of state and to deny that France had ever offered these rebels and adventurers any encouragement or promise of political recognition. If the federal government could be convinced of these points, then there would be no question of recognizing the validity of the rebels' claim to the protection of France, once they fell into the hands of the federal government.[40]

Writing to Jaudenes a little later, Quesada urged him to insist that the federal government force the Georgia officials to round up not only the Spanish citizens in refuge there, but also all Americans who, through active participation or by offering asylum to the rebels, were involved in the activities against Spain. He encouraged Jaudenes to persevere until Randolph agreed to send orders to the federal forces in Georgia to march against the enemy. In this way the uncoöperative attitude of Governor Mathews would be circumvented and the situation resolved. Jaudenes was to lay most of the blame for the success of the rebel attacks on the Spanish posts on Mathews, for, as Quesada reasoned, if the governor of Georgia had complied with earlier requests to return the refugees to East Florida, there would have been no armed rebellion. By permitting these men to stay in Georgia, Mathews encouraged them to believe that the local authorities really favored their schemes to attack East Florida.[41]

Morales, never one to be particularly diplomatic in his language, had sent several very unflattering characterizations of Governor Mathews to Las Casas. He declared that although the governor of Georgia was personally responsible for the many insults to Spanish authority, he continued to maintain his innocence. At one point the acting governor said of Mathews, "He is weak in will power and lacking in energy, as he does not have the troops to make himself respected."[42] Ironically enough these very words, to a lesser degree, fitted Morales himself.

However feeble may have been Mathews' efforts to curb the enthusiasm of some of his Georgia friends, they appeared to be enough to satisfy his own conscience. He no doubt desired to have the entire matter rest there, hoping that as conditions changed, the difficulties would resolve themselves. But in this he was doomed to disappointment, just as he had been in 1794. Once again he was to feel the full weight of federal disapproval. When the news of the passage of the Georgia Land Act of 1795 reached Philadelphia, all official eyes were turned to this new problem in Georgia. Washington and his Cabinet were greatly aroused by this speculative action of doubtful legality. The news of this act, together with the memory of Mathews' inactivity during the Oconee incident in 1794 and the subsequent reports of the events of the summer of 1795, was enough to convince the secretary of state that the time was rapidly approaching when the federal government would have to intervene once again in the Georgia frontier troubles. Jaudenes and Viar continued to shower Randolph with the latest accounts of events as reported to them from St. Augustine. These reports included not only accounts of the activities of Clark, but also those of the rebels, of French privateers and their illegal seizures and sales, of runaway slaves, of illegal navigation of the St. Mary's River, and many other items of lesser interest.

Some of the federal officials in Georgia were alarmed by the tension in the southern part of the state. They sent dispatches to Philadelphia as well as to the state officials in Augusta. Colonel Gaither, the commander of the federal troops in the state, wrote to Mathews in the middle of August informing him of the role being played by Americans in the rebel attacks on East Florida. He pointed out that some were actually enrolled in the militia regiment of Captain Randolph. He further declared that his powers from the federal government gave him authority to request the Spanish authorities to arrest and surrender any American soldier found in East Florida.[43] As was to be expected, Mathews expressed surprise to learn that members of the Georgia militia were deserting to help in the rebellion. He urged Colonel Gaither to continue his investigation.[44] Mathews also mentioned receiving a dispatch from James Seagrove about the rebellion in East Florida. He mentioned his orders issued that very day to Captain Jonas Fauche requiring him to raise some of his detachment of mounted dragoons. Fauche was then to hurry to Camden County to assist the local magistrates in maintaining law and order along the St. Mary's River.[45] Mathews neglected to inform the federal commander at St. Mary's that he had received the first dispatch from the secretary of state on the subject of preventing citizens of the United States from aiding the rebels. Mathews' next letter was to Camden County to inform the local magistrates of Fauche's mission. He warned them, however, that the military force was not to be under their command. The governor requested that a copy of this letter be sent to St. Augustine at the earliest opportunity to show Quesada that the state of Georgia was taking the necessary measures to maintain peace along the St. Mary's River.[46]

For some reason the letter sent by Morales to Mathews on July 6, protesting against the attitude of the citizens of southern Georgia, was delayed in transmission to Augusta and was not received until early in September. Mathews' reply denied any previous knowledge of the attack on Juana and pointed out that those taking part were citizens of Florida and not of Georgia. He denied that any of these rebels had crossed into Georgia with the booty and prisoners seized at the Spanish post. He suggested that they were still hiding in the northern part of the Spanish province. All the steps taken to prevent any movement of forces to East Florida were mentioned by Mathews, and he included a copy of his orders to Fauche.[47] Two months later, in defending his actions in a letter to Las Casas, the governor of Georgia wrote, "My orders to Captain Fauche were given the 24th day of August which was seventeen days previous to my receiving any information from East Florida, on the subject of the insurrection."[48] This was indeed a case of splitting hairs, although Mathews was correct in that he had actually received no information directly from St. Augustine and had dispatched Fauche and his dragoons to Camden County on the basis of the news contained in the letters from Gaither and Seagrove. Yet the impression that Mathews wished to give the governor general was that the very first news received about the rebellion had come after he had sent Fauche to the south. If this had been true, then the orders to Fauche would prove how eager Mathews was to prevent any trouble from occurring along the frontier. It must also be borne in mind that at least one of the letters from the secretary of state was received in Augusta before August 24.[49] It is very doubtful that Las Casas was taken in by Mathews' professions of innocence.

CHAPTER XII

PEACE RESTORED

As soon as word was circulated that Clark was definitely planning a second move against East Florida, some of the former rebels seized the opportunity to renew their attacks across the St. Mary's River. They crossed the river in small groups of two or three, usually under cover of darkness, and raided isolated plantations along the river bank. Most of these attacks were made against the homes of the settlers who had refused to participate in the earlier rebel plans and who had professed loyalty to Spain. This would indicate that revenge was the motive for the renewal of hostility. As a rule, the purpose of the raids was to obtain food, cattle and horses, and valuable household property and to make off with unguarded Negro slaves. A typical raid was made on the home of Daniel Plummer in late September.[1] Two former citizens of East Florida, William Ashley and William Downs, crossed the river in a canoe and appeared suddenly in the Plummer house, just as the master was preparing to retire after a long ride from St. Augustine. Plummer and his wife were held at pistol point for several hours while the two bandits debated what to do with them. All the while they insulted Plummer, mocked his wife, and threatened to kill him in her presence. The pleas of the woman saved her husband's life, and the two bandits finally departed after forcing Mrs. Plummer to fill a saddlebag with food, drink, and some of the family silver. On the way back to the canoe, they saw three of the plantation slaves whom they proceeded to seize. With this loot, Ashley and Downs returned to Georgia, where it was reported that they sold the slaves.[2] Following the accepted pattern, Quesada sent a protest to the officials in Camden County requesting the return of the stolen property and the arrest of the culprits. He expressed extreme displeasure at the ease with which the rebels reëntered Georgia, at the freedom they enjoyed within the state, and at the willingness of people to purchase stolen property. Such apparent dereliction of duty on the part of the Georgia law officers was a direct insult to the King of Spain, since it exemplified the contempt with which they regarded the rights of his subjects. Quesada defended the friendly policy of Spain toward the United States, asserting, "Not even the slightest reason for anger has ever been given by this government to the state of Georgia."[3]

Captain Andrew Atkinson was sent to St. Mary's with the governor's

[1] For notes to chap. xii, see pp. 174–177.

letter, and with another written in the same vein to be forwarded to Mathews. Atkinson was chosen as emissary because of his knowledge of English and because of a long-standing friendship with Captain Nicholl and other officers in the region. Although Atkinson was unable to obtain a pledge of assistance from either of the magistrates, he managed to hold a long conversation with Nicholl and learned much about recent events on the northern bank of the river. Upon Atkinson's return to St. Augustine, the governor requested him to read an account of his experiences before a junta held on October 9. Atkinson was able to tell the gathering of the arrival of Fauche and his fifty dragoons late in August with orders from Mathews to prevent further aid being given those involved in the plans of either Clark or the rebels. But he questioned the real value of this little force, as some of the dragoons had been seen crossing to the south bank of the river on foraging expeditions in direct violation of orders from Augusta. He reported that Nicholl had located Clark with his forces on a sizable hummock in the middle of a swampy area, at a spot accessible from one direction only. Seventy persons, including several rebels from East Florida, were reported to be with the general. Among the rebels was John McIntosh. According to another rumor, Lang was said to be on the way to Clark's headquarters with about thirty men. But Atkinson was happy to report that the largest force, numbering approximately seven hundred, had disbanded upon the arrival of Fauche's detail.[4] The governor complimented Atkinson on having obtained such a large amount of important information.

After listening to this report, some of the members were convinced that an immediate assault was called for. If this were done, they reasoned, Clark could be defeated and driven off before the arrival of additional support, and before any form of French assistance could materialize. Also, such a plan, if carried out successfully, might end the threat to the province before the sympathetic population along the St. John's River could make up their minds to aid the enemy. But Quesada preferred to follow a cautious policy, pointing out the dangers that might ensue if the Spanish forces met with defeat. As he reasoned, the number of men who might join Clark in the next week or so was unknown, and Howard's forces might meet with overwhelming numbers. In spite of encouraging reports from Charleston, it was not yet certain that Clark's recruiting efforts in the central part of Georgia had been unsuccessful. In the event of a Spanish defeat, the entire frontier would lie open, necessitating a retreat to the very gates of St. Augustine. The troops then available in the province were not sufficient to be divided into two separate forces, one to attack Clark, and one to defend the St. John's River. According to Quesada, there were but 391 regular veteran troops capable of bearing arms, the other 500 being incapacitated by illness or other reasons. The frontier militia had but a handful of suitable mounts, and even these were old and half starved owing to lack of care. If Clark's position were to be attacked successfully, a large force of cavalry was essential.[5]

After this portentious report by the governor, the other members reversed their decision, agreeing that no assault could be contemplated until the Spanish forces were regrouped, until Howard was reinforced, until a sea and land blockade could be established along the St. Mary's River, and until all routes to Clark's headquarters from Georgia could be cut. Quesada was optimistic, expressing the belief that when these steps were taken, most of Clark's followers would drift back to the north, recrossing the river into Georgia. This might bring an end to the whole affair without the necessity of using Spanish forces.[6]

Once these plans had been agreed to, the junta took up the question of putting them into effect. It was decided to call in all the available militia, to arm all available free Negroes, and to draw a force of a hundred veteran soldiers from the various posts in the province.[7] A small force of artillery with full equipment was to be drawn from the garrison of the town. The sloop *Santa Mónica* and the gunboat *San Augustín de Patrón* were to sail north and anchor in the St. Mary's River to prevent communication between Clark's force and St. Mary's, with explicit orders to sink any craft that refused to turn back to the American shore. A small schooner belonging to John Leslie was to be loaded with all necessary supplies of food and ammunition. It was deemed wiser to use the sea route because hostile bands of Indians were known to be haunting the road north of the St. John's River. Andrew Atkinson with four militiamen was to proceed at once to the St. Mary's River to reconnoiter Clark's position and, if possible, to talk to the general in an effort to convince him of the futility of his cause. It was decided to send an account of these projected plans to Camden County. Orders were therefore issued to Sergeant Spicer Christopher of the militia to prepare the dispatch boat for the trip to St. Mary's.[8]

In this dispatch to Georgia, Quesada openly accused the local law officers of having failed to carry out their duties in so far as the Clark expedition was concerned. He also accused them of failing to support Fauche in carrying out Mathews' orders. He expressed the hope that the situation might be remedied at once, in time to prevent further complications. A complete recapitulation of events since the beginning of the year was enclosed to refresh the memory of the justices. The letter concluded with a rather pointed question: "Are the United States at war with Spain?" Quesada expressed the belief that a negative answer was in order, and that the Georgia magistrates had a great deal of explaining to do.[9]

Atkinson and Christopher departed as soon as the necessary papers and letters were drawn up. Shortly after reaching the St. Mary's River at a spot nearly opposite the village of Coleraine, Atkinson's little party met some of Clark's supporters, but neither party committed a hostile act. In the meantime, orders had been issued to carry out the decisions of the junta to collect a sizable force to drive Clark from his refuge. Howard had been present at the meeting and therefore was thoroughly acquainted with the plans. The necessary preparations were quickly made and Howard set out, probably on October 15, to march overland to the river. The naval force departed at the same time in order to meet him at the rendezvous. Little difficulty was experienced in reaching the destination on the river, since Clark appeared to be making no effort to scout the Spanish advance. On October 20, a scouting party under Captain Hall was ambushed near "Cryers"[10] by a group of eighteen to twenty armed men, probably some of Clark's force. After a brief and bloodless skirmish, the attackers were driven off and disappeared into the swamps. When Atkinson heard of this, he sent a dispatch to Quesada stressing the need for more men and additional supplies, if he and Hall were to continue to patrol in advance of Howard's force.[11]

When Howard finally reached the position supposedly held by Clark and his men, the hummock was found to be entirely deserted save for the ashes of several camp fires. Evidence showed the group of men to be much smaller than had been first reported to St. Augustine. No trace of an armed force could be found in the neighborhood, and it was decided that the group encountered by Hall was, in truth, the remnant of Clark's force attempting to retreat to the river. For the third time in a year, Howard had led his forces north to drive out an enemy and, for the third time, the enemy had chosen to melt away without putting up any sort of fight. Once again the plans of Quesada appeared to have succeeded.

The complete success of Howard's campaign against Clark's force depended partly upon the actions of Fauche and his dragoons on the north bank of the river. If Fauche had not coöperated with the Spanish force, the enemy would have been able to recross the river unhindered and reform in Georgia, possibly to try another assault on East Florida. Fauche, however, was a good soldier and endeavored to coöperate with Howard as far as his orders from Mathews would permit. Unfortunately, these did not give him much opportunity to use his initiative in making decisions. The governor had leaned over backward in his attempt to prevent any unpleasantness between Fauche and the citizens supporting Clark's cause. He had urged the captain to inquire into the matter of the citizenship of the leaders of the forces involved. If they claimed to be French and were serving under legally granted commissions, they were to be treated honorably since the United States was a neutral in the war between France and Spain. The interpretation of "honorable treatment" was so uncertain that Fauche was given virtually a free hand in this matter. However, if these officers were "self-created," then Fauche was forbidden to take matters into his own hands. He was to turn them over to the local magistrates and then send a complete report to Augusta.[12] It will be seen that the governor was putting too much faith in the patriotism of the local justices, particularly since they were known to be sympathetic to Clark and the French cause.

Once Fauche had received his orders from Mathews, he lost no time in advancing to the St. Mary's River, reaching the vicinity of Temple late in August. Uncertain as to the size of the forces opposing him, he was careful not to engage his detachment in a skirmish.[13] He encountered no large number of armed men north of the river. The few persons that he did meet denied knowledge of Clark's whereabouts or plans. Some of the local residents refused to give him information on any topic, and were unwilling to sell supplies to the militia. At one point, near Temple, Fauche was challenged by a mounted picket, and at another time, a group of the local inhabitants shouted insults at his men, referring to them as a band of "mad-caps." His scouts reported an abandoned camp site on the Spanish side of the river and he ordered several of them across the river to make a thorough investigation.[14] It is quite likely that this was the site of Lang's camp of the preceding year at Mills Ford. There was nothing to show whether Clark had as yet led his men across the river into Spanish territory or was still lurking in Georgia. As Fauche found very little of importance to report to Mathews, he finally decided to proceed in an easterly direction along the river to St. Mary's in order to deliver the governor's letter to the Camden County magistrates. No sooner had he reached the town than he was forced to use his authority to prevent a group of armed men from crossing into Spanish territory. According to his official report, "We proceeded to the town of St. Mary's, and there took a boat full of armed men, whom we brought before the civil authority, and they were discharged, finding no law of the State, nor of the Union, which they had violated."[15] Doubtless this was one of the events that later angered the Spanish authorities. Fauche made no effort to press the matter further, choosing to abide by Mathews' orders to coöperate with the local authorities, not antagonize them.

Later, when Fauche was informed of the imminent departure of several boatloads of provisions for an unidentified destination, he refused to issue orders to seize the boats. As he wrote later, "I could find nothing in my instructions which authorized me in interrupting any commercial transaction."[16] He reached this decision even though it was established that the provisions had been paid for with gold and silver coins of foreign origin. Fauche communicated with the French consul in St. Mary's, asking him whether or not the French government had any troops under arms within the boundaries of Georgia. This was to be the test of Clark's assertion that he and his men were under the protection of the French Republic and that he was a commissioned officer in the French army. Suares, the consul, appeared before a justice of the peace and swore that there were no authorized French troops within the United States. Both the justices and Fauche accepted this statement without asking Suares whether he considered Coleraine and the region west of the line of 1790 to be outside the United States. Adet's subsequent report on the East Florida expedition substantiated Suares' statement that there were no armed men under French colors in the United States. The French minister further declared that Clark was not acting under a French commission in the fall of 1795, since all commissions issued by Genêt and Mangourit in 1793 and 1794 had been rescinded when Fauchet arrived in the United States. He did admit, however, that Clark and some of his men were wearing the three-colored cockade. If, as Adet wrote, he had decided to throw the full support of France behind Clark's plans in spite of the rumors of impending peace between that Republic and Spain, the conquest of East Florida would have been completed in a matter of fifteen days.[17] In spite of this blunt denial made by the French minister that Clark was operating directly under French orders, certain portions of Adet's report to Paris show that Clark may have thought that he was assisting the French cause either officially or unofficially. At a later date, in discussing the ultimate collapse of Clark's venture of 1795, Adet reported to the minister of foreign relations.

Secretly disposed toward his success, the government of Georgia executed the orders that the executive of United States had sent to curb this hostile emigration only with slowness; but this deference should have ceased when he [Mathews] saw this enterprise abandoned by France; and ever since then he had his troops on the march in order to disperse the reassembled forces and to allow criminal justice [to act] in its free course against men armed in violation of American neutrality.

To abandon these warriors reassembled in the name of Liberty, since a great number of them were former soldiers of the war of independence now ruined by the financial system of Hamilton, to the steel of the Spaniards, to the scaffolds of the Americans, or to misery, would have been equally impolitic and unjust.

Impolitic: the English might have extended a hand to turn this revolution to their profit.

Unjust: it [revolution] was undertaken for us, and if some men had been attracted by the hope of plunder or of rewards, a great number also had followed only the inspiration of liberty.[18]

Adet concluded his report with the information that the French consul in Charleston was trying to solicit funds to send some of Clark's followers to Haiti to assist in the struggle against the English. He admitted offering a contribution of 400 gourdes, but under an assumed name. From this evidence, it appears that the French minister felt a certain amount of responsibility for the destitution of the members of Clark's small force. It is impossible to tell whether this feeling was prompted by a sense of guilt, or by humanitarianism.

Fauche appeared to be thoroughly satisfied with Suares' reply.[19] He then sent a dispatch to Clark to inform him of the stand taken by the federal government on the violation of Spanish territory by citizens of the United States. Writing thirty years later, he attempted to recall the contents of this letter. According to him, the letter began:

The president and the cabinet in Washington [sic], it is credibly asserted, are unanimously determined to recommend a strict neutrality with the European belligerents, and you can best judge, what weight such recommendations will have with Congress. The insurgents of the Floridas cannot alone contend with Spain; the agent of the French government here denies that the French government hath any troops here or near here. If Congress should pass a law materially penal against armaments which are authorized by no government, where will be their's; where will be your country?[20]

As far as Fauche was concerned, the declaration of Suares put an end to any claim that Clark might make that he and his men represented an official portion of the French army. If captured, they could not claim immunity as soldiers of an ally of the United States.

It was at this point that Fauche and Nicholl received a letter from Quesada, thanking them for their assistance. As he wrote, "It had contributed to the extermination of the projects of General Clark and his followers in association with the rebellious subjects of the King my master, against the territory of his dominions."[21] He went on to praise Mathews for sending Fauche to Camden County, referring to the governor's "honorable and upright proceedings and mode of thinking." This was one of the rare occasions when Quesada had a kind word to say for Mathews. He concluded his letter to Fauche on a hopeful note, writing, "I have the honor of offering myself at your disposal with lively wishes of rendering you services, and I am persuaded that you will continue to accede as far as your forces will permit you to the prosperous issue of our mutual desires and maintenance of the pacific disposition of the government of the two powers."[22]

This letter was received in St. Mary's four or five days after it was written by Quesada. Fauche wrote a short reply to thank the governor for his expressions of gratitude.[23] According to Fauche's later account of the military events of 1795, another letter from St. Augustine arrived at nearly the same time, requesting further information on the location and size of Clark's forces. Apparently Fauche interpreted this to be a request for military assistance. He replied that he was unable to supply the desired information as he was in complete ignorance of these facts. He suggested that any further reinforcements to the forces of Clark would probably come from East Florida, referring, no doubt, to Lang and his friends.[24]

The pleasure with which Quesada welcomed the advent of Fauche's dragoons was further expressed in a dispatch sent to Mathews. The governor of East Florida had only one complaint, claiming that the arrival of these dragoons had driven Clark across the St. Mary's River into his province. He declared that Clark was unwilling to come in direct conflict with Fauche's force. Once across the river and in the territory of Spain, he would be safe from the American force. Changing his tone, Quesada admitted that it was on the advice of Fauche and Nicholl that he had decided to muster his forces for an attack on Clark before reinforcements could arrive.[25] Quesada closed his letter with the hope that Mathews would continue to take effectual steps against Clark's forces and against Lang and his rebel friends.[26] The latest information located the remnant of the rebel band near Coleraine.

At practically the same time, Colonel Gaither wrote Mathews that the rebels and their Georgia allies were entrenched in a spot near Temple, and that more men were expected to arrive momentarily.[27] This report may have referred to Clark's force, for Gaither did not differentiate between this and the rebel force. From the available information it is impossible to tell when Clark moved south of the river, although it may have occurred early in October. An undated dispatch from Captain Randolph to Mathews gave the first definite news that the general had actually crossed into East Florida. The letter began, "It gives me much satisfaction to find that General Clark and his adherents are defeated in their unlawful attempts, and that peace and tranquillity is again restored to the United States."[28] Obviously Randolph, who never liked Clark, professed to believe that the affairs of East Florida did not concern the United States.

Fauche was not so certain that Clark's departure from Georgia assured the return of peace and quiet. The captain moved west along the northern bank of the river in order to coöperate with Howard's forces which were reported to be approaching from the south. Fauche finally halted near the settlement at Temple, which was not far from Mills Ford where the main highway from St. Augustine crossed the river. He hoped that by remaining at this advantageous spot, he might be able to seize any of Clark's men attempting to retreat to Georgia. A few of the general's men tried to scout Fauche's position near Temple. They were bold enough to engage the dragoons in conversation. Two of them were seized and later handed over to the magistrates at St. Mary's, who immediately released one for lack of evidence. The other was found to be a deserter from the militia force under Lieutenant Vaughan at Burnt Fort,[29] and Fauche ordered him to stand a military trial. The court-martial found him guilty and sentenced him to run the gantlet. At the same time, local informers told Fauche the names of some of those involved in the attack on San Nicolás, but as most of them were Floridians rather than Americans, the magistrates refused to aid him in apprehending them. The captain was not particularly alarmed, however, as he had been reliably informed that none of these men were still in Georgia.

What caused Fauche more worry than Clark's activities was the continued hostility shown him and his dragoons by the local citizenry. He wrote the governor, "There have been a great many exertions made by the New-Floridians and their well wishers to raise discontent amongst my command. Their last expedient has been to procure letters from Upper Country, informing them that there was late news come from the secretary of war, imputing that my troops will not get paid for their former services, etc."[30] He was also worried at times by the sympathetic way in which some of his own men spoke of the schemes of Clark

and the rebels. There were times when it appeared as though some preferred to join the French cause. In his memoirs, he wrote:

> Being myself in the United States service, I issued an order to the troops then
> under my command, [neither] to join nor counternance either party. Soon after-
> wards, some mounted the French cockade, even one of my subaltern officers left the
> United States service to join the French. This led to a single combat [duel] between
> a then French officer and myself, after which I experienced no further defection.[31]

A few days later, three more men donned the French cockade, and
Fauche warned them that they were violating the neutrality of the
United States and were guilty of desertion. According to his memoirs,
"On the next day the detachment was fully American."[32]

Little else of interest occurred, and Fauche expressed the opinion
that Clark's forces had already melted away, possibly before the start
of Howard's move to the St. Mary's River.[33] Strangely enough, Howard
expressed the same opinion at nearly the same time. He wrote to Fauche
to tell him of the disappearance of all hostile forces along the frontier.
In reply, Fauche congratulated the colonel on his prompt action, assuring him that there was no possibility that the enemy would regroup in
Georgia. He said that the local population was tired of constant turmoil
and uncertainty.[34] Neither Fauche nor Howard seemed to associate the
collapse of Clark's schemes with the announcement of Suares that
France did not recognize or support the expedition. When Adet described the termination of Clark's venture, he declared that it had been
due solely to the neutral stand taken by the French agents in the United
States. He expressed utter contempt for Mathews and the Georgia officials who had done nothing until threatened by the federal government.[35]

When a few armed men finally did appear on the northern bank of
the St. Mary's River, Fauche seized four of them. Apparently one was
the notorious Daniel McGirt, long wanted in East Florida for illegal
trading in horses and cattle, and then under indictment in Georgia for
having been involved in the theft of several Negro slaves in Liberty
County.[36] Fauche surrendered him to the magistrates in St. Mary's for
a preliminary examination before jailing him to await further instructions from Augusta. A few days after the apprehension of McGirt,
Howard sent a letter to Fauche to tell him of the collapse of Clark's
expedition against East Florida. He stated that there were still isolated
groups of whites and Indians plundering plantations on both sides of
the river. He identified McGirt as the leader of one of these bands with
headquarters near Coleraine. A request was made that Fauche seize

McGirt and turn him over to a Spanish representative in St. Mary's.[37] Although Fauche recognized the justice of Howard's request, he refused to comply until the magistrates could make a decision in the matter.

He presented Howard's letter about McGirt to the magistrates in St. Mary's. The evidence contained therein was sufficient to convict the rebel, but the law officers refused to indict him because of the question of his nationality. Since he claimed to be an American, no evidence of crimes committed in a foreign country could be admitted in an American court as the basis for an indictment. As a result, he was ordered dismissed and set free. Fauche sent this information to Howard to show why he could not surrender McGirt.[38] When Fauche wrote his memoirs, he declared that he had had another reason for refusing to surrender his prisoner. This concerned what he had considered a gross breach of faith on the part of the authorities in St. Augustine. In May, two deserters from St. Augustine fled to Savannah where they were apprehended and lodged in the local jail.[39] At the request of Quesada, they were returned to St. Augustine, but only after the Spaniards had promised not to inflict physical punishment on them. No sooner had they been returned to East Florida than they were found guilty of desertion and hanged.[40]

As soon as the news of the McGirt case reached Quesada, he sent a letter to Philadelphia requesting Jaudenes to approach the secretary of state on the matter of obtaining justice.[41] The governor was busily engaged in putting his affairs in order since ill health had forced him to ask to be relieved of his duties. Hence he could not devote much time and effort to the problems of the frontier. One of his last dispatches to Jaudenes contained copies of all documents received from Mathews dealing with the events in Camden County during the summer and fall of 1795. He stated that the situation along the St. Mary's River was once again normal and that the need for federal intervention had passed.[42]

The refusal of the magistrates to indict the prisoner McGirt, and their order for his release, annoyed Mathews even more than it had Quesada. He was not slow in expressing his great displeasure. It appeared to him that the evidence against McGirt for crimes committed in Georgia was certainly sufficient for an indictment. The governor addressed a letter to Fauche in which he wrote, "If that nefarious villain McGirt is still lurking in Camden, have him secured and brought with you under guard to this place [Augusta]...."[43] The governor hoped that the evidence against the culprit would make a deeper impression on the magistrates in Richmond County than it had in Camden County. In spite of the governor's orders, McGirt was never again brought before a court in Georgia, and it appears that he made great haste to leave the state.[44]

Aside from the McGirt case, Mathews was much pleased with the preliminary reports of the outcome of Fauche's activities along the St. Mary's River. He cautioned, however, against too close coöperation with Howard. He wrote:

> With regard to the letter you refer to, from a subject of his Catholic Majesty's, saying that it is in your power to restore peace and order to the government, this is a subject I think which required great caution, and should you take it at all, your first step should be to inform Captain Atkinson or some other of his Catholic Majesty's subjects.[45]

He urged Fauche to wait for an official request before offering to lend assistance. The letter continued.

> It must afford real satisfaction to the human heart to be the means of relieving the necessities or distress, but in this instance great precaution is required to convince them that we are actuated from pure motives of justice toward the interests and happiness of their government and which I trust, if you interfere at all, will be the line of your conduct.[46]

The governor of East Florida also expressed great pleasure upon hearing that the troubles appeared to be over. When he finally reported the withdrawal of Clark's forces to Las Casas, he declared that the fundamental reason for the collapse of the enterprise of the old general lay in the rumored peace negotiations between France and Spain.[47] If Clark was really sincere in his avowed attachment to the French cause, the possibility of a European peace must have caused him dismay for it would mean the ruin of his plans. So reasoned Quesada in his letter to Havana. The end of Clark's activities and the news of the signing of the Treaty of Basle occurred at virtually the same time. Relieved that the frontier situation was once again normal, Quesada informed the governor general early in November that he was returning the three companies of Cuban Infantry to Havana.[48] Once again it appeared that a combination of Quesada's caution and Howard's vigor had resulted in the reëstablishment of peace and quiet within the province, all achieved without the loss of a single man. Spain certainly had not lost face diplomatically, and her military prestige had not suffered.

Perhaps the most remarkable aspect of the joint attempt to dislodge Clark and the rebels was the absence of friction between the armed forces of Spain and the United States. Both Fauche and Howard exhibited the greatest desire to coöperate and maintain friendly relations. The only incident of any magnitude to mar this show of coöperation involved Captain Randolph. He asserted that his dispatch boat on the St. Mary's River had been interfered with and that one of his aides was being held prisoner by the Spaniards. Howard was requested to investigate the matter and obtain the release of the prisoner. Not satisfied with this demand, Randolph threatened to blockade the river, to seize a Spanish schooner and gunboat then at anchor, and to protest formally to President Washington.[49] Upon hearing this, Mathews wrote to the magistrates in Camden County requesting a thorough investigation of Randolph's charges and appropriate action if they were verified.[50] There is no evidence available to show just how this matter was settled. Quesada made no mention of it in his reports to Las Casas, and there is no indication that Jaudenes ever received orders to protest to the federal government over the abusive language employed by Randolph.

For some time after the military phase was concluded, negotiations were continued in an effort to apprehend and punish those guilty of engineering the recent disturbances. Quesada was particularly anxious to discover what the state of Georgia intended to do with the refugees from East Florida still living along the northern bank of the St. Mary's River. Many of these men had declared their intention to remain in the United States, even at the risk of losing their property in Spanish territory. The question seemed to hinge on whether the authorities in Georgia felt themselves bound to turn these men over to Quesada upon his request. It was obvious from the first that the local magistrates had not the slightest intention of so doing, and Mathews was reluctant to take steps to force the issue. In writing to Quesada, he avoided making direct reference to the residence of any Spanish subjects in Georgia. Possibly irked by this studied effort to evade the issue, Quesada pointed out that all fugitive citizens should be returned to East Florida as "state criminals."[51] Mathews might have been able to continue disregarding the issue of the return of these men, had it not been for the unwelcome arrival of Colonel Kindelan with letters from Las Casas and Quesada. This officer arrived in Augusta on November 11 and immediately presented the governor with Las Casas' dispatch of August 21 which dealt with the development of the frontier problem up to that date.[52] In addition, he brought Quesada's letter of October 12 which contained the news of Clark's move to the south bank of the St. Mary's River.

The letter from Las Casas spoke in glowing terms of the abilities of his emissary and stated that he had wide powers to negotiate with

Mathews on all matters. Perhaps Las Casas was resorting to sarcasm when he urged Mathews to take the steps necessary to bring about a quick solution to the problem, unless the United States was already at war with Spain. The governor general knew very well that such was not the case, for he had been informed of the preliminary negotiations already underway in Spain between his government and the United States. The tone of the dispatch from the governor general both surprised and offended Mathews. In an attempt to justify his stand, Mathews wrote, "I can with great truth assure Your Excellency that nothing in my power shall be wanting to punish a general,[53] colon [sic][54] and any of his Majesty's subjects who have, or may attempt to take refuge in this state, with designs to disturb the power of your government, or plundering the property of your peacable [sic] subjects."[55] Hoping to convince Las Casas of his desire to be coöperative, Mathews continued,

This will be delivered to Your Excellency by Colonel Kindelan, with whom I have conversed, candidly and unreservedly, on the subject of his mission; and who I hope and trust is impressed fully with the idea, and will inform Your Excellency to that effect, of my most sincere wish of the most friendly relations with the provinces of East and West Florida over which you preside.[56]

Several meetings were held during which the two men exchanged their views. After each of these meetings, written résumés were exchanged in English and Spanish so that each man could compare what had been said with what the other thought had been said. The governor obviously wanted to impress the Spaniard with his willingness to discuss every phase of each problem. Uncertain how far this coöperation might lead, he asked the attorney general of the state to give an opinion on what he as governor was bound by law to do about those citizens of Georgia who had taken part in the rebellion in East Florida. In a long reply, the law officer set forth as a cardinal principal of the law of nations that no one nation could permit its citizens to aid those of a second nation in open rebellion. Those guilty should be punished since their actions could easily lead to a declaration of war. He urged Mathews to issue warrants at once for the arrest of all citizens of Georgia known to have assisted the rebels. His report concluded:

It is particularly unfortunate for this state and perhaps for the United States that that part of Georgia bordering on the domains of his Catholic Majesty is infested with vile and abandoned characters who alternately pursue plunder and robberies within the territory of each country; and possibly it may be a cause of wonder and astonishment in the officers of the Spanish government that those offenders cannot be punished in a summary way by the government of America; but we ought to hope that a spirit of liberality will induce them to consider the great difference in the nature of the two governments, and to believe that while we ought mutually to deplore the depravity of those wretches, we ought not to impute to a nation the faults of individuals.[57]

Mathews wrote at once to Fauche, ordering him to act upon the advice of the attorney general. Sensing possible trouble, he warned the captain to keep a constant watch on the local population, and to have some soldiers accompany him at all times. He included a letter for the magistrates in St. Mary's in which he did not mince words, saying, "The unpleasant situation this state has been placed in, from the conduct of some of his Catholic Majesty's subjects, that have taken refuge in Camden County, and the imprudence of some of our own citizens, makes it requesite that the full power of the laws and government should be exerted to punish such abuses, and guard against such inconveniences in the future."[58]

Kindelan expressed the opinion that Mathews was not being definite enough in his promises of future action and continued to press for more drastic steps. Such references to laxity on his part and to the failure of the state government to function properly irked the governor. He retorted angrily, "I now repeat that he [Clark] is no officer of the state, or of the United States, that an insurrection had actually been committed and existed in East Florida, by your own subjects, and that Clark and his followers were invited and enticed out of the state by them."[59] This was a slight exaggeration, since it is doubtful that Clark ever needed to be "enticed" into making war on Spain.

Still not convinced, Kindelan wrote Mathews again, requesting a further statement on his future plans for the apprehension of rebels. The governor, showing great patience, complied and began by restating the background of the entire situation. He continued:

It is painful to be informed that the magistrates of Camden have been remiss in carrying into execution my orders respecting such of his Catholic Majesty's subjects as have taken refuge in that county. You may be assured that the neglect shall be inquired into and a proper remedy applied; and that any of the citizens of Georgia, who have been aiding or abetting the revolt of your subjects, or any others who may have taken residence with us for the purpose of disturbing the peace of your government shall be proceeded against in terms of the laws of the United States, and that such property as has been taken and now remains in the hands of the captors or their abettors shall be restored.[60]

He concluded his letter with a startling bit of information, declaring:

The circumstances you refer to respecting Clark and other citizens of Georgia, exciting your subjects to rebellion and acts of hostility I think wrong [*sic*] stated;

he and they were, if I am rightly informed, solicited by the Cherokees to take a part with them and aid an insurrection; by this act they have forfeited the protection of this state, and in some degree their allegiance to the United States, and should they return, will be punished according to their demerits. If they fall into your hands, you well know how to treat them.[61]

This was the first and only reference to the Indians as a cause of the troubles of 1795, and there is little evidence to support such an allegation. The promise of legal action against all Georgians involved with the rebels was never kept, since not one suspect was ever brought to trial. Kindelan's subsequent departure shows that he was satisfied with the progress that he and the governor had made toward the ultimate solution of the frontier problems.

A short time later, in defending his actions during 1795 before the state legislature, the governor made it clear that his willingness to negotiate with Kindelan had not sprung from a desire to remain at peace with Spain but from fear of what might happen if Kindelan, unsuccessful in Augusta, had continued his negotiations in Philadelphia. His message read in part, "The colonel was instructed, if he did not receive that satisfaction from me which this subject required, to proceed to Philadelphia and make known to the President of the United States, his complaint."[62] Mathews knew that any action taken then by the federal government would have been more drastic than that contemplated at the time of the Trans-Oconee affair. Washington and his Cabinet were known to be anxious to avoid any disagreements that might delay the successful conclusion of the negotiations then in progress in Madrid. That the governor wanted to forestall such a move was shown by the speed with which he informed the secretary of war of the end of the revolt in East Florida, the dispatch of Fauche on a peace mission to Camden County, and the successful outcome of his conversations with Kindelan.[63] In an effort to impress the legislature, Mathews emphasized the success of his recent negotiations, declaring, "I had it in my power to convince the colonel that . . . the government had pursued measures to prevent our citizens from aiding or abetting their revolted subjects."[64]

The governor found it necessary to defend himself so vigorously before the legislature because of the determination of the newly elected body to wipe out the stigma of the Yazoo land frauds of the previous year. Since Mathews had signed the original bill, albeit reluctantly, he realized that he was to be one of the chief targets of the legislative investigation. This later proved to be so, and Mathews' political career was blighted. There was, however, an even more pressing reason. In the eyes of many, he was no longer the legal governor of Georgia and had not been since his term of office expired on November 6, 1795. The legislative session of 1794 had been busy with an attempted revision of the state constitution and had broken up in dissention without having selected a new governor. This, and the removal of the seat of government from Augusta to Louisville at the beginning of January, 1796, led to great confusion in political affairs. Since he had no legal successor, Mathews continued in office until the new legislature could select a governor. After much confusion, General Jared Irwin was chosen on January 15 and took office immediately. Therefore the legality of Mathews' actions between November 6 and January 15 was open to doubt.

Curiously enough, even as Mathews was being replaced by Irwin as governor of Georgia, a similar change of officials was in progress in East Florida. The recurrent illness of Quesada finally convinced Las Casas that he should accept the governor's request to be relieved of his duties. In writing to Spain, Las Casas pointed out that Quesada had served faithfully for more than five years during a very hectic period. More than nine months elapsed between the dispatch of this report to Spain and the receipt of the order relieving Quesada. Finally, on February 27, 1796, Quesada wrote James Murphy, the Spanish vice-consul in Charleston,[65] that permission to return to Spain had at last arrived, and that he was about to depart, leaving the duties of governor in the hands of Morales, who had often served as acting governor. The new governor, Enrique White, formerly governor of West Florida, was expected to reach St. Augustine in the summer. On March 12 Morales wrote Murphy to inform him that he had actually taken over the duties of governor.[66] White arrived from Pensacola on June 5 and assumed full command of the province on June 20.[67]

Thus, in the first three months of 1796, both George Mathews and Juan Nepomuceno de Quesada, the two opposing leaders during the troubled years of 1794 and 1795, retired from the scene, the former with his administration under fire and his honor besmirched, the latter with the approbation of his commanding officers and with the knowledge that he had kept the borders of his province inviolate.

CHAPTER XIII

IN RETROSPECT

THE EVENTS ALONG the Georgia-Florida frontier in the years from 1793 to 1796 may well fade into insignificance if compared with the momentous social impact of the French Revolution, the violence of the protracted European conflict, or the bitter factional struggle within the United States over Hamilton's fiscal policies. It is doubtful that the events discussed in this study made much impression on the mind of the American public of that time. The numbers involved were small, the theater of operations restricted, and the immediate results negligible. Perhaps the ardent and loyal Georgia or Florida historian might understandably overemphasized the importance of these events in influencing the negotiations between the United States and Spain.[1]

Nevertheless, this frontier struggle did represent an important phase in the relations between the United States, France, and Spain. Also, it was more or less typical of the struggle over a large number of questions then being waged between the nascent federal government and the older and more established state governments. Finally, it represented an early episode in what is often referred to as the "Westward Movement." It might be suggested with cautious reservation that this frontier struggle constituted a very early expression of what was later to be called "Manifest Destiny." In general, the frontier problems presented in this study represent but a small bit in the vast mosaic of American history. An examination of a small piece of the mosaic, however, can sometimes lead to an understanding of the entire pattern.

In 1793, the United States had been confronted for the first time in its short history with a general European conflict in which it desired to take no part, but in which it nevertheless became involved. Widespread dislike for England was manifest on nearly every side, while her ally Spain was the particular object of distrust among the population of Georgia. On the other hand, the first impulse of many Americans was to accept the French Revolution as a European extension of the spirit of 1776. The path of neutrality would have been difficult enough to follow without the highhanded actions of the French ministers in the United States. Genêt's assumption that popular will would overcome presidential reluctance led him to overstep the bounds of diplomatic behavior. The activities of Mangourit and the French agents in Georgia,

---

[1] For notes to chap. xiii, see p. 177.

and of the latter on Amelia Island, were carried on in open defiance of the express desires of the President and of the laws of the Congress. The angry tone of official correspondence received in Charleston and Augusta from Philadelphia gave warning of the President's growing impatience. There can be little doubt that he was alarmed lest the protracted negotiations with Spain over commercial concessions in New Orleans and the Indies and over boundary settlements should be jeopardized by hostile acts committed along the Georgia-Florida frontier.[2]

The unsuccessful attempt of various groups within the United States to seize, occupy, and hold portions of East Florida in the years 1793 to 1796 was but the first of several such efforts. The first of these frontier skirmishes did not result in the occupation of Spanish territory by the troops of the United States as did the so-called "wars" in 1812 and 1817. The fundamental reason for all the attacks was the same: the desire to rid the area of Spanish control and thus bring the province under the authority of the United States. In the 1790's an effort was made to hide behind the skirts of France, then at war with Spain. It is doubtful that the enthusiasm shown for French republicanism was more than camouflage to mislead the French minister and his agents. Men like George Mathews, Samuel Hammond, and Elijah Clark wanted to see Spain and England humbled, regardless of the method employed. All were resentful of the influence exercised by Spain over certain of the southeastern Indian tribes. All troubles experienced by Georgia with these Indians were ascribed to the Spanish desire to plague the United States. Hammond, in particular, believed that these Indians could be induced to change sides by playing upon their former French affiliations.

Closely allied with the problem of Spanish influence among the Indians was the question of the differences of opinion between the federal and state governments on how to handle Indian matters. Washington's stand that the Indian problem fell solely within the jurisdiction of the federal government was bitterly opposed by the Georgia authorities, who claimed that it was a local matter and hence purely a state problem. Whereas the federal agents attempted to reach satisfactory agreements with the Indians through the granting of pensions, subsidies, and concessions, Georgia tried to solve the problem by matching violence with violence, and murder with murder. Governor Mathews believed that the elimination of Spanish control in the southeast would deprive the Indians of their chief source of assistance. This would bring a swift end to the Indian problem and a halt to federal meddling in state affairs.

Differences between state and federal governments were evident in other fields: the extent to which the federal government might coerce the individual state in an effort to prevent recruiting for a foreign army; the right of the secretary of the treasury to enforce the terms of the neutrality proclamation through the collectors of the customs; and finally, the extent to which federal militia could be employed within a state to enforce federal regulations. This last problem was one that caused great bitterness in Georgia, although each time the president reluctantly ordered the use of federal forces, the state government acquiesced. Its ultimate triumph in each altercation with Georgia indicated the growing strength of the new federal government.

Finally, the willingness of American settlers to move to East Florida, even under restrictive Spanish control, the ease with which Elijah Clark recruited men to settle in the Indian lands across the Oconee River, and the eagerness of Americans to purchase land in Georgia's western domains showed that the westward surge of the new nation was well under way. The move from the Old South into the borderlands to the west and southwest was already in progress during the Revolution. Many of the men involved in the frontier difficulties in the 1790's were not natives of Georgia, but came from states farther north. Governor Mathews was not a native of the state which twice selected him as its chief executive.[3] The leaders of the so-called rebellion of 1795 in East Florida came from north of the Savannah River. The check received in 1795 to this move to the south of the St. Mary's River was but momentary, for American settlers once again began crossing the river a few years later. The province became an American territorial possession in 1821.

The desire of many Americans to see East Florida become not only a haven for settlers but also an American possession was the cause of much of the support given the rebels. The later attempts at annexation were attributable directly to this desire to change flags. In a way, the road to the Mississippi River and New Orleans in 1795 appeared to lead through St. Augustine and Pensacola. Later events, however, showed that Florida was to be by-passed on the march to the southwest.

For Spain, the troubles along the Florida frontier in the 1790's were but another of the many attempted encroachments on her colonial possessions. Although the local authorities tried to draw the attention of the home government to the need to guard against the growing power of the new state lying along the Atlantic coast, the main causes for alarm in Madrid appeared to be the fear of the French Revolution and its implications, the apprehension lest France attempt to regain her lost colonial empire, and the attitude of England toward Spanish dominance, particularly in the Caribbean area. Even when the governor general of Cuba wrote of the urgency of taking steps to strengthen Spanish control of East Florida, the King's ministers limited their action to praising Las Casas and Quesada for what they had already done to defend the province.[4] Although the disturbances along the St. Mary's River did focus attention on the need for certain boundary settlements, it was the changing picture in Europe and the conclusion of the Jay Treaty that finally stirred the government of Charles IV into action.

If the troublesome frontier problems and the difficulty of maintaining Spanish authority over the region did not cause much worry in Madrid, they certainly did in St. Augustine and Havana. Both Quesada and Las Casas believed that the problem of restoring peace to the frontier region was a matter of great importance to Spain. Quesada, more than Las Casas, realized the latent danger in the growing giant to the north. He was clever in his use of the channels of diplomatic correspondence and in his employment of a small military force at crucial moments. Although Quesada's forces far outnumbered the American and rebel groups, the long defense line made the efficient use of Spanish troops essential. The governor was most fortunate in having Colonel Howard as commander of the frontier, a man upon whom he could rely with complete confidence. The diplomatic pressure applied by Quesada and Las Casas to the federal government through the Spanish representatives in Philadelphia did more than anything else to convince Washington of the need to coerce the Georgia authorities into taking drastic action to curb the enthusiasm of certain citizens. Quesada's diplomatic offensive and military defensive were rewarded with complete success, for the territorial integrity of the province was preserved without the need to shed blood.

It can be asserted justifiably that the difficulties along the St. Mary's River in the years 1793 to 1796 reflected to some degree the vital problems of the day: the struggle between federal and state governments; the confused state of the foreign affairs of the United States; the ever-present Indian controversy; the growing movement toward the west; and, finally, the struggle of Spain to maintain control over the peripheral parts of her American colonial empire.

NOTES TO CHAPTER I

EARLY HISTORY

[1] This river was so called because of its discovery on May 1. It is presumably the same as the present St. John's River.

[2] For an account of this voyage, see Thomas Hackit, ed., *The true and last discoverie of Florida, made by Captain John Ribault in the yeare 1562*, The Hakluyt Society Publications, no. 7 (London, 1854), pp. 91–115.

[3] For an account of the massacre of the French, see Gonzalo Solis de Meras, *Pedro Menéndez de Avilés*, J. T. Connor, ed. and trans., Florida State Historical Society Publications, no. 3 (DeLand, Florida, 1923), pp. 80–137.

[4] *Ibid.*, p. 83.

[5] For an account of the reasons that lay behind the founding of Pensacola, see William Edward Dunn, *Spanish and French Rivalry in the Gulf Region of the United States, 1678–1702*, University of Texas Bulletin, no. 1705, Studies in History, no. 1 (Austin, Texas, 1917), pp. 146–184.

[6] For a brief account of the attack by Sir Francis Drake, see George R. Fairbanks, *History of Florida from Its Discovery by Ponce de Leon, in 1512, to the Close of the Florida War in 1842* (Philadelphia, 1871), pp. 159–161. For the adventures of Captain John Davis, see Alexander Olivier Exquemelin, *The Buccaneers of America, 1648–1685* (London, 1924), pp. 77–79.

[7] There were two Spanish attacks on the English settlements in the Carolinas, one in 1676, against the Ashley River region, and the other in 1678, against Port Royal Island. See Hugh McCall, *The History of Georgia, containing Brief Sketches of the most Remarkable Events up to the Present Day.* [1784] (Atlanta, 1909), pp. 3–6. See also Verner W. Crane, *The Southern Frontier, 1670–1732* (Durham, North Carolina, 1928).

[8] Edward McCrady, *The History of South Carolina under the Proprietary Government, 1670–1719* (New York, 1897), pp. 377–386.

[9] *Ibid.*, pp. 392–394. For a firsthand account of this expedition, see "An account of what the army did, under the command of Col. Moore, in his expedition last winter, against the Spaniards and Spanish Indians," Boston *News*, May 1, 1704, reprinted in B. R. Carroll, *Historical Collections of South Carolina* (New York, 1836), II, 573–576.

[10] McCrady, *op. cit.*, pp. 396–401.

[11] October, 1739.

[12] Fairbanks, *op. cit.*, pp. 191–206, 208–209; and McCall, *op. cit.*, pp. 101–105, 133–134.

[13] Fairbanks, *op. cit.*, pp. 206–208; and McCall, *op. cit.*, pp. 122–132.

[14] Fairbanks, *op. cit.*, pp. 210–224. See Charles L. Mowat, *East Florida as a British Province, 1763–1784*, University of California Publications in History, vol. 32 (Berkeley, 1943).

[15] It is reported that effigies of Samuel Adams and John Hancock were hanged and burned in St. Augustine in 1776. Herbert B. Fuller, *The Purchase of Florida, Its History and Diplomacy* (Cleveland, 1906), p. 17.

[16] In August, 1779, during a debate in the Continental Congress over the impending treaty with Spain, George Mathews of Georgia insisted that the word "Floridas" be

included in the amendment by which Spain would guarantee to the United States possession of Canada, Nova Scotia, and Bermuda. Francis Wharton, ed., *The Revolutionary Diplomatic Correspondence of the United States* (Washington, 1889), III, 274–275.

[17] Wilbur Henry Siebert, *Loyalists in East Florida, 1774–1785*, Florida State Historical Society Publications, no. 9 (DeLand, Florida, 1929), I, 137–180.

[18] The Altamaha River had been established as the southern boundary of the royal grant to Oglethorpe, and it remained the unofficial boundary until the acquisition of Florida by England in 1763. McCall, *op. cit.*, p. 17.

[19] E. Merton Coulter, *Georgia: A Short History* (Chapel Hill, North Carolina, 1947), p. 181. See John Richard Alden, *John Stuart and the Southern Colonial Frontier . . . 1754–1775*, University of Michigan Publications, History and Political Science, Vol. XV (Ann Arbor, 1944).

[20] Camden County was created in 1776 by a consolidation of the parishes of St. Patrick and St. Mary's which had been laid out in 1765.

[21] James Thomas Vocelle, *History of Camden County, Georgia* (St. Mary's, Georgia, 1914), pp. 21–35.

[22] According to a contemporary report, the total population of East Florida in May, 1787, was 1390, of which nine hundred were whites. "Discourse of José Salcedo relative to the cession of East Florida to the English, August 20, 1788," printed in Arthur Preston Whitaker, ed. and trans., *Documents Relating to the Commercial Policy of Spain in the Floridas with Incidental Reference to Louisiana*, Florida State Historical Society Publications, no. 10 (DeLand, Florida, 1931), p. 81. See also, Joseph B. Lockey, "The St. Augustine Census of 1786," *Florida Historical Quarterly*, XVIII (1939), 11–31.

[23] Vicente Manuel de Céspedes to Marqués de la Sonora (minister of the Indies), May 12, 1787, printed in Whitaker, *op. cit.*, p. 53.

[24] *Spanish Land Grants in Florida* (Tallahassee, Florida, 1940), I, xxi.

[25] Juan Nepomuceno de Quesada assumed the duties of governor in July, 1790, replacing Céspedes. He retained this office until February, 1796, when he was recalled because of illness.

[26] The Ashleys had settled near St. Patrick in Camden County in 1785, while the McIntosh family established themselves at Refuge Plantation. Vocelle, *op. cit.*, pp. 34 ff.

[27] Juan Nepomuceno de Quesada to Conde de Lerena (minister of marine), November 15, 1791, printed in Whitaker, *op. cit.*, p. 157.

[28] By the end of 1791, some of the new settlers had already returned to the United States. *Ibid.*, p. 161.

[29] The correspondence between Governor Quesada and the Spanish consuls in the United States during 1794 is filled with references to the problem of runaway slaves. E.F.P., 102 K 8.

[30] Coulter, *op. cit.*, pp. 181–182.

[31] The Augusta *Chronicle and Gazette of the State* (Augusta, Georgia), January 4, 1794.

[32] Coulter, *op. cit.*, p. 183. For a short biography of Edward Telfair, see *D.A.B.*, XVIII (1943), 361–362.

[33] Fauchet, the French minister who replaced Citizen Genêt, discussed this Spanish policy in a letter to France in 1794. "Commissioners to Minister of Foreign Affairs, May 28, 1794," A.H.A. *Report*, 1903, II, 356–357.

[34] Francisco Luis Héctor, Baron de Carondelet, a native of Flanders and a member of an ancient Burgundian family, the former governor of Guatemala, arrived in Louisiana late in 1791, and assumed his duties on January 1, 1792.

[35] See Alexander Moultrie to Dr. Benjamin Farrar, January 24, 1790, and Alexander Moultrie to John MacGillivray, February 19, 1790, A.G.I., P.C., 202.

[36] For an excellent account of the Yazoo sales, see Charles H. Haskins, "The Yazoo Land Companies," A.H.A. *Papers*, V (1891), 59–103.

[37] This Scottish trading-house had been given permission by the Spaniards to continue operations after the transfer of the Floridas to Spain. For many years official negotiations with the Indians were carried on through the agents of this concern.

[38] For a brief summary of the life and diplomatic career of Edmund Charles Edouard Genêt, see *D.A.B.*, VII (1931), 207–209. Genêt reached Charleston on April 8, 1793.

[39] "Mémoire pour servir d'instruction au Citoyen Genêt Adjutant-Général-Colonel, allant en Amérique en qualité de Ministre Plénipotentiaire de la République Française près le Congrès des États-Unis, Décembre, 1792," A.H.A. *Report*, 1896, I, 967.

[40] For a short biography of George Rogers Clark, see *D.A.B.*, IV (1943), 127–130.

[41] For a short biography of William Moultrie, see *ibid.*, XIII, 293–294. His brother, John, was appointed lieutenant governor of East Florida in 1771.

[42] For Elijah Clark, see Louise Frederick Hays, *Hero of Hornet's Nest: A Biography of Elijah Clark, 1733 to 1799* (New York, 1946).

NOTES TO CHAPTER II

MANGOURIT'S PREPARATIONS IN CHARLESTON

[1] The proclamation was issued on April 22, obviously before the news of the French declaration of war on Spain had reached Philadelphia, since only Austria, Prussia, Sardinia, Great Britain, and the United Netherlands were named as the opponents of France. James Daniel Richardson, ed., *A Compilation of the Messages and Papers of the Presidents, 1789–1897* (Washington, 1896–1899), I, 156–157.

[2] Michel Ange Bernard de Mangourit (1752–1829) was a diplomat and writer of some note. For a short account of his life and career, see Pierre Larousse, *Grand Dictionnaire Universel du XIX Siècle* (Paris, 1866–1890), X, 1673. For a sketch of Mangourit's diplomatic career, see also Masson, *Le Départment des Affaires Etrangères pendant la révolution* (Paris, 1877), pp. 323–325, printed in Frederick J. Turner, ed., "Correspondence of the French Ministers to the United States, 1791–1797," A.H.A. *Report*, 1903, II, 930–932.

[3] Mangourit received his credentials on September 3, 1792. "French Consular Agents in the United States, 1791–1850," *Franco-American Review*, I (1936), 85.

[4] Little appears to be known of the individual whose name appears variously as Tintiniac, Tinteniac, and Dantignac. It is possible that he belonged to the famous French family of Tinténiac, although most of its members were royalists. From his

own letters, he apparently fought in the American Revolution and later settled down on a plantation on the Edisto River.

⁵ Michel Ange Bernard de Mangourit to Tintiniac [n.d.], enclosed in Mangourit to Edmund Charles Edouard Genêt, June 14, 1793, A.H.A. *Report*, 1897, p. 581.

⁶ Gaspard Monge (minister of marine) to Mangourit, February 11, 1793, enclosed in Mangourit to Genêt, June 14, 1793, *ibid.*, p. 582.

⁷ Dantignac [*sic*] to Mangourit, June 6, 1793, enclosed in Mangourit to Genêt, June 14, 1793, *ibid.*, pp. 582–583. The Edisto River rises near Columbia, the capital of South Carolina, and flows to the southeast, emptying into St. Helena Sound some thirty miles southwest of Charleston.

⁸ Mangourit to Genêt, June 14, 1793, *ibid.*, p. 580.

⁹ Mangourit to Genêt, August 6, 1793, *ibid.*, p. 587.

¹⁰ The minister of marine had written Genêt, "You will find enclosed, Citizen, 300 letters of marque which you can distribute to all American privateers who desire to put to sea against the English, Dutch, Russians, Prussians, and Austrians." *Actes et mémoires concernent les négociations qui ont eu lieu entre la France et Les Etats-Unis de l'Amérique, depuis 1793 jusqu'à la conclusion de la convention du 30 Septembre, 1800* (London, 1807), I, 12.

¹¹ See Charles Marion Thomas, *American Neutrality in 1793* (New York, 1931).

¹² Mangourit to Captain Branzon (master of the *Las Casas*), February 11, 1794, A.H.A. *Report*, 1897, pp. 612–613. As early as April, 1793, Governor Moultrie had issued orders to close all inns that were being used as rendezvous for volunteers in the French service. *City Gazette and Daily Advertiser* (Charleston), April 16, 1793. It is doubtful that any effort was made to enforce these regulations, since the number of volunteers in the summer of 1793 was fairly large.

¹³ Quesada to José de Jaudenes and José Ignacio de Viar (Spanish representatives in Philadelphia), December 3, 1793, E.F.P., 102 K 8.

¹⁴ A careful reading of Genêt's instructions reveals the vague skeleton of the results expected of the new French minister. See "Memoire pour servir d'instruction au Citoyen Genêt ... ," A.H.A. *Report*, 1896, I, 967.

¹⁵ See Frederick J. Turner, ed., "Correspondence of Clark and Genêt," A.H.A. *Report*, 1896, I, 930–1107; Frederick J. Turner, "The Origins of Genêt's Projected Attack on Louisiana and the Floridas," *American Historical Review*, III (1898), 650–671; and Marc de Villiers du Terrage, *Les dernières Années de la Louisiane Française* (Paris [n.d.]), p. 365.

¹⁶ Genêt had ample time to discuss his plans with Mangourit during the eleven days the two were together in Charleston.

¹⁷ Genêt to minister of foreign affairs, April 16, 1793, A.H.A. *Report*, 1903, II, 213.

¹⁸ Mangourit to Genêt, June 17, 1793, *ibid.*, p. 584.

¹⁹ Little seems to be known about William Tate. He was a native of South Carolina and served as a lieutenant in the American Revolution. For Mangourit's glowing account of Tate's character and military capabilities, see Mangourit to Fauchet, March 30, 1794, *ibid.*, p. 646.

²⁰ Genêt's commission to William Tate, 1793, *ibid.*, p. 599. Mangourit presented Tate with his commission late in September. On October 1, the French consul sent the colonel a lengthy dispatch with explicit instructions how and where to recruit men, and what to promise them in the way of wages and division of future spoils. Mangourit to William Tate, October 1, 1793, enclosed in Tate to the Directory,

September 17, 1796, *ibid.*, 1897, pp. 672–675. For some general remarks on Tate's projected plan against New Orleans or West Florida, see Mangourit to William Tate, October 1, 1795, Tate to Charles Lecroix (minister of foreign affairs), December 6, 1795, and Tate to the Directory, September 17, 1796, *ibid.*, pp. 671–674.

[21] "Mangourit Correspondence," *ibid.*, pp. 590–591.

[22] Mangourit to Genêt, April 24, 1793, *ibid.*, p. 575.

[23] Mangourit to Genêt, April 28, 1793, *ibid.*, p. 578.

[24] Samuel Hammond was born September 21, 1757, in Richmond County, Farnham Parish, Virginia. He came to Savannah after the revolution and entered politics. During the Creek War, he held the rank of colonel in the state militia. After serving as representative in Congress in 1802, he was appointed military and civil governor of upper Louisiana (Missouri) in 1805. After moving to South Carolina, he held the offices of surveyor general and later secretary of state. He died in 1824. John A. Chapman, *History of Edgefield County from the Earliest Settlement to 1897* (Newberry, South Carolina, 1897).

[25] "Mangourit Correspondence," A.H.A. *Report*, 1897, p. 589.

[26] Except for Mangourit's remarks, nothing is known of Major Bert. The consul wrote that Bert was born in Alsace, that he had been associated with the legion "Armond," and that he was a prudent and valiant republican patriot. Mangourit to Genêt, June 19, 1793, *ibid.*, pp. 584–585.

[27] *Ibid.*

[28] Mangourit to Genêt, July 1, 1793, *ibid.*, p. 585.

[29] Mangourit to Edward Telfair, July 25, 1793, as quoted in Executive Department Minutes, August 21, 1793, D.A.H.G.

[30] Mangourit to Genêt, August 6, 1793, A.H.A. *Report*, 1897, p. 588.

[31] Genêt sent approximately two score dispatches to Paris early in October covering all phases of his activities in the United States, in order to counter any protests that Jefferson might have sent by way of the American minister in Paris.

[32] Genêt to minister of foreign affairs, October 7, 1793 [no. 11 of that date], A.H.A. *Report*, 1903, II, 265.

[33] Mangourit to Genêt, October 19, 1793, *ibid.*, 1897, p. 602.

[34] *City Gazette and Daily Advertiser* (Charleston), November 5, 1793.

[35] Mangourit to Genêt, November 3, 1793, A.H.A. *Report*, 1897, pp. 603–604.

[36] Among those suspected of assisting Mangourit was Stephen Drayton, the private secretary of Governor Moultrie, and a member of a highly respected South Carolina family.

[37] A committee had been appointed on December 2 to investigate these rumors of enlistments, and on December 6 it was reported that, "The avowed purpose for which these troops are now raising is to rendezvous in the State of Georgia and from thence to proceed into the Spanish dominions with a view to conquest or plunder as their strength might enable or opportunity might tempt them." Report of the Committee in the House, December 6, 1793, *Journal of the House*, pp. 380–386. See also *Journal of the Senate*, pp. 36–38, Historical Commission of South Carolina, Columbia. The proclamation of Governor Moultrie is to be found printed in the *City Gazette and Daily Advertiser* (Charleston), December 14, 1793.

[38] See *Journal of the House*, pp. 426–429, 621–622, 625; and Alexander Moultrie, *An Appeal to the People, on the Account of a Certain Public Body in South Carolina, Respecting Colonel Drayton and Colonel Moultrie* (Charleston, 1794).

[39] The Augusta *Chronicle and Gazette of the State* (Augusta, Georgia), December 21, 1793.

[40] Mangourit to Bournonville (secretary of legation), February 24, 1794, A.H.A. *Report*, 1897, p. 621.

[41] An extract from a letter written in Charleston, appearing in a Philadelphia newspaper, indicated that there were those in South Carolina who hoped to see Governor Moultrie impeached for treason. *Gazette of the United States* (Philadelphia), December 23, 1793.

[42] Mangourit to Genêt, January 14, 1794, A.H.A. *Report*, 1897, pp. 604–605.

[43] *Ibid.*, p. 605.

[44] "Proposals for enlistment in the French service [1793]," D.A.H.G. It is possible that this document was similar to the one seized among the papers of Abner Hammond, which bore the date, July 24, 1793. Luis de Las Casas (governor general of Cuba) to Ambrosio José Negrette, Conde de Campo Alange (secretary of state for war and Indies), April 6, 1794, A.G.I., S.D., 2563. If these are both copies of the same document, the original must have been written several months before the seizure of the Charleston copy.

[45] "Proposals for enlistment in the French service [1793]," D.A.H.G.

[46] Mangourit did not give the details of how or by whom this decision was reached, although he did use the expression, "we have decided on April 10 next." Mangourit to Genêt, March 5, 1794, A.H.A. *Report*, 1897, p. 627. However, several weeks earlier, he had indicated that the date of the rendezvous had already been set. Mangourit to Genêt, February 17, 1794, *ibid.*, p. 619. An undated letter from Samuel Hammond, probably written in February, suggested April 10 as a possible date for the rendezvous. Samuel Hammond to Mangourit [n.d.], *ibid.*, p. 596.

[47] Projet de traité avec les Indiens Creeks que le Colonel leRoi Hammond est chargé de faire avec eux, *ibid.*, pp. 591–593.

[48] *Ibid.*, p. 593.

[49] Instructions données aux Colonels des légions révolutionnaires d'Amérique et de Floride, Wm Tate et Samuel LeRoi Hammond, le 4 Mars, present mois, lequelles serviront de baze fondamentale aux discours que prononceront leurs agens, près les Nations Indiennes, *ibid.*, pp. 623–625.

[50] Mangourit to Leroy Hammond (uncle of Samuel Hammond), March 6, 1794, *ibid.*, p. 594.

[51] Note des troupes actuelles au service depuis St. Augustin de la Floride à la rivière Ste. Marie, *ibid.*, pp. 596–597.

[52] Mangourit to Genêt, February 7, 1794, *ibid.*, pp. 606–608.

[53] Mangourit to Captain Branzon, February 11, 1794, *ibid.*, pp. 612–613.

[54] Jefferson to Genêt [n.d.], as printed in Paul Leicester Ford, ed., *The Writings of Thomas Jefferson* (New York, 1892–1899), VI, 429.

[55] For information on the four commissioners, see Turner, "Correspondence of the French Ministers to the United States, 1791–1797," A.H.A. *Report*, 1903, II, 288–289, footnotes.

[56] A letter from Fauchet, dated December 22, 1794, expressed the hope that his ship might be able to depart from Brest on the following morning. Jean Antoine Joseph Fauchet to minister of foreign affairs, December 22, 1793, *ibid.*, p. 301.

[57] Rapport sur les causes du rappel du Cit. Mangourit ... [November 19, 1793], *ibid.*, 1897, p. 658.

[58] Mangourit to Genêt, February 10, 1794, *ibid.*, p. 638.

[59] "Portions of the Journal of André Michaux, Botanist . . . ," *Proceedings of the American Philosophical Society*, XXVI (1889), 102.

[60] *Ibid.*, p. 108.

[61] Mangourit to Genêt, March 23, 1794, A.H.A. *Report*, 1897, p. 638.

[62] Mangourit to Fauchet, March 25, 1794, *ibid.*, pp. 636–638.

[63] Fauchet's proclamation appeared on March 27, 1794, in the *City Gazette and Daily Advertiser* (Charleston).

[64] Report of assembly of leaders of the expedition at Charleston, March 29, 1794, A.H.A. *Report*, 1897, pp. 629–632.

[65] Bert to Mangourit, March 30, 1794, *ibid.*, pp. 647–648.

[66] Mangourit to Fauchet, March 30, 1794, *ibid.*, p. 645.

[67] Mangourit to Fauchet, March 31, 1794, *ibid.*, pp. 648–650.

[68] Mangourit to Hammond, April 4, 1794, and Address to the Floridians to be issued at St. Mary's, April 10, 1794, *ibid.*, pp. 651–656.

[69] Commissioners to minister of foreign affairs, May 20, 1794, *ibid.*, pp. 659–661.

[70] Fauchet to minister of foreign affairs, May 20, 1794, *ibid.*, 1903, II, 345.

NOTES TO CHAPTER III

SAMUEL HAMMOND AND FRENCH PREPARATIONS IN GEORGIA

[1] General order, April 11, 1793, order book of Major General John Twiggs, p. 43, G.H.S.

[2] John Twiggs to Telfair, July 19 and September 8, 1793, G.H.S.

[3] Colonel LeRoy Hammond, the uncle of Samuel and Abner, had commanded a regiment of irregular troops in the Revolutionary War. Samuel Hammond served under his uncle for several years. Stella M. Drumm, "Samuel Hammond," *Missouri Historical Society Collections*, IV (1923), 420.

[4] Commissioners to minister of foreign affairs, May 20, 1794, A.H.A. *Report*, 1897, p. 660.

[5] Mangourit to Fauchet, March 25, 1794, *ibid.*, pp. 636–638. Mouchet was later given a commission by Mangourit appointing him commissioner of war and controller of expenses for the East Florida expedition. Commission to Mouchet, March 25, 1794, enclosed in Mangourit to Mouchet, March 26, 1794, *ibid.*, pp. 641–642.

[6] *City Gazette and Daily Advertiser* (Charleston), January 3, 1794.

[7] *Columbian Centinel* (Boston), February 8, 1794.

[8] Mangourit to Genêt, November 3, 1793, A.H.A. *Report*, 1897, p. 603.

[9] S. Hammond to Mangourit, February 1 (?), 1794, *ibid.*, p. 597.

[10] List of troops near the St. Mary's, 1794, *ibid.*, p. 596.

[11] The seat of Wilkes County in the east-central part of Georgia.

[12] S. Hammond to Mangourit, February, 1794, and S. Hammond to Mangourit (?), February 12, 1794, A.H.A. *Report*, 1897, pp. 596 and 613.

[13] S. Hammond to Mangourit, February, 1794, *ibid.*, p. 596.

[14] Bert to Mangourit, February 15, 1794, *ibid.*, p. 616.

[15] *Ibid.* The writer's allusion to settlers fleeing East Florida referred to those suspected of being involved in the schemes of Abner Hammond who managed to elude the Spanish authorities.

[16] Mangourit to Genêt, March 5, 1794, *ibid.*, p. 627.

[17] Hammond to Mangourit, March 19, 1794, *ibid.*, p. 635.

[18] *Ibid.*, pp. 635–636.

[19] Hammond to Mangourit, March 19, 1794, *ibid.*, p. 636.

[20] Hays, *op. cit.*, p. 246. This may have been the same banquet held at the order of the state legislature at which the governor and the adjutant general presided. George White, *Historical Collections of Georgia* (New York, 1854), p. 624. The legislative act ordering the holding of this celebration appeared in the Augusta newspapers on December 14. The Augusta *Chronicle and Gazette of the State* (Augusta, Georgia), December 14, 1793.

[21] Elijah Clark to George Mathews, February 18, 1794 (photostatic copy), D.A.H.G.

[22] Executive Department Minutes, p. 72, *ibid.*

[23] Clark to Tate, February 21, 1794, *ibid.*

[24] *Ibid.*

[25] One authority states that Mangourit persuaded Clark to join the French schemes in the summer of 1793, issuing him a commission as major general in the French army, at a salary of $10,000. However, no proof of this statement is offered. William F. Keller, "The Frontier Intrigues of Citizen Genêt," *Americana*, XXXIV (1940), 581.

[26] Affidavit of William Jones, February 6, 1794 (English translation), G.H.S.

[27] Situated in Greene County at the confluence of the Oconee and Apalachee rivers.

[28] Thomas Houghton (justice of the peace) to Mathews, March 16, 1794, D.A.H.G.

[29] Regina Katherine Crandall, "Genêt's Projected Attack on Louisiana and the Floridas, 1793–1794," MS (University of Chicago, 1902), p. 144.

[30] Quesada to Mathews, January 23, 1794, *A.S.P.*, *F.R.*, I, 426–427, and Mathews to Quesada, February 21, 1794, L.B.M., pp. 34–36, D.A.H.G.

[31] The Augusta *Chronicle and Gazette of the State* (Augusta, Georgia), February 8 and 15, 1794.

[32] L.B.M., pp. 66–67, D.A.H.G.

[33] Mathews to secretary of war, February 19, 1794, *ibid.*

[34] Mathews to senators and representatives of Georgia, February 19, 1794, *ibid.*

[35] Mathews to adjutant general of Georgia, February 24, 1794, L.B.M., p. 39, *ibid.* See also *City Gazette and Daily Advertiser* (Charleston), March 27, 1794.

[36] L.B.M., pp. 66–67, D.A.H.G. The proclamation appeared officially in the Augusta *Chronicle and Gazette of the State* (Augusta, Georgia) on March 8, and in the *Georgia Gazette* (Savannah, Georgia) on March 13. In neither case was there any editorial comment.

[37] Mangourit to Hammond, April 4, 1794, A.H.A. *Report*, 1897, p. 653.

[38] Coleraine was a small village on the St. Mary's River in the westernmost part of Camden County, and only a few miles from Charlton County. In 1794, Coleraine lay west of the "temporary line" of the treaty of 1790. The ruins of Temple Church still stand seven miles east-south-east of Coleraine, and approximately one and one-half miles north of the St. Mary's River.

[39] W. Winterbotham, *An Historical, Geographical, Commercial, and Philosophical View of the American United States, and of the European Settlements in America and the West Indies* (London, 1795), III, 273.

[40] Luis de Las Casas y Aragorri to Campo Alange, May 18, 1794, A.G.I., S.D., 2563, and *City Gazette and Daily Advertiser* (Charleston), April 26, 1794.

[41] This probably refers to the report of the justices of the peace in Greene County accusing some of Clark's men of illegal acts, and to the presentments of the grand jury in Burke County.

[42] James Seagrove was appointed federal agent to the Creek Indians, probably in 1791. See secretary of war to James Seagrove, February 20, 1792, *A.S.P.*, *I.A.*, I, 249–250.

[43] It is impossible to identify Old King, as the name "King" was in common usage among the Creek Indians.

[44] From a letter written on April 2, 1794, at Fort Independence on the St. Mary's River, and printed in the *Gazette of the United States* (Philadelphia), May 24, 1794.

[45] The *Herald* (New York), May 6, 1794, and Constant Freeman to secretary of war, April 18, 1794, as printed in the *Herald* (New York), June 4, 1794.

[46] Probably the fort at St. Mary's often referred to as Fort St. Tammany.

[47] Henry Gaither to secretary of war, April 13, 1794, as printed in the *Herald* (New York), June 4, 1794.

[48] Constant Freeman was the agent of the Department of War in Georgia.

[49] M. Williamson to Captain Thomas Martin, April 9, 1794, as printed in the *Herald* (New York), May 14, 1794.

[50] Henry Knox to governor of Georgia [n.d.], as printed in the *Herald* (New York), May 14, 1794.

[51] Quesada to Benjamin Moodie (British consul in Charleston), May 9, 1794, E.F.P., 102 K 8.

[52] G. W. Foster (justice of the peace of Greene County) to Clark, April 24 and 27, 1794, and Clark to Foster, April 27, 1794, D.A.H.G. See also *City Gazette and Daily Advertiser* (Charleston), May 1 and 6, 1794, and June 11, 1794.

[53] The two men, John Watkins, a notorious gambler, and Theoderic Scott, an engraver, claimed to be the leaders of a gang of about forty men. The two men escaped from the jail in Savannah on May 18 and fled to South Carolina where they were eventually apprehended and returned to Georgia. *City Gazette and Daily Advertiser* (Charleston), June 11, 1794.

[54] Letter of John Holland, April 26, 1794, as printed in the *Herald* (New York), May 6, 1794.

NOTES TO CHAPTER IV

COUNTERMEASURES IN EAST FLORIDA

[1] Luis de Las Casas y Aragorri was governor general of Cuba from 1790 to 1796. For a short biography, see *Diccionario Enciclopedico Hispano-Americano de Literatura, Ciencias y Artes* (Barcelona, 1888–1889), IV, 863–864.

[2] Las Casas to Campo Alange, March 21, 1793, A.G.I., S.D., 2562.

[3] Juan Vicente de Guemes Pacheco y Padilla, Conde de Revilla Gigedo (viceroy of Mexico) to Campo Alange, April 30, 1793, *ibid.*, 2578.

[4] Quesada to Las Casas, June 10, 1793, A.G.I., P.C., 1437.

[5] Quesada to Jaudenes and Viar, June 7, 1793, E.F.P., 102 K 8.

[6] Quesada to Las Casas, March 14, 1793, enclosed in Las Casas to Campo Alange, April 10, 1793, A.G.I., S.D., 2562.

[7] Colonel Carlos Howard held the position of private secretary to Governor Céspedes from 1784 to 1790. He was retained in that post by Governor Quesada until

early in 1793. When Richard Lang, temporary commander of the northern frontier since the murder of Enrique O'Neill, proved unsatisfactory, Quesada recommended Howard for that position at an annual salary of 1,500 pesos. This appointment was approved by Las Casas in the spring of 1793, although Howard had been carrying out the duties of the office since February. Howard was of Irish and Spanish extraction.

[8] Carlos Howard to Quesada, August 22, 1793, enclosed in Quesada to Las Casas, September 9, 1793, A.G.I., S.D., 2561.

[9] Richard Lang came to East Florida in 1790, probably from Camden County, Georgia, where his father, Isaac Lang, had settled in 1783. On November 1, 1790, Governor Quesada granted Lang 400 acres of land at White House Plantation near Mills Ford on the southern bank of the St. Mary's River. He was appointed temporary justice of the peace and militia commander of the region lying between the Nassau and St. Mary's rivers. *Spanish Land Grants*, III, 30. The name of Lang often appears as Lane or Land in the Spanish records.

[10] Howard to Quesada, August 22, 1793, enclosed in Quesada to Las Casas, September 9, 1793, A.G.I., S.D., 2561.

[11] Quesada to Las Casas, September 9, 1793, *ibid.*

[12] Covachicha (Spanish agent) to Quesada, August 9, 1793, enclosed in Quesada to Las Casas, August 28, 1793, and Jaudenes and Viar to Las Casas, October 1, 1793, both enclosed in Las Casas to Campo Alange, October 26, 1793, *ibid.*

[13] Las Casas to Quesada, October 23, 1793, A.G.I., S.D., 2561.

[14] Quesada to Las Casas, November 21, 1793, A.G.I., P.C., 1437.

[15] Howard to Quesada, November 25, 1793, enclosed in Quesada to Las Casas, December 10, 1793, *ibid.*

[16] *City Gazette and Daily Advertiser* (Charleston), October 10, 1793, enclosed in Bernardo Sanchez (Spanish consul in Charleston) to Quesada, October 19, 1793, enclosed in Quesada to Las Casas, December 11, 1793, *ibid.*

[17] Quesada to Las Casas, December 11, 1793, *ibid.*

[18] William Jones came to East Florida early in 1792 and established his home on the southern bank of the St. John's River on a plantation formerly owned by Robert Pritchard. On February 24, 1793, the governor granted Jones title to 216 acres near the site of present-day South Jacksonville. His plantation was developed rapidly during the first year. Inventory of the property of William Jones, July 22, 1795, E.F.P., 295; Affidavit of William Jones, February 6, 1794 (English translation), G.H.S.; and Thomas Frederick Davis, *History of Early Jacksonville, Florida....* (Jacksonville, 1911), p. 17.

[19] For one person's views, see Testimony of David Garvin, February 10, 1794, enclosed in Las Casas to Campo Alange, April 8, 1794, A.G.I., S.D., 2563.

[20] Reuben Pitcher, a former citizen of the United States, came to East Florida, probably in 1790, and settled near the St. Mary's River. Late in 1793, he became embroiled in difficulties with the Spanish authorities and fled to Georgia, where he became one of Samuel Hammond's chief assistants in the recruiting program early in 1794.

[21] John Houston McIntosh, a member of the famous family of General Lachlan McIntosh of Revolutionary War fame, left Camden County, Georgia, late in 1790, and settled on Spring Hill Plantation on the southern bank of the St. John's River,

about seven miles from Cow Ford. He apparently enjoyed the governor's confidence since he was appointed to a minor governmental position.

[22] William Plowden came to East Florida, probably from Georgia, in 1791, and settled in St. Augustine where he was permitted to purchase a large house in the Calle de la Marina.

[23] John Peter Wagnon settled in St. Augustine, possibly in 1792, where he apparently carried on some sort of trade. He owned a small house in the town which he was forced to sell the next year.

[24] Las Casas to Campo Alange, February 12 and 13, 1794, A.G.S., Guerra, 7235.

[25] Although Las Casas reported that Samuel Hammond's commission was dated June 24, 1793, it is unlikely that it was actually issued to him at that date. When Genêt left Charleston, he handed Mangourit a large number of signed commissions with the name left blank. Hammond's was probably one of these. Las Casas to Campo Alange, February 13, 1794, *ibid.*

[26] *Ibid.*

[27] Walter Charlton Hartridge, ed., *The Letters of Don Juan McQueen to His Family, Written from Spanish East Florida, 1791–1807* (Columbia, South Carolina, 1943), p. 21. See also Hays, *op. cit.*, p. 245.

[28] White, *op. cit.*, p. 553.

[29] When the reports from Las Casas reached Madrid, a meeting of the Council of State was held, at which time it was decided that McIntosh was guilty of having given moral support to the plans of Samuel Hammond. Actas del Consejo de Estado, meeting of May 2, 1794, A.H.N., Estado, 923.

[30] Quesada to Las Casas, January 3, 1794, enclosed in Las Casas to Campo Alange, February 12, 1794, A.G.S., Guerra, 7235.

[31] Colonel Sebastian Kindelan y Oregan was at one time the sergeant major of the Mexican Infantry Regiment and was stationed at Havana in the spring of 1794. In addition, he appears to have had some connection with the Royal Engineers. He enjoyed the confidence of the governor general. The convicts were to work on digging trenches and on repairing Fort San Marcos.

[32] Benjamin Moodie (British consul in Charleston) to Quesada, March 22, 1794, E.F.P., 102 K 8.

[33] Juan McQueen [John McQueen] to the Misses McQueen, February 9, 1794, as printed in Hartridge, *op. cit.*, p. 21.

[34] *City Gazette and Daily Advertiser* (Charleston), February 18, 1794.

[35] The Augusta *Chronicle and Gazette of the State* (Augusta, Georgia), February 15, 1794.

[36] *City Gazette and Daily Advertiser* (Charleston), February 27, 1794.

[37] Declaration of Quesada, December 12, 1794, *Spanish Land Grants*, III, 78.

[38] Timothy Hollingsworth was born in North Carolina in 1755, and was living in East Florida in 1784. In 1790, he was granted title to a 900-acre plantation, known as Mulberry Grove. He served in the rural militia with the rank of captain.

[39] Quesada to Diego de Gardoqui, August 10, 1794, A.G.I., S.D., 2643.

[40] Bartolomé Morales to Las Casas, May 27, 1795, A.G.I., P.C., 1438.

[41] Howard to Morales, June 7, 1794, enclosed in Morales to Las Casas, June 9, 1794, *ibid.*

[42] Ataque de San Augustin de la Florida, 1794, E.F.P., photostatic copy in archives of Fort San Marcos National Monument Library.

[43] Diary of John Hambly, 1794, A.G.I., S.D., 2563.

[44] Quesada to Las Casas, June 23, 1794, enclosed in Las Casas to Campo Alange, September 29, 1794, *ibid.*

[45] Las Casas to Campo Alange, May 18, 1794, *ibid.*

[46] Among the British agents in the United States who rendered particular service to Governor Quesada and Governor General Las Casas were John Wallace in Savannah, James Shoolbred and Benjamin Moodie in Charleston, and John Hamilton in Norfolk.

[47] Quesada to Mathews, January 7, 1794, enclosed in Quesada to John Wallace (British consul in Savannah), January 7, 1794, E.F.P., 102 K 8.

[48] Quesada to Jaudenes and Viar, January 8, 1794, *ibid.*

[49] Quesada to Mathews, January 22, 1794, enclosed in Quesada to Wallace, January 22, 1794, and Quesada to Jaudenes and Viar, January 22, 1794, *ibid.*

[50] Quesada to Jaudenes and Viar, February 4, 1794, *ibid.*

[51] Wallace to Quesada, February 13, 1794, *ibid.*

[52] Mathews to Wallace, February 21, 1794, enclosed in Wallace to Quesada, March 6, 1794, *ibid.*

[53] Wallace to Quesada, March 6, 1794, *ibid.*

[54] *Ibid.*

[55] Wallace to Quesada, April 16, 1794, *ibid.*

[56] Howard to S. Hammond, March 23, 1794, enclosed in Howard to Wallace, March 23, 1794, *ibid.*

[57] Mathews to Quesada, February 21, 1794, L.B.M., D.A.H.G.

[58] Quesada to Wallace, April 28, 1794, E.F.P., 102 K 8.

[59] Quesada to Moodie, April 28, 1794, *ibid.*

[60] Wallace to Quesada, April 26, 1794, *ibid.*

[61] The prisoners held in St. Augustine were released in late April or early May, when the governor agreed to allow them to be set free upon the posting of sufficient bail. José de Ortega to Quesada, April 29, 1794, enclosed in Ortega to Las Casas, May 21, 1794, A.G.I., P.C., 152B. Lang spent nearly two months in the Royal Hospital where he ran up a $300 medical bill. He was finally freed upon agreeing to pay his account as soon as he could liquidate some of his holdings. However, he hastened across the St. Mary's River and then defied Quesada to collect the $300. Quesada to Mathews, March (?), E.F.P., 108 D 9.

NOTES TO CHAPTER V

TRANS-OCONEE AFFAIR

[1] Jacob Townshend, a trader among the Creeks, reported that Clark had actually gone to Philadelphia to see Fauchet. Jacob Townshend to William Panton, July 14, 1794, *Georgia Historical Quarterly*, XXIV (1940), 259.

[2] Mathews to John Clark, May 4 and 6, 1794, L.B.M., D.A.H.G.

[3] Hays, *op. cit.*, pp. 260–261.

[4] General Jared Irwin was born in Mecklenburg County, North Carolina, and came to Georgia at an early age. He served in the Revolutionary War and became one of the leading military and political figures in the state. He served as governor from 1796 to 1798 and 1806 to 1809.

[5] Mathews to secretary of war, August 19, 1794, *A.S.P., I.A.*, I, 495, and White, *op. cit.*, p. 686.

[6] Diary of John Hambly, June to August, 1794, A.G.I., S.D., 2563.

[7] Thomas Houghton was one of the justices of the peace in Greene County and was foreman of the first grand jury selected in that county.

[8] The "men of ill repute" may have been a reference to the two counterfeiters who had been apprehended after joining Clark's force in the spring. Houghton to Mathews, May 20, 1794, D.A.H.G.

[9] Houghton to Mathews, May 20, 1794, *ibid.*, and White, *op. cit.*, p. 687.

[10] Elijah Clark to David Adams, May 17, 1794, D.A.H.G.

[11] Fort Twiggs was a public blockhouse on the east bank of the Oconee River just below the mouth of Shoulderbone Creek.

[12] Robert Raines to Attorney General Elholm, May 27, 1794, and William Melton to Mathews, May 22, 1794, D.A.H.G.

[13] Fort Fidius was a federal militia post on the east bank of the Oconee River about eight miles south of the present city of Milledgeville, at a spot then referred to as Rock Landing.

[14] Mathews to secretary of war, August 19, 1794, *A.S.P., I.A.*, I, 495.

[15] Mathews to Jared Irwin, July 22, 1794, D.A.H.G. See also White, *op. cit.*, p. 686.

[16] *Columbian Centinel* (Boston), July 26, 1794. The period of 16 months and 12 days referred to the remainder of Mathews' term of office as governor.

[17] *Ibid.*, June 14, 1794.

[18] Mathews to Captain James Armstrong, October 1, 1794, L.B.M., D.A.H.G.

[19] Mathews to Seagrove, August 13, 1794, *ibid.*

[20] Wilkes County lies just east of Greene County. The county seat is the town of Washington.

[21] Mathews to George Walker, and Mathews to Judge Stith, July 26, 1794, L.B.M., D.A.H.G.

[22] Lucian Lamar Knight, *Georgia's Landmarks, Memorials and Legends* (Atlanta, 1914), II, 112.

[23] Jonas Fauche was of French descent and apparently lived in or near Savannah. At one time, he was engaged as a school teacher, instructing in French. He held the position of captain in the state militia and was a trusted friend of Governor Mathews.

[24] Mathews to Jonas Fauche, July 20, 1794, *A.S.P., I.A.*, I, 496.

[25] According to one authority, the four justices were R. Worsham, Robert Christmas, Gibson Wooldridge, and William Bell. White, *op. cit.*, pp. 686–687.

[26] *A.S.P., I.A.*, I, 496; White, *op. cit.*, p. 687; and Knight, *op. cit.*, II, 113. It appears to be impossible to ascertain the precise date upon which Clark made his visit to the Wilkes County authorities, although it must have been before August 21 when a letter from the general mentioning his exoneration was printed on the editorial page of a Savannah newspaper. *Southern Centinel and Gazette of the State*, August 21, 1794.

[27] Thomas P. Carnes (militia officer) presented a copy of the proceedings in the Clark case to the governor and his council. Executive Department Minutes, August 19, 1794, D.A.H.G.

[28] Secretary of war to Mathews, July 28, 1794, *A.S.P., I.A.*, I, 501.

[29] Mathews to secretary of war, August 5, 1794, *ibid.*, p. 502.

[30] Alexander Hamilton was acting secretary of war during a short absence of Knox from Philadelphia.

[31] Hamilton to Mathews, September 25, 1794, *A.S.P., I.A.*, I, 502.

[32] Diary of John Hambly, 1794, A.G.I., S.D., 2563.

[33] Mathews to headmen of Creeks, August 11, 1794, *A.S.P., I.A.*, I, 497.

[34] Freeman to secretary of war, September 29, 1794, *ibid.*, p. 500.

[35] Knight, *op. cit.*, II, 110.

[36] *Ibid.*

[37] George Walton was born in Virginia and moved to Georgia where he practiced law. He was a delegate to the Continental Congress, 1776–1779, and 1780–1781. He was one of the three men from Georgia who signed the Declaration of Independence. He also signed the Articles of Confederation. He was elected governor in 1779 and again in 1789. Later he became judge of the superior court. Governor Telfair appointed him attorney general in 1793. He later served in the United States Senate.

[38] Augusta, the capital of Georgia in 1793, is now the seat of Richmond County.

[39] Judge Walton's charge to the grand jury of Richmond County, August 26, 1794, *A.S.P., I.A.*, I, 498–499.

[40] John Y. Noel (attorney general) to Mathews, August 27, 1794, G.H.S.

[41] Noel to Mathews, *op. cit.*

[42] General John Twiggs was one of Georgia's leading guerrilla leaders during the Revolutionary War. He was the ranking militia general in 1794.

[43] Mathews to secretary of war, August 30, 1794, *A.S.P., I.A.*, I, 497.

[44] Mathews to John Clark, August 29, 1794, D.A.H.G.

[45] The Augusta *Chronicle and Gazette of the State* (Augusta, Georgia), September 6, 1794.

[46] *Ibid.*

[47] *Ibid.*, September 13, 1794.

[48] As far as can be ascertained, this document was actually completed and adopted by the Committee of Safety, but no copy has ever been found, and none of the later writers were able to claim having seen the original. Clark to Committee of Safety, September 5, 1794, D.A.H.G.; Houghton to Mathews, May 20, 1794, *ibid.; and A.S.P., I.A.*, I, 500.

[49] Clark to Committee of Safety, September 3, 1794, *A.S.P., I.A.*, I, 501.

[50] Clark had written a long letter to the *Southern Centinel and Gazette of the State* in which he defended his actions, declaring, "If federal treaties, or acts of the Georgia assembly are considered law, I must be justified in all my proceedings." *Southern Centinel and Gazette of the State* (Savannah), August 21, 1794.

[51] Mathews to Twiggs, September 17, 1794, D.A.H.G.

[52] Mathews to secretary of war, October 12, 1794, *A.S.P., I.A.*, I, 499.

[53] The new federal battery at Savannah had been enlarged and rebuilt by Paul Hyacinte Perrault, temporary engineer for the United States Army. Knox to Paul Hyacinte Perrault, April 19, 1794 and Perrault to Knox, May 4, 1794, *A.S.P., M.A.*, I, 102.

[54] Brigadier General James Gunn was appointed to the United States Senate in 1789 and held that position until his death in 1801. He became deeply involved in the Yazoo Land Company scandals in 1795.

[55] Thomas Peter Carnes, a major in the state militia, was elected to Congress in 1793. He was a member of the convention which drew up the Constitution of 1798.

[56] Freeman to secretary of war, September 29, 1794, *A.S.P., I.A.*, I, 500.

[57] Twiggs to Mathews, October 2, 1794, D.A.H.G.

[58] Irwin to Clark, September 25, 1794, *ibid.*

[59] Clark to Irwin, September 24, 1794, *ibid.*

[60] Mathews to secretary of war, October 12, 1794, *A.S.P., I.A.*, I, 499.

[61] *Ibid.*

[62] Clark to Dr. McDonald, December 9, 1794, G.H.S.

[63] Absolom H. Chappell, *Miscellanies of Georgia, Historical, Biographical, Descriptive, Etc.* (Atlanta, 1874), pp. 33–55. This part of Chappell's work constitutes a long and extremely extravagant encomium of General Clark.

NOTES TO CHAPTER VI

SPANISH REACTION

[1] Wallace to Quesada, April 16, 1794, in E.F.P., 102 8 K.

[2] Quesada to Wallace, May 12, 1794, *ibid.*

[3] Quesada to Jaudenes and Viar, May 14, 1794, *ibid.*

[4] Jaudenes and Viar to Quesada, June 14, 1794, *ibid.*

[5] John Leslie to Panton, June 6, 1794, original in Meleise H. Cruzat Collection, F.H.S.

[6] Panton to Leslie, June 29 and 30, 1794, *ibid.*

[7] Francisco Luis Héctor, Baron de Carondelet, to Gardoqui, April 25, 1794, in A.G.I., S.D., 2643.

[8] Howard to Quesada, June 20, 1794, enclosed in Quesada to Las Casas, July 18, 1794, in A.G.I., P.C., 1438. Cumberland Island lies just to the north of the St. Mary's River, off the coast of Camden County, Georgia.

[9] Andrew Atkinson, a native of Northampton County, Virginia, settled in Camden County, Georgia, in 1785. He came to East Florida, possibly in 1792, and soon attained the rank of captain in the urban militia. In 1820, he was living in Philadelphia.

[10] Andrew Atkinson to Howard, June 20, 1794, enclosed in Howard to Quesada, June 23, 1794, in A.G.I., P.C., 1438. Amelia Island lies south of the mouth of the St. Mary's River, parallel to the coast of East Florida. The St. Mary's River empties into the Atlantic between Cumberland and Amelia islands.

[11] Knox to Perrault, April 19, 1794, in *A.S.P., M.A.*, I, 102.

[12] Perrault to Knox, May 4, 1794, and Knox to secretary of the treasury, July 9, 1794, *ibid.*

[13] Timothy Pickering to the President, January 16, 1796, *ibid.*, pp. 110–111.

[14] Atkinson to Howard, June 20, 1794, in A.G.I., P.C., 1438.

[15] *Ibid.*

[16] Mathews to Quesada, June 17, 1794, and secretary of war to Mathews, May 14, 1794, both enclosed in Quesada to Las Casas, June 28, 1794, *ibid.*

[17] Quesada to Mathews, June 23, 1794, *ibid.*

[18] Quesada to chief of Cowetas and others, June 23, 1794, *ibid.*

[19] Quesada to Las Casas, July 18, 1794, *ibid.*

[20] John Burrows to John McQueen, July 13, 1794, enclosed in McQueen to Quesada, July 15, 1794, enclosed in Quesada to Las Casas, July 18, 1794, *ibid.*

[21] Sarah McIntosh to John McIntosh, October 24, 1794, printed in White, *op. cit.*, pp. 552–553.

[22] Declaration of Leven Gumby, July 17, 1794, enclosed in Quesada to Las Casas, July 18, 1794, *ibid.*

[23] Quesada to Las Casas, July 18, 1794, *ibid.*

[24] Las Casas to Quesada, September 17, 1794, A.G.I., P.C., 1438.

[25] Hillabee or Hillibies was an Upper Creek town near the Chattahoochee River.

[26] Jacob Townshend to Panton, July 14, 1794, in D. C. Corbitt, ed. and trans., "Papers Relating to the Georgia-Florida Frontier, 1784–1800," *Georgia Historical Quarterly,* XXIV (1940), 259.

[27] Enrique White was governor of West Florida, under the direct command of the governor of Louisiana. He later replaced Quesada as governor of East Florida in 1796, a position he held until 1811.

[28] Panton to Enrique White [n.d.], in Corbitt, "Papers Relating to the Georgia-Florida Frontier, 1784–1800," *Georgia Historical Quarterly,* XXIV (1940), 261.

[29] White to Carondelet [n.d.], enclosed in Carondelet to Las Casas, October 30, 1794, A.G.I., P.C., 152 B.

[30] Carondelet to Las Casas, October 30, 1794, *ibid.*

[31] Carondelet to Las Casas, September 17, 1794, *ibid.*

[32] Carondelet to Las Casas, October 30, 1794, *ibid.*

[33] Panton to Carondelet, September 16, 1794, A.G.I., P.C., 203.

[34] Panton to Carondelet, September 30, 1794, *ibid.,* 153.

[35] Las Casas to Quesada, October 17, 1794, *ibid.,* 1438.

[36] Diary of John Hambly, June–August 1794, A.G.I., S.D., 2563.

[37] Jack Kinnard to Quesada, July 23, 1794, enclosed in Quesada to Las Casas, September 11, 1794, A.G.I., P.C., 1438. Kinnard was a Lower Creek chief who attempted to assume the position of McGillivray, after the latter's death in 1793. Kinnard leaned toward friendship with the United States. His home lay between the Flint and Chattahoochee rivers.

[38] *Ibid.*

[39] Quesada to Jaudenes and Viar, October 22, 1794, E.F.P., 102 K 8.

[40] Quesada to Las Casas, September 11, 1794, A.G.I., P.C., 1438.

[41] Quesada to Jaudenes and Viar, October 22, 1794, *ibid.*

[42] Quesada to Jaudenes and Viar, September 3, 1794, E.F.P., 102 K 8.

[43] Quesada to Las Casas, October 22, 1794, A.G.I., P.C., 1438.

[44] *Georgia Gazette* (Augusta), May 21, 1795.

[45] Mathews to Armstrong, October 1, 1794, D.A.H.G.

[46] Howard to Quesada, October 27, 1794, A.G.I., P.C., 1438.

[47] Quesada to Jaudenes and Viar, November 10, 1794, E.F.P., 102 K 8, and Quesada to Las Casas, November 10, 1794, *ibid.*

NOTES TO CHAPTER VII

RENEWED ALARMS

[1] John MacQueen or McQueen, was born and brought up in North Carolina. He apparently abandoned his family and entered East Florida under the terms of the royal order of May 3, 1790. He was in command of a force of volunteers raised in 1792 to apprehend the elusive William Augustus Bowles. As a result of this service, he was recommended for the post of captain in the rural militia. Las Casas finally

approved the recommendation. Las Casas to Campo Alange, May 7, 1793, A.G.I., S.D., 2562.

[2] The names of three children of Richard Lang, one of William Plowden, and one of Daniel McGirt appear in the baptismal records of St. Augustine Parish. *Roman Catholic Records, St. Augustine Parish, White Baptisms, 1784–1799* (Tallahassee, Florida, 1941), entry 133 on p. 30, entry 350 on p. 91, entry 351 on p. 92, entry 372 on p. 97, and entry 511 on p. 123.

[3] Quesada to Las Casas, March 18, 1793, enclosed in Las Casas to Campo Alange, April 9, 1793, A.G.I., S.D., 2562.

[4] Las Casas to Gardoqui, June 1, 1793, *ibid.*

[5] Quesada to Las Casas, August 28, 1793, *ibid.*, 2561. Fauchet claimed that most of these people were escaped criminals or debtors. Fauchet to commissioners of foreign relations, February 2, 1795, A.H.A. *Report*, 1903, II, 556.

[6] Las Casas to Quesada, October 23, 1793, A.G.I., S.D., 2562.

[7] This information was included in the will of John McIntosh's wife, Sarah Simons McIntosh, dated March 26, 1793. Deed book for years 1793 and 1794 (typewritten brief in St. Augustine Historical Society), p. 41.

[8] Wagnon purchased this house from Andrew Lewis Dewes on March 30, 1793. *Ibid.*, p. 37. It was quickly resold. *Ibid.*, p. 128.

[9] The house was purchased from Valentine Fitzpatrick on June 20, 1794, and the new owner at once secured a large mortgage to guarantee future payments. *Ibid.*, p. 275.

[10] Comments on the local militia are to be found in Howard to Richard Lang, August 20, 1793, enclosed in Howard to Quesada, August 22, 1793, enclosed in Quesada to Las Casas, September 9, 1793, A.G.I., S.D., 2561, and Howard to Morales, June 7, 1795, enclosed in Morales to Las Casas, June 9, 1795, A.G.I., P.C., 1438.

[11] Several of these complaints are mentioned in Howard to Quesada, August 22, 1793, A.G.I., S.D., 2561.

[12] Quesada to Las Casas, September 9, 1793, *ibid.*

[13] Howard to Lang, August 20, 1793, enclosed in Howard to Quesada, August 22, 1793, enclosed in Quesada to Las Casas, September 9, 1793, *ibid.*

[14] Morales to Las Casas, June 4, 1795, A.G.I., P.C., 1438.

[15] Bartolomé Morales had been intendant of Louisiana before being sent to East Florida in 1791 as the commanding officer of the 3d Battalion of Cuba. He then held the rank of lieutenant colonel. Quesada's poor health forced him to relinquish his political and military duties to Morales, and the duties of the *Real Hacienda* to Gonzalo Zamorano, the auditor of St. Augustine. Quesada to Acosta, April 30, 1795, E.F.P., 78.

[16] Jones requested that his family be allowed to visit his daughter, Abner Hammond's wife, at her home in Georgia. Morales permitted Jones to go only after exacting an oath of allegiance and good faith. Morales to Las Casas, June 4, 1795, A.G.I., P.C., 1438.

[17] For a comprehensive account of the Georgia land sales, see Haskins, "The Yazoo Land Companies," A.H.A. *Papers*, V, no. 4, (1891), 59–103.

[18] Chief Mad Dog was one of the leading Creek chiefs and a close friend of Alexander McGillivray. He usually favored the United States in preference to Spain. Mad Dog lived at Tuckebatches on the Tallapoosa River.

[19] Howard to Quesada, January 18, 1795, enclosed in Quesada to Las Casas, January 20, 1795, A.G.I., P.C., 1438.

[20] This figure appears to have been approximately correct. Atkinson to Howard, January 17, 1795, enclosed in Howard to Quesada, January 18, 1795, enclosed in Quesada to Las Casas, January 20, 1795, *ibid.*

[21] This report later turned out to be false, since Clark's total purchases of land amounted to 56,000 acres, and those of his son, John, to 28,000. *A.S.P., P.L.*, I, 141.

[22] Wallace to Quesada, January 23, 1795, enclosed in Quesada to Las Casas, February 10, 1795, A.G.I., P.C., 1438.

[23] Las Casas to Quesada, March 10, 1795, *ibid.*

[24] General James Jackson was one of the leading figures in Georgia history. For a short biography, see *D.A.B.* (1943), IX, 544–545. Jackson resigned his seat in the United State Senate in order to return to Georgia to be a candidate for the state legislature from Chatham County. He and his friends carried on a vigorous campaign against the land law of 1795, which resulted in his election and in a measure to the rescinding of the obnoxious act. When the rescinding act was passed in February, 1796, twenty years of litigation began. See Robert Preston Brooks, *History of Georgia* (Atlanta, 1913), pp. 157–163.

[25] Morales to Las Casas, May 6, 1795, A.G.I., P.C., 1438.

[26] Lang had presented his "account" to Quesada at an earlier date, and had received no reply. The governor forwarded a copy of this letter to Mathews, saying that Lang had fled to Georgia, and that the whole problem was one for the Georgia officials. Mathews replied that Lang still claimed his Spanish citizenship, and hence was not under Georgia's laws. It was after this indirect rebuff from Quesada that Lang sent his second and more demanding letter to the governor of East Florida. Quesada to Mathews, October 8, 1795, D.A.H.G.

[27] Lang to Quesada, May 18, 1795, enclosed in Morales to Las Casas June 4, 1795, A.G.I., P.C., 1438.

[28] George Fleming to Morales, May 30, 1795, enclosed in Morales to Las Casas, June 4, 1795, *ibid.*

[29] On March 10, Quesada sent a letter to Mathews, by way of the justices of the peace in Camden County, protesting against the actions of Lang. Quesada to Mathews, October 8, 1795, D.A.H.G.

[30] Quesada finally permitted Susana Plowden to take her children to Georgia, but not until after the confiscation of all her belongings.

[31] Susana Plowden to governor [Quesada], June 1, 1795, enclosed in Morales to Las Casas, June 4, 1795, A.G.I., P.C., 1438.

[32] *Junta de guerra*, June 2, 1795, enclosed in Morales to Las Casas, June 4, 1795, *ibid.*

[33] Howard to Morales, June 7, 1795, enclosed in Morales to Las Casas, June 9, 1795, *ibid.*

[34] William Plowden denied all the reports concerning his activities that were being circulated along the frontier. He said these were malicious rumors concocted by a personal enemy named Forrester. Plowden to governor of Florida, June 19, 1795, enclosed in Morales to Las Casas, June 28, 1795, *ibid.*

[35] Quesada had expressed some apprehension in letters to Las Casas in November, 1794, and January, 1795. Quesada to Las Casas, November 20, 1794, and Quesada to Las Casas, January 20, 1795, *ibid.*

[36] Quesada to Las Casas, January 20, 1795, *ibid.* Anastasia Island lies between St. Augustine and the Atlantic Ocean.

[37] The captured schooner was the property of Gordon and Company of the Bahamas. Atkinson to Howard, January 17, 1795, enclosed in Howard to Quesada, January 18, 1795, enclosed in Quesada to Las Casas, January 20, 1795, *ibid.* These French supporters were probably those left behind on Amelia Island when the *Las Casas* left the St. Mary's region in April, 1794.

[38] Atkinson to Howard, January 17, 1795, enclosed in Howard to Quesada, January 18, 1795, enclosed in Quesada to Las Casas, January 20, 1795, *ibid.*

[39] Howard to Quesada, May 7, 1795, enclosed in Morales to Las Casas, May 27, 1795, *ibid.*

[40] Morales to Las Casas, May 27, 1795, *ibid.*

[41] Howard gave a complete account of these troop withdrawals in his letter to Morales. Howard to Morales, June 7, 1795, *ibid.*

[42] Morales to Las Casas, May 27, 1795, *ibid.*

[43] Testimony of John McQueen, May 27, 1795, enclosed in Morales to Las Casas, May 27, 1795, *ibid.*

[44] Genêt purchased a farm on Long Island, and later one in Rensselaer County, where he lived until his death in 1834. He married Cornelia Clinton Toppen, the daughter of the governor of New York.

[45] George Fleming was one of the most respected Anglo-Saxon residents of East Florida. He married Sophia Philipina Maria Dominga, the daughter of Francisco Felipe Fatio, the largest landowner along the St. John's River. Fleming held a commission as captain in the militia and was entrusted with the task of supplying the province with fresh beef. He also held the position of alderman in St. Augustine.

[46] Fleming to Morales, May 30, 1795, enclosed in Morales to Las Casas, June 4, 1795, A.G.I., P.C., 1438.

[47] Alexander McDonell to governor [Quesada], June 9, 1795, enclosed in Morales to Las Casas, June 9, 1795, *ibid.*

[48] Fleming to Morales, May 30, 1795, enclosed in Morales to Las Casas, June 4, 1795, *ibid.*

[49] The junta was held on June 2, 1795. Report of *junta de guerra*, June 2, 1795, enclosed in Morales to Las Casas, June 4, 1795, *ibid.*

[50] Howard to Morales, June 7, 1795, enclosed in Morales to Las Casas, June 9, 1795, *ibid.*

[51] Morales to Las Casas, June 9, 1795, *ibid.*

[52] John Burrows (justice of the peace in St. Mary's) to Atkinson, June 5, 1795, enclosed in Morales to Las Casas, June 10, 1795, *ibid.*

[53] Peck Cornel to Quesada, June 1, 1795, enclosed in Morales to Las Casas, June 10, 1795, *ibid.*

[54] Captain John F. Randolph was in command of a small force of cavalry in the federal post at Coleraine. He was frequently accused by the Spaniards of assisting those hostile to the peace of the frontier. He also held the office of sheriff of Camden County in 1793 and 1794.

[55] Morales to Las Casas, June 10, 1795, A.G.I., P.C., 1438.

[56] Howard acknowledged the receipt of these orders in a note to Morales. Howard to Morales, June 23, 1795, enclosed in Morales to Las Casas, June 28, 1795, *ibid.*

[57] Nathan Atkinson, brother of Andrew, came from Northampton County, Virginia, and settled in Camden County, Georgia, in 1785. He made frequent trips to East Florida to visit his brother.

[58] Nathan Atkinson to Howard, June 21, 1795, enclosed in Howard to Morales, June 23, 1795, enclosed in Morales to Las Casas, June 28, 1795, *ibid.*

[59] The owner of the Mère Mitchele, a Mr. Booth, was present at the meeting of the "Republican Society" and spoke to Andrew Atkinson about the plans for his ship. Atkinson to Howard, June 23, 1795, enclosed in Howard to Morales, June 23, 1795, enclosed in Morales to Las Casas, June 28, 1795, *ibid.*

[60] *Ibid.*

[61] Howard to Morales, June 23, 1795, enclosed in Morales to Las Casas, June 28, 1795, *ibid.*

[62] Morales to Las Casas, June 28, 1795, *ibid.*

[63] Morales to Quesada, June 27, 1795, *ibid.*

[64] Las Casas to Campo Alange, September 19, 1795, A.G.I., S.D., 2564.

[65] Morales to Las Casas, June 28, 1795, A.G.I., P.C., 1438.

[66] Quesada to Mathews, October 8, 1795, D.A.H.G.

[67] Lang to Quesada, May 18, 1795, enclosed in Morales to Las Casas, June 4, 1795, A.G.I., P.C., 1438.

[68] *Columbian Centinel* (Boston), June 20, 1795.

[69] *Ibid.*

[70] Mathews to justices of inferior court of the County of Camden, August 24, 1795, L.B.M., D.A.H.G.

NOTES TO CHAPTER VIII

BORDER REBELLION IN EAST FLORIDA

[1] Quesada to Jaudenes and Viar, June 9, 1795, E.F.P., 103 L 8.

[2] Jaudenes to Edmund Randolph, July 2, 1795, and Randolph to Jaudenes, July 6, 1795, *ibid.*

[3] See in particular, Morales to Las Casas, June 9, 1795, A.G.I., P.C., 1438.

[4] Las Casas to Governor of Florida, July 8, 1795, enclosed in Las Casas to Campo Alange, July 10, 1795, A.G.I., S.D., 2564.

[5] Las Casas to Quesada, July 13, 1795, enclosed in Las Casas to Campo Alange, August 22, 1795, *ibid.*

[6] Juana was a small outpost approximately nine miles north of St. Augustine. It stood on one of the banks of Juana Creek, a tributary of North River, on the road to the St. John's and St. Mary's rivers. The garrison consisted of one officer, one noncommissioned officer, and thirteen enlisted men. Howard to Morales, July 4, 1795, enclosed in Morales to Las Casas, July 5, 1795, A.G.I., P.C., 1428.

[7] Various reports differed as to the actual number of men involved. In the report of the junta held on August 14 in Havana, the governor general spoke of sixty-two attackers. Report of junta, August 14, 1795, H.E.H.L., MSS 107–112. One of the garrison captured at Juana, Sergeant McCoulloth, was later released by Lang, and reported the number of the men in the rebel camp to be between forty and fifty. Howard to Morales, July 4, 1795, enclosed in Morales to Las Casas, July 5, 1795, A.G.I., P.C., 1428.

[8] Most of the cattle belonged to George Fleming, and constituted the meat supply of the province. As a result of this loss, he informed the governor that it would be impossible to fulfill his contract to supply the usual quota of fresh meat. Fleming to Morales, July 3, 1795, enclosed in Morales to Las Casas, July 4, 1795, *ibid.*

[9] A complete account of the attack can be pieced together from the lengthy set of dispatches sent to Madrid by the governor general. Las Casas to Campo Alange, August 22, 1795, A.G.I., S.D., 2564.

[10] Lang to governor of Florida, July 3, 1795, enclosed in Morales to Las Casas, July 5, 1795, A.G.I., P.C., 1428. Howard indicated that he believed this camp to be within the bounds of East Florida, Howard to Morales, July 4, 1795, enclosed in Morales to Las Casas, July 5, 1795, *ibid.*

[11] Peter Carne held a commission as captain in the rural militia.

[12] This Burnett could have been either John or Robert Burnett, both sons of David Burnett, a resident of East Florida. Both the young men had been militiamen in Howard's frontier force.

[13] Lang certainly was in command of the forces on July 3, for he then signed himself as "Commander of St. Marys." Lang to Howard, July 3, 1795, enclosed in Howard to Morales, July 4, 1795, enclosed in Morales to Las Casas, July 5, 1795, A.G.I., P.C., 1428.

[14] Peter Carne to Howard, June 30, 1795, enclosed in Howard to Morales, June 30, 1795, enclosed in Morales to Las Casas, July 4, 1795, *ibid.*

[15] Howard to Morales, June 30, 1795, enclosed in Morales to Las Casas, July 4, 1795, *ibid.*

[16] Morales to John King (justice of the peace at St. Mary's) and Burrows, July 3, 1795, and Morales to Mathews, July 3, 1795, both enclosed in Morales to Las Casas, July 4, 1795, *ibid.*

[17] Cook to Morales, July 2, 1795, enclosed in Morales to Las Casas, July 4, 1795, *ibid.*

[18] Fleming to Morales, July 3, 1795, enclosed in Morales to Las Casas, July 4, 1795, *ibid.*

[19] Other agents confirmed the rumor of Clark's reappearance near the St. Mary's River.

[20] Hall (captain in militia) to Howard, July, 1795, enclosed in Howard to Morales, July 4, 1795, enclosed in Morales to Las Casas, July 5, 1795, *ibid.*

[21] Howard to Morales, July 4, 1795, enclosed in Morales to Las Casas, July 5, 1795, *ibid.*

[22] This was in lieu of Howard's suggestion to build a small fort on the north bank of the St. John's River to protect the approaches to the ford.

[23] The *Conquest* was a twenty-gun brig under the command of Captain John McCockburn. The prize schooner, *Micaela*, carried ten guns.

[24] *Junta de guerra*, July 4, 1795, enclosed in Morales to Las Casas, July 5, 1795, A.G.I., P.C., 1428.

[25] Morales to Las Casas, July 5, 1795, *ibid.*

[26] Inventory of William Lane, July 23, 1795, E.F.P., 295. Sebastian Antonio Verazaluze was a Basque, coming from Guetaria in the province of Guipuscoa. His name sometimes appears as Berazaluze or Beracaluze.

[27] *Florida Times-Union*, trade edition, January, 1890, as quoted in Davis, *Jacksonville*, p. 11.

[28] Quesada forwarded a complete account of the events of July 9 to Havana. Quesada to Las Casas, July 25, 1795, A.G.I., P.C., 1428.

[29] Pellicier was a member of the Catalan Light Infantry Company.

[30] Quesada to Las Casas, July 25, 1795, A.G.I., P.C., 1428.

[31] Maas was a soldier in the regiment of the Dragoons of America.

[32] McIntosh had been released from Morro Castle by Las Casas and had been permitted to return to East Florida. According to Davis, McIntosh was "a turbulent man, of restless and reckless disposition," who had spent his time in prison devising methods of wreaking revenge on the Spaniards. Davis, *Jacksonville*, pp. 15–16.

[33] Quesada to Las Casas, July 25, 1795, enclosed in Las Casas to Campo Alange, August 25, 1795, A.G.I., S.D., 2564.

[34] Córdoba held the rank of captain in the 3d Cuban Regiment which comprised the garrison of St. Augustine.

[35] Panqua was a member of the same regiment.

[36] Quesada to Las Casas, July 25, 1795, enclosed in Las Casas to Campo Alange, August 25, 1795, A.G.I., S.D., 2564.

[37] Remedios was the ranking artillery officer in East Florida and also a member of the governor's inner council.

[38] Catafal was a member of the Mountain Fusiliers.

[39] A complete account of the military preparations and of the personnel involved is to be found in Quesada to Las Casas, July 25, 1795, enclosed in Las Casas to Campo Alange, August 25, 1795, A.G.I., S.D., 2564.

[40] Quesada to Las Casas, July 25, 1795, enclosed in Las Casas to Campo Alange, August 25, 1795, *ibid.*

[41] In addition, Howard reported that many of the militiamen were prone to mistreat and underfeed their mounts, particularly if the mounts belonged to the crown.

[42] Quesada to Las Casas, July 25, 1795, enclosed in Las Casas to Campo Alange, August 25, 1795, A.G.I., S.D., 2564.

[43] Quesada to Henry Grant (Spanish agent in Charleston), July 17, 1795, E.F.P., 103 L 8.

NOTES TO CHAPTER IX
AMELIA ISLAND AFFAIR

[1] [Andrew] Atkinson to Howard, January 18, 1795, enclosed in Howard to Quesada, January 18, 1795, enclosed in Quesada to Las Casas, January 20, 1795, A.G.I., P.C., 1438.

[2] Although the rumors about this fleet later turned out to be false, the French consul in Charleston was attempting to arouse interest in an assault on East Florida. Pierre Auguste Adet to minister of foreign relations, February 9, 1796, A.H.A. *Report*, 1903, II, 827.

[3] Howard to Quesada, May 7, 1795, enclosed in Morales to Las Casas, May 27, 1795, A.G.I., P.C., 1438.

[4] Fleming to Morales, May 30, 1795, enclosed in Morales to Las Casas, June 4, 1795, *ibid.*

[5] Pedro Diaz Berrio was the ranking officer of the engineers in East Florida and was a member of the governor's inner council.

[6] Pedro Diaz Berrio to Quesada, December 10, 1794, enclosed in Las Casas to Campo Alange, July 10, 1795, A.G.I., S.D., 2564.

[7] Report of the junta of June 2, 1795, enclosed in Morales to Las Casas, June 4, 1795, A.G.I., P.C., 1438.

[8] Morales to Las Casas, June 4, 1795, *ibid.*

[9] Talbot Island lies parallel to the seacoast and six miles north of the mouth of the St. John's River. It is about ten miles long and is separated from the mainland by a wide, marshy area traversed by many narrow tidal creeks. The northern end of the island lies directly south of the southern end of Amelia Island, and the two are about five miles apart, separated by the waters of Nassau Sound.

[10] This force consisted of a sergeant, a corporal, and twelve privates. Howard to Morales, June 7, 1795, enclosed in Morales to Las Casas, June 9, 1795, A.G.I., P.C., 1438.

[11] *Ibid.*

[12] [Andrew] Atkinson to Howard, June 23, 1795, enclosed in Howard to Morales, June 23, 1795, enclosed in Morales to Las Casas, June 28, 1795, *ibid.*

[13] Morales to Las Casas, June 28, 1795, *ibid.*

[14] Quesada to Jaudenes and Viar, July 17, 1795, E.F.P., 103 L 8.

[15] Quesada to Las Casas, July 25, 1795, A.G.I., P.C., 1438.

[16] Howard to Quesada, July 12, 1795, enclosed in Quesada to Las Casas, July 25, 1795, enclosed in Las Casas to Campo Alange, August 25, 1795, A.G.I., S.D., 2564.

[17] Pierre Auguste Adet reached Philadelphia on June 15, 1795, replacing the previous minister, Fauchet.

[18] Adet to minister of foreign relations, February 9, 1796, A.H.A. *Report*, 1903, II, 827.

[19] Samuel Fulton was a close associate of General George Rogers Clark, and was placed in command of a part of the latter's cavalry force in 1794. He visited France in the winter of 1794–1795 and was granted a commission as colonel in the republican army. For an interesting account of Fulton's career on the frontier, see Frederick Jackson Turner, "The Policy of France toward the Mississippi Valley in the Period of Washington and Adams," *American Historical Review*, X (1905), 270, footnote.

[20] Adet to minister of foreign relations, February 9, 1796, A.H.A. *Report*, 1903, II, 828.

[21] *Ibid.*, pp. 828–829, and Adet to minister of foreign affairs, February 9, 1796, *ibid.* 1897, pp. 661–666.

[22] Morales to Las Casas, June 4, 1795, enclosed in Las Casas to Campo Alange, July 10, 1795, A.G.I., S.D., 2564.

[23] Unfortunately Las Casas failed to send any of the required materials with his orders to construct the fort.

[24] Las Casas to governor of Florida, July 8, 1795, enclosed in Las Casas to Campo Alange, July 10, 1795, A.G.I., S.D., 2564.

[25] The vessels actually departed from Havana on July 20 with the coast-guard sloop *Favorito*, and reached St. Augustine a few days later. Quesada to Las Casas, July 29, 1795, A.G.I., P.C., 1438.

[26] Las Casas to governor of Florida, July 8, 1795, enclosed in Las Casas to Campo Alange, July 10, 1795, *ibid.*

[27] Las Casas to Campo Alange, July 10, 1795, *ibid.*

[28] Las Casas to governor of Florida, July 13, 1795, enclosed in Las Casas to Campo Alange, August 22, 1795, A.G.I., S.D., 2564.

[29] Las Casas to Campo Alange, August 22, 1795, *ibid.*

[30] Report of the junta of August 14, 1795, *ibid.*

[31] Las Casas to Mathews, August 21, 1795, *ibid.*

[32] This dispatch was brought to Havana by the *Favorito* which had completed its assignment to accompany the *Flecha* and *San Antonio* to St. Augustine.

[33] Quesada to Las Casas, July 25 and 29, 1795, enclosed in Las Casas to Campo Alange, August 25, 1795, A.G.I., S.D., 2564.

[34] Quesada to Las Casas, July 29, 1795, A.G.I., P.C., 1438.

[35] Fort George was on the northern bank of the St. John's River not far from its mouth. It was but a few miles distant from the southern tip of Talbot Island.

[36] Quesada to Las Casas, July 31, 1795, enclosed in Las Casas to Campo Alange, August 25, 1795, A.G.I., S.D., 2564.

[37] [Andrew] Atkinson to Howard, July 29, 1795, enclosed in Howard to Quesada, July 30, 1795, enclosed in Quesada to Las Casas, July 31, 1795, enclosed in Las Casas to Campo Alange, August 25, 1795, *ibid.*

[38] Howard forwarded Quesada a complete account of the attack on Amelia Island. Howard to Quesada, August 10 and 11, 1795, enclosed in Quesada to Las Casas, August 14, 1795, enclosed in Las Casas to Campo Alange, October 23, 1795, *ibid.*

[39] Pedro de la Guardia Saenz to Quesada, August 3, 1795, enclosed in Quesada to Las Casas, August 14, 1795, enclosed in Las Casas to Campo Alange, October 23, 1795, *ibid.*

[40] Howard to Quesada, August 11, 1795, enclosed in Quesada to Las Casas, August 14, 1795, enclosed in Las Casas to Campo Alange, October 23, 1795, *ibid.*

[41] Berrio to Quesada, July 24, 1795, enclosed in Quesada to Las Casas, September 12, 1795, enclosed in Las Casas to Campo Alange, October 23, 1795, *ibid.*

[42] Morales to Quesada, August 25, 1795, enclosed in Quesada to Las Casas, September 12, 1795, enclosed in Las Casas to Campo Alange, October 23, 1795, *ibid.*

[43] The two naval vessels under Captain Saenz remained at St. Augustine despite the order of the governor general, because Quesada believed that the need for them was not yet at an end.

[44] Morales to Quesada, September 4, 1795, and Saenz to Quesada, September 7, 1794, both enclosed in Quesada to Las Casas, September 12, 1795, enclosed in Las Casas to Campo Alange, October 23, 1795, A.G.I., S.D., 2564.

[45] Quesada to Las Casas, July 13, 1794, *ibid.*

[46] Morales to Quesada, August 31, 1795, enclosed in Quesada to Las Casas, September 4, 1795, enclosed in Las Casas to Campo Alange, October 13, 1795, *ibid.*

[47] Las Casas to Campo Alange, October 13, 1795, *ibid.*

[48] Quesada to Las Casas, September 12, 1795, enclosed in Las Casas to Campo Alange, October 23, 1795, *ibid.*

[49] Las Casas to Campo Alange, October 23, 1795, *ibid.*

[50] The Treaty of Basle was signed by the French and Spanish representatives on July 22, 1795, and was ratified in Paris and Madrid early the next month. George Friedrich von Martens, ed., *Receuil des Principaux Traités d'Alliance de Paix, de Trêve, de Neutralité, de Commerce, de Limites, d'Exchange*, etc. ... (Göttingen, 1791–1801), VI, 124–128.

[51] Las Casas to Campo Alange, October 23, 1795, A.G.I., S.D., 2564.

[52] Las Casas to Campo Alange, November 13, 1795, *ibid.*

[53] Las Casas to Pedro Pablo Abarca de Bolea, Conde de Aranda (former prime minister), April 26, 1796, *ibid.*, 2565.

[54] George Mathews of Georgia was instrumental in bringing about the so-called "Patriot War" in 1812-1813 during which Amelia Island was occupied by federal forces. See T. Frederick Davis, "United States troops in Spanish East Florida, 1812-13," *Florida Historical Quarterly*, IX (July, 1930), 3-23; IX (Oct., 1930), 96-116; IX (Jan., 1931), 135-155; IX (April, 1931), 259-278; and X (July, 1931), 24-40. For an account of the 1817 rebellion under Sir Gregor MacGregor, see Joseph B. Lockey, "The Florida Intrigues of José Alvarez de Toledo," *Florida Historical Quarterly*, XII (April, 1934), 145-178; D. C. Corbitt, "The Return of Spanish Rule to the St. Marys and the St. Johns, 1813-1821," *Florida Historical Quarterly*, XX (July, 1941), 47-68; and Rufus Kay Wyllys, "The Filibusters of Amelia Island," *Georgia Historical Quarterly*, XII (Dec. 1928), 297-325.

[55] Las Casas to Araoz, October 4, 1795, and Las Casas to Campo Alange, October 23, 1795, *ibid.*

NOTES TO CHAPTER X
PUNISHMENT OF THE REBELS

[1] Decree of July 16, 1795, E.F.P., 295.

[2] *Ibid.*

[3] Quesada to Howard, July 20, 1795, *ibid.*

[4] Howard to Quesada, July 22, 1795, *ibid.*

[5] Bernardo Joseph Segui to Quesada, July 22, 1795, *ibid.* It is quite likely that Juan Machogui was the John Magee or McGee who had come to East Florida from Georgia a few years earlier.

[6] Inventory of William Jones, July 22, 1795, *ibid.*

[7] "Cerro fuente."

[8] Inventory of John McIntosh, July 26, 1795, *ibid.*

[9] Inventories of George Knolls, July 26, 1795, and James Leslie, July 29, 1795, *ibid.*

[10] Inventory of Francis Goodwin, July 31, 1795, *ibid.* Later records show that not only was Goodwin allowed to return to East Florida, but that he was also permitted to resume residence on his old plantation, "Strawberry Hill." *Spanish Land Grants*, III, 193.

[11] Decree of August 3, 1795, enclosed in Quesada to Segui, August 3, 1795, E.F.P., 295.

[12] Quesada to Las Casas, July 29, 1795, A.G.I., P.C., 1428.

[13] *Ibid.*

[14] Quesada to Las Casas, July 31, 1795, enclosed in Las Casas to Campo Alange, August 25, 1795, A.G.I., S.D., 2564.

[15] Quesada to Jaudenes, August 11, 1795, E.F.P., 103 L 8.

[16] The complete list of names appeared in the decree of August 3, 1795, *ibid.*

[17] *Ibid.*

[18] Those arrested by Segui were John Simpson, Cornelius Griffiths, Joseph Rains, and Cornelius Rains. These men were transported to St. Augustine on August 10 to permit Quesada to interrogate them personally.

[19] See sales manifests dated August 16, September 1 and 6, 1795, E.F.P., 103 L 8.

[20] Quesada to Segui, August 25, 1795, *ibid.*

[21] Decree of October 2, 1795, enclosed in Quesada to Segui, October 2, 1795, *ibid.*

[22] Decree of October 31, 1795, enclosed in Quesada to Segui, October 31, 1795, *ibid.*

[23] Hollingsworth's wife requested the return of certain items of property, declaring that they did not belong to her husband. By a decree of December 6, 1795, Quesada ordered these things returned to her, on the ground that the *Recopilación* forbade the seizure of a wife's goods for an act of her husband. Decree of December 6, 1795, *ibid.*

[24] Attachment order, August 3, 1795, *ibid.*

[25] Decree of September 2, 1795, *ibid.*

[26] Receipt of sales, August 22, 1795, *ibid.*

[27] Decree of November 6, 1795, *ibid.*

[28] Receipt of sales, November 25, 1795, *ibid.*

[29] Half a dozen lengthy documents dealing with the disposal of these slaves are to be found among the papers of Miguel Yznardi, a merchant of St. Augustine who was put in charge of the slave auctions. He was later accused of having allowed several slaves to escape and of having mistreated and undernourished others, so that several died before December, 1797. *Ibid.*

[30] Marixal to governor, January 19, 1797, *ibid.*

[31] Segui to Governor Enrique White, October 21, 1797, *ibid.*

[32] Enrique White was the governor of West Florida before his appointment to succeed Quesada in St. Augustine. He reached East Florida on June 5, 1795, and took over his duties on June 20. See White to Murphy, June 20, 1795, *ibid.*, 103 L 8.

[33] *Spanish land grants,* III, 30, and IV, 107.

NOTES TO CHAPTER XI

REAPPEARANCE OF ELIJAH CLARK

[1] Morales to Las Casas, May 27, 1795, A.G.I., P.C., 1438.

[2] Morales to Las Casas, June 4, 1795, *ibid.*

[3] It later developed that the Creek chiefs who had gathered on the west bank of the Altamaha River and who were associated with Clark in Morales' report, actually were there to discuss the possibility of a new treaty for land cessions to Georgia. They had no connection with Clark or with any venture hostile to the Spanish cause. Alexander McDonnell to governor of East Florida, June 9, 1795, *ibid.* This discussion with the Indians broke down and no further land cessions were made until 1802.

[4] Fleming to Morales, June 7, 1795, enclosed in Morales to Las Casas, June 9, 1795, *ibid.*

[5] Howard to Morales, June 7, 1795, enclosed in Morales to Las Casas, June 9, 1795, *ibid.*

[6] White to Carondelet [n.d.], 1795, *ibid.*, 153.

[7] Carondelet to Villebeuve, September 10, 1795, *ibid.*

[8] Howard to Morales, June 7, 1795, enclosed in Morales to Las Casas, June 9, 1795, *ibid.*, 1438.

[9] Testimony of John McQueen, May 27, 1795, enclosed in Morales to Las Casas, May 27, 1795, *ibid.*

[10] The Augusta *Chronicle and Gazette of the State,* April 4, 1794.

¹¹ Not all the emigrés from the French islands were in sympathy with the cause of the Republic. This unsympathetic group was a constant thorn in the side of the republican ministers to the United States. Ternant objected to the hostility of some of these refugees, writing, "I am sadly affected by the conduct of the inhabitants of Ste. Domingo who have taken refuge here. They make haughty declarations against our revolution, and some of them do not blush to drink the health of the Duke of Brunswick at their tables and at dinners in the local inns." Ternant to minister of foreign affairs, November 1, 1792, A.H.A. *Report*, 1903, II, 163.

¹² Quesada to Jaudenes and Viar, June 9, 1795, E.F.P., 103 L 8.

¹³ Randolph to Jaudenes, July 6, 1795, *ibid.*

¹⁴ The total number of federal troops in Georgia late in November, 1794, amounted to 146, exclusive of officers. Knox to Senate, November 25, 1794, A.S.P., M.A., I, 68. A year later, the number had shrunk to 78, although large reinforcements were reported to be on the way. Pickering report, December 12, 1795, *ibid.*, 109.

¹⁵ Jaudenes and Viar to Morales, July 29, 1795, E.F.P., 103 L 8.

¹⁶ [Nathan] Atkinson to Howard, June 21, 1795, enclosed in Howard to Morales, June 23, 1795, enclosed in Morales to Las Casas, June 28, 1795, A.G.I., P.C., 1438.

¹⁷ Howard to Morales, July 4, 1795, enclosed in Morales to Las Casas, July 5, 1795, *ibid.*

¹⁸ Quesada to Jaudenes and Viar, July 17, 1795, E.F.P., 103 L 8.

¹⁹ Quesada to Las Casas, July 25, 1795, A.G.I., P.C., 1438.

²⁰ Quesada to Las Casas, July 29, 1795, *ibid.*

²¹ Morales to Las Casas, September 18, 1795, *ibid.*, 1439. Morales apparently was not very familiar with the geography of Georgia, for this distance of 400 miles is more than twice the distance from the St. Mary's River to Augusta, and is just about equal to the distance between that river and Raleigh, North Carolina.

²² It is probable that Suares, the French consul, had just received news of the negotiations underway at Basle, although he could scarcely have received a report of the actual ratification of the final draft of the treaty by the National Convention on August 1.

²³ Morales to Las Casas, September 18, 1795, A.G.I., P.C., 1439.

²⁴ Morales to Saenz, September 10, 1795, enclosed in Morales to Las Casas, September 18, 1795, *ibid.*

²⁵ Saenz to Morales, September 10, 1795, enclosed in Morales to Las Casas, September 18, 1795, *ibid.*

²⁶ Morales to Saenz, September 10, 1795, enclosed in Morales to Las Casas, September 18, 1795, *ibid.*

²⁷ James Murphy to Quesada, August 31, 1795, E.F.P., 103 L 8. This report differed radically from one that Adet sent his government. The French minister claimed that Clark already had 600 men with him, including some cavalry, and that there were 1,500 more ready to aid him. The Creek Indians were supposed to be coming to the St. Mary's "wearing cockades." Adet to minister of foreign relations, February 9, 1796, A.H.A. *Reports*, 1897, pp. 661–666.

²⁸ Saenz to Morales, September 10, 1795, enclosed in Morales to Las Casas, September 18, 1795, A.G.I., P.C., 1439. At the moment of making this decision, unknown to Saenz, a second letter from Murphy was on the way to St. Augustine with the report that the twenty-four-gun French frigate then in the harbor at Charleston was

being laid up indefinitely, because of the dearth of suitable crew members. Murphy to Quesada, September 2, 1795, E.F.P., 103 L 8.

[29] Las Casas to Campo Alange, October 23, 1795, A.G.I., S.D., 2564.

[30] Report of junta, October 9, 1795, enclosed in Quesada to Las Casas, October 26, 1795, A.G.I., P.C., 1439. Las Casas claimed that Clark first crossed the "frontier" in August, basing this report on Spain's claim to the lands west of the Altamaha River. Las Casas to Campo Alange, October 23, 1795, *ibid.*

[31] Carondelet to Villebeuve, September 30, 1795, *ibid.*, 212.

[32] Major Thomas Skrine, a member of the Camden County militia, was a close friend of Clark, and had taken part in the adventures of 1794.

[33] Quesada to Jaudenes, September 10, 1795, E.F.P., 103 L 8.

[34] Quesada to Mathews, September 10, 1795, enclosed in Quesada to Murphy, September 10, 1795, *ibid.*

[35] Quesada to Jaudenes, September 10, 1795, *ibid.*

[36] The activities of Randolph and his militiamen had long been under suspicion by the Florida authorities. He had been accused in September, 1794, of having participated with some of his men in a raid across the St. Mary's River, at which time a herd of cattle, some horses, and a Negro were stolen. Quesada to Las Casas, November 20, 1794, and Quesada to Jaudenes, September 10, 1795, A.G.I., P.C., 1438.

[37] Morales to King and Burrows, July 3, 1795, enclosed in Morales to Las Casas, July 4, 1795, *ibid.* Once again official protests availed nothing.

[38] Quesada to Jaudenes, August 11, 1795, E.F.P., 103 L 8.

[39] An appeal by Quesada to Mathews in March for the return of Lang and Plowden to East Florida had failed. At that time, Quesada declared that these two men were a "diabolical menace" to the peace of the frontier. Quesada to Jaudenes, September 10, 1795, *ibid.*, and Quesada to Mathews, October 8, 1795, D.A.H.G.

[40] Quesada to Jaudenes, September 10, 1795, E.F.P., 103 L 8.

[41] *Ibid.*

[42] Morales to Las Casas, September 18, 1795, A.G.I., P.C., 1428.

[43] Gaither to Mathews, August 20, 1795, L.B.M., D.A.H.G.

[44] Mathews to Gaither, August 24, 1795, *ibid.*

[45] Mathews to Fauche, August 24, 1795, *ibid.*

[46] Mathews to justices of inferior court of the County of Camden, August 24, 1795, *ibid.*

[47] Mathews to Morales, September 10, 1795, *ibid.*

[48] Mathews to Las Casas, November 11, 1795, *ibid.*

[49] Randolph to Jaudenes, July 6, 1795, E.F.P., 103 L 8.

NOTES TO CHAPTER XII
PEACE RESTORED

[1] The Plummer plantation was north of Nassau River, near the present village of Hero. A small stream flowing into Nassau River near Hero bears the name of Plummer, as does the swamp from which it flows.

[2] Declaration of Daniel Plummer, September 30, 1795, enclosed in Quesada to Las Casas, October 26, 1795, A.G.I., P.C., 1439.

[3] Quesada to King and Burrows, October 3, 1795, D.A.H.G.

⁴ Report of junta, October 9, 1795, enclosed in Quesada to Las Casas, October 26, 1795, A.G.I., P.C., 1439.

⁵ Quesada to junta, October 9, 1795, enclosed in Quesada to Las Casas, October 26, 1795, *ibid.*

⁶ Report of junta, October 9, 1795, enclosed in Quesada to Las Casas, October 26, 1795, *ibid.*

⁷ It was estimated that there would be about one hundred mounted militiamen. Most of the free Negroes were to be under the command of John McQueen, who was given the task of arming them. *Ibid.*

⁸ *Ibid.*

⁹ Quesada to magistrates of Camden County, October 9, 1795, enclosed in Quesada to Las Casas, October 26, 1795, *ibid.*

¹⁰ The reference to "Cryers" presumably was to the plantation of Thomas Cryer. Quesada had granted him five hundred acres on November 6, 1790, in the region between the St. Mary's and Nassau rivers. *Spanish Land Grants,* III, 30.

¹¹ [Andrew] Atkinson to Quesada, October 20, 1795, enclosed in Quesada to Las Casas, October 26, 1795, A.G.I., P.C., 1439.

¹² Mathews to Fauche [August 24], 1795, D.A.H.G.

¹³ Quesada to Jaudenes, October 9, 1795, E.F.P., 103 L 8.

¹⁴ This may have been the origin of Atkinson's report that some of Fauche's men had appeared on the south bank of the river.

¹⁵ His report did not specify whether the suspects were American or residents of East Florida. Fauche to Bevan, February 5, 1825, G.H.S.

¹⁶ *Ibid.*

¹⁷ Adet to minister of foreign relations, February 9, 1796, A.H.A. *Report,* 1903, III, 829.

¹⁸ Adet to minister of foreign relations, February 9, 1796, *ibid.* 1897, pp. 661–666.

¹⁹ Suares appeared before Thomas King of the inferior court of Camden County. This interview with Suares occurred some time before October 1, as Fauche mentioned it in a letter of that date to the governor. Mathews to Fauche, October 26, 1795, D.A.H.G.

²⁰ Writing thirty years later in 1825, Fauche was in error as to the site of the national capital in 1795. Also, he failed to recall that the President had issued a neutrality proclamation in 1793. Fauche to Bevan, February 5, 1825, G.H.S.

²¹ Quesada to Captains Abemial Nicholl and Jonas Fauche, October 9, 1795, D.A.H.G.

²² *Ibid.*

²³ Fauche to Quesada, October 14, 1795, *ibid.*

²⁴ Fauche to Bevan, February 5, 1825, G.H.S.

²⁵ Quesada claimed that Atkinson had spoken to Fauche and Nicholl, and that they had advised an immediate assault on Clark's position. This meeting took place when Atkinson was dispatched to St. Mary's on October 3 with Quesada's letter to King and Burrows. Quesada to Mathews, October 12, 1795, D.A.H.G.

²⁶ As Quesada indicated, this letter was entrusted to Colonel Sebastian Kindelan, who was on his way to confer with Mathews, having been sent from Havana by Las Casas. *Ibid.*

²⁷ However, Gaither did not mention the presence of Clark, and he merely said, "near Temple," which could easily mean as far west as Coleraine. Gaither to Mathews, September 29, 1795, *ibid.*

[28] The governor acknowledged the receipt of Randolph's letter of October 5, and summarized the contents in a short reply to the militia captain. Mathews to Randolph, October 28, 1795, *ibid.*

[29] A small militia post standing near the Great Satilla River.

[30] Fauche to Mathews, October 17, 1795, G.H.S.

[31] Fauche to Bevan, February 5, 1825, *ibid.*

[32] *Ibid.*

[33] Fauche had reported to Mathews as early as October 1 that there appeared to be little of interest taking place, and that his task in Camden County seemed to be an easy one. Mathews to Fauche, October 26, 1795, D.A.H.G.

[34] Fauche to Howard, October 31, 1795, G.H.S.

[35] Adet to minister of foreign relations, February 9, 1796, A.H.A. *Report*, 1903, III, 829.

[36] Quesada summed up the charges against McGirt in a letter to Jaudenes. Quesada to Jaudenes, November 6, 1795, E.F.P., 103 L 8. Mathews acquainted Fauche with McGirt's activities in Liberty County in a letter of November 15. Mathews to Fauche, November 15, 1795, L.B.M., D.A.H.G.

[37] Howard to Fauche, October 31, 1795, and Fauche to Bevan, February 5, 1825, G.H.S.

[38] Fauche to Howard, November 2, 1795, *ibid.*

[39] The Augusta *Chronicle and Gazette of the State*, May 27, 1795.

[40] Fauche to Bevan, February 5, 1825, G.H.S.

[41] Quesada to Jaudenes, November 6, 1795, E.F.P., 103 L 8.

[42] Quesada to Jaudenes, January 7, 1796, *ibid.*

[43] Mathews to Fauche, November 15, 1795, D.A.H.G.

[44] There is uncertainty as to the subsequent history of Daniel McGirt. Knight asserts that McGirt was ill and retired to Sumter District in South Carolina, where he soon died. Knight, *op. cit.*, II, 498. This theory has been adopted by other writers of Georgia history in their short mentions of McGirt. However, among the land grants from the governors of East Florida, there is one dated November 20, 1797, in which Governor White gives Daniel McGirt permission to return and settle on the lands of his father. *Spanish Land Grants*, I, 219. In addition, there is an entry in the church records that a son of Daniel McGirt and Susana Ashley, John Robert McGirt, was born in St. Augustine on September 4, 1798. *Roman Catholic Records*, II, 123. From these two entries, it appears to be fairly certain that McGirt returned to East Florida to settle down, although he may have gone back to South Carolina at a later date.

[45] Mathews to Fauche, November 4, 1795, D.A.H.G.

[46] Mathews was probably referring to the correspondence that had passed back and forth between Fauche and Howard. Mathews to Fauche, November 4, 1895, D.A.H.G.

[47] Quesada to Las Casas, October 26, 1795, enclosed in Las Casas to Campo Alange, December 16, 1795, A.G.I., S.D., 2564.

[48] Quesada to Las Casas, November 7, 1795, *ibid.*

[49] Randolph to Howard, November 1, 1795, G.H.S.

[50] Mathews to justices of the inferior court of Camden, November 15, 1795, D.A.H.G.

[51] Quesada to Mathews, October 12, 1795, enclosed in Quesada to Las Casas, October 30, 1795, A.G.I., P.C., 1439.

[52] Las Casas to Mathews, August 21, 1795, A.G.I., S.D., 2564.

[53] This probably referred to General Elijah Clark.

[54] This may have referred to Colonel Samuel Hammond.

[55] Mathews to Las Casas, November 11, 1795, L.B.M., D.A.H.G.

[56] *Ibid.*

[57] George Walker to Mathews, November 14, 1795, D.A.H.G.

[58] Mathews to justices of the inferior court of Camden, November 15, 1795, L.B.M., *ibid.*

[59] Mathews to Kindelan, November 15, 1795, *ibid.*

[60] Mathews to Kindelan, November 17–18, 1795, *ibid.*

[61] *Ibid.*

[62] Message of Mathews, January 14, 1796, *ibid.*

[63] Mathews to secretary of war, November 19, 1795, *ibid.*

[64] Message of Mathews, January 14, 1796, *ibid.*

[65] James Murphy held the office of Spanish vice-consul in Charleston, South Carolina, during the 1790's. His duties included watching over Spanish interests in Georgia. He usually employed the Spanish version of his name, Diego Morphy, when writing to the Spanish authorities in St. Augustine and Havana.

[66] Morales to James Murphy, March 12, 1796, E.F.P., 103 L 8. Morales reported to Murphy that he had been ordered to return to Spain as soon as Governor White arrived from Pensacola to assume the duties of his office. Morales to Murphy, February 27, 1796, *ibid.*

[67] White to Viar, June 7, 1796, and White to Murphy, June 20, 1796, *ibid.*

NOTES TO CHAPTER XIII

IN RETROSPECT

[1] After discussing Clark's efforts to assist Samuel Hammond in 1794, Mrs. Hays writes that "Spain, convinced of the power of the United States to take Florida and the Louisiana territory, graciously agreed to remove their troops from the soil claimed by Georgia and open the Mississippi to navigation to the western settlers." Hays, *op. cit.*, pp. 254–255. It is doubtful that the frontier episodes of 1793–1796 had as great influence on settling the boundary disputes as did international events, particularly the conclusion of the Jay Treaty in 1794.

[2] See Samuel Flagg Bemis, *Pinckney's Treaty: A Study of America's Advantage from Europe's Distress, 1783–1800* (Baltimore, 1926).

[3] George Mathews was a native of Virginia.

[4] Actas del Consejo de Estado, May 2, 1794, A.H.N., Estado, 923.

BIBLIOGRAPHY

BIBLIOGRAPHY

The broad question of French interest in the revolutionizing of Spanish America, and more particularly in the seizure of Louisiana, has been given considerable attention by several leading historians. Genêt and his attempts to arouse anti-Spanish sentiment in the Ohio Valley have received perhaps the greater part of this attention, while the projected attack on the Spanish in East Florida has received the least. Little more than passing mention has been made of this latter scheme. Even the major histories of the United States and of Franco-American diplomatic relations either ignore this episode or pass it off as "a lesser portion of the Genêt schemes." When the East Florida project is mentioned, reference is usually made either to the Turner collections of French diplomatic correspondence or to the selection of American and Spanish documents printed in the *American State Papers*. As far as I know, there are no monographs on the East Florida venture. The documentary collections from the Spanish archives have received only passing consideration.

The purpose of this bibliography is to present a selected group of materials concerned directly with this study. Since, as has been pointed out, the vast majority of general histories of the United States offer nothing of importance, they will be ignored. The same is generally true of many of the state, county, and municipal histories of Florida, Georgia, and South Carolina. A large number of these were consulted in the preparation of this study, and only the more useful works will be listed in the bibliography. Even the works limited to Florida during the eighteenth century hardly mention the projected attack on St. Augustine and the rebellion of 1795. The few references are seldom documented and are usually inaccurate.

In order to achieve some logical classification of the material to be presented in this bibliography, the following arbitrary method of division has been adopted: Manuscripts; Printed material: 1. Documents, 2. Guides to archival and documentary collections, 3. Articles in periodicals, 4. Biographies, 5. General works; Contemporary newspapers.

MANUSCRIPTS

In general, the manuscript materials can be grouped under two major headings: those coming originally in one form or another from Spanish archives, and those to be found in the original in the Georgia archives. The first group often contains Spanish translations of documents originally written in English, while the second contains a small number of English translations of Spanish dispatches. In each case, an attempt was made to locate and utilize the original document in order to avoid translation errors.

The materials from the Spanish archives consist of a vast amount of official and semiofficial correspondence between the governor of East Florida and the representatives of the Spanish government in Philadelphia, the governor general in Havana, and the governor of Georgia. In addition, there are many dispatches to and from various military, naval, and political leaders in East Florida and Georgia, as well as records of the more important meetings of the *juntas de guerra* in St. Augustine and Havana. The larger part of the correspondence between the governor of East Florida and the Spanish representatives in Philadelphia is to be found in the various boxes of the East Florida Papers in the Library of Congress in Washington. This same repository yields the official account of the rebellion of 1795 in East Florida. Correspondence between St. Augustine and Havana is located primarily in the

Archivo General de Indias, Papeles Procedentes de Cuba, while the dispatches from Havana to Madrid are to be found in the same collection, Santo Domingo. These documents were used in microfilm copy either from the Library of Congress, or from the North Carolina Historical Commission, the latter through the kindness of the P. K. Yonge Library of Florida History, at Gainesville, Florida. Much overlapping occurs in the last two groups because the governor general attempted to forward copies of all documents from St. Augustine with his personal reports to Spain.

The Department of Archives and History in Atlanta, Georgia, yields a quantity of interesting material on the subject of this study, little of which has ever been used. Here are to be found the letter books of the early governors of Georgia, the unprinted journals of the upper and lower houses of the state legislature, and a mass of miscellaneous correspondence between the governors and many state and federal officials, as well as with the governor of East Florida and the governor general in Havana. Many of the letters from the governor of Georgia to the secretaries of state and war are to be found printed in the *American State Papers*. Fragments of several unprinted diaries and a few scattered letters are to be found in the Georgia Historical Society in Savannah.

There are two excellent selections of the Panton and Leslie letters, the Admiral Greenslade and Meleise H. Cruzat collections, now on loan to the Florida Historical Society in St. Augustine. Certain of the ecclesiastical, real estate, and deed records of St. Augustine have been transcribed and are now available in bound manuscript form in the St. Augustine Historical Association Library.

Archivo General de Indias, Seville.

Papeles procedentes de Cuba, *Legajos* 152A, 152B, 153, 202, 203, 1428, 1437, 1438, 1439, 1442, 2354.

These *legajos* contain a large body of correspondence between the governor of East Florida and his superiors in New Orleans and Havana from 1790 to 1796. Included in this material are copies of dispatches and reports from the local military and political figures in East Florida, as well as copies of official orders from Madrid to St. Augustine by way of Havana.

For correspondence of Carondelet and Las Casas, see *legajos* 152A and 152B.

For correspondence of Quesada and Las Casas, see *legajos* 1437, 1438, 1439, and 1442.

For an account of the rebellion of 1795 and the methods taken to suppress it, see *legajo* 1439.

For an account of Elijah Clark and the Trans-Oconee Republic, see *legajo* 203. Santo Domingo, *Legajos* 2560–2567, 2578, 2588, 2642, 2643.

These *legajos* contain primarily the correspondence between Las Casas and the government in Madrid from 1791 to 1797. Included in these dispatches to Madrid are copies of letters from East Florida, New Orleans, and Philadelphia.

For Quesada's account of the physical condition of East Florida in 1791, see *legajo* 2642.

For a copy of the diary of John Hambly, see *legajo* 2563.

For an extensive account of the rebellion of 1795, see *legajo* 2564.

Archivo General de Simancas, Simancas.

Sección de Guerra, *Legajos* 6916 and 7235.

For the views of the Spanish government on the Abner Hammond case and the ensuing events, see *legajo* 7235.

Archivo Histórico Nacional, Madrid.

Sección de Estado, *Legajos* 923 and 3888.

Legajo 923 contains the minutes of the Council of State during the first half of 1794. The meeting held on May 2, 1794, was devoted to the Abner Hammond case and the steps that should be taken to prevent further violations of East Florida.

Archivo Nacional de Cuba, Havana.

Legajos 1, 3, 14, 21, and 34.

These *legajos* contain copies of some of the East Florida materials to be found in the AGI, PC. In addition, there are dispatches from New Orleans to Havana dealing with the growing French "peril" in 1792 and 1793. There are several reports on the activities of Elijah Clark west of the Oconee River in 1794.

East Florida Papers, Library of Congress, Washington.

Boxes 25 L 2, 37 K 8, 78, 102 K 8, 103 L 8, 108 D 9, 293, 294, 295.

The East Florida Papers represent practically the entire story of that province from the retrocession to Spain in 1784 to the final occupation by the United States in 1821. No complete index has ever been made of this vast collection of documents, although a large number of the boxes have been given general category labels.

For the correspondence of Quesada with Las Casas during 1793, 1794, and 1795, see boxes 25 L 2 and 37 K 8.

For the correspondence of Quesada with Spanish agents and consuls in the United States, see boxes 102 K 8, 103 L 8 and 108 D 9.

For correspondence between Quesada and Georgia officials, see box 108 D 9.

For information on land grants made to foreigners between 1785 and the end of the Spanish period, see box 153 J 12.

For the minutes of juntas held in St. Augustine, see box 277.

For a complete report of the rebellion of 1795, and the trial of the rebels and the seizure of their goods, see boxes 293–296.

Florida Historical Society, St. Augustine.

Among the Panton and Leslie papers in the Admiral Greenslade and Meleise H. Cruzat collections are several letters written by Panton from Pensacola in 1794. These letters indicate to some extent the fear felt that the Creek Indians might desert their Spanish allies for the Franco-American cause.

Georgia, Department of Archives and History, Atlanta.

Executive Department Minutes, 1793–1794.

Here is to be found a copy of a part of the proceedings against Elijah Clark in August, 1794.

Journals of the lower house, 1793–1794.

Journals of the upper house, 1793–1794.

These contain information on the official position of the State of Georgia during the frontier problems of 1794.

Letter book of Governor Mathews, 1793–1796.

This collection of material contains copies of letters to and from Quesada in East Florida as well as many letters dealing with Elijah Clark and his expedition across the Oconee River. It is possible to obtain a fairly clear picture of the governor's views on the responsibility of the citizens of Georgia in this problem. Some of the dispatches to and from the federal government are printed in the *American State Papers, Foreign Relations* and *Indian Affairs*.

Letter book of Governor Telfair, 1791–1793.

Here are to be found letters dealing with the problem of maintaining friendly relations with the Spanish in East Florida, while keeping a watchful eye on their allies, the Creek Indians.

Miscellaneous letters and military dispatches.

In this collection are a large number of dispatches dealing with eye-witness accounts of Elijah Clark's movements in 1794, as well as military reports on the activities along the St. Mary's River in 1795, during the period of the rebellion in East Florida.

Georgia Historical Society, Savannah.

Order book of General Twiggs, 1791–1794.

This contains fragmentary material on the campaign against Elijah Clark's settlement across the Oconee River in 1794.

Letter of Jonas Fauche to Joseph Bevan, 1825.

The writer gives a complete account of his recollections of the events of 1794 and 1795 when he was commander of a force of militia along the St. Mary's River.

Henry E. Huntington Library, San Marino, California.

MSS 107–115, 117, 118, 151, 157–162.

These documents are copies of a part of the correspondence between Havana and Madrid in 1794 and 1795. They deal with the use of Spanish warships to assist in driving the rebels from their positions along the St. Mary's and St. John's rivers.

Massachusetts Historical Society, Boston.

Henry Knox papers.

These contain letters to Jefferson expressing the views of the writer on the activities of Genêt in 1793.

The National Archives, Washington.

Division of the State Department Archives, Miscellaneous Letters, September–November, 1793.

A letter from Dr. James O'Fallon to Captain Herran describes the progress made by George Rogers Clark in rounding up a force of westerners to attack the Spanish in New Orleans.

St. Augustine Historical Society, St. Augustine.

Deed book of St. Augustine for years 1793 and 1794.

Real Estate Records of St. Augustine and East Florida before the American Occupation in 1821.

From these records can be gleaned much information concerning certain of the settlers in East Florida who had come to that province from the United States before the troubles of 1794 and 1795.

South Carolina Historical Society, Charleston.

Timothy Pickering papers.

These contain letters expressing concern over the strained relations between the United States and France in 1793. Also included is a letter to Jefferson of January 7, 1793, in which the writer questions the character of Genêt.

South Carolina State Historical Commission, Columbia.

Journal of the House, 1793.

Journal of the Senate, 1793.

These journals contain interesting debates on certain prominent South Carolinians accused of assisting the enlistment of Americans for the service of France.

University of Chicago Library, Chicago.

Crandall, Regina Katherine. "Genêt's Projected Attack on Louisiana and the Floridas, 1793–1794." MS, University of Chicago, 1902.

Woodfin, Maude Howlett. "Citizen Genêt and His Mission." MS, University of Chicago, 1928.

These two unprinted theses contain fairly comprehensive studies of Genêt's activities on behalf of the republican government of France. The Florida problem, however, is given very cursory attention, largely because of the failure to make use of the Spanish materials, as well as those collections of documents to be found in the Georgia repositories.

PRINTED MATERIAL

1. DOCUMENTS

Actes et mémoires concernant les négociations qui ont eu entre la France et Les États-Unis de l'Amérique, depuis 1793, jusqu'à la conclusion de la convention du 30 Septembre, 1800. London, 1807. 3 vols.

Contains dispatches from the minister of marine to Genêt enclosing blank letters of marque to be distributed to American ship captains.

Adams, John. *The Works of John Adams, Second President of the United States.* Boston, 1850–1856. 10 vols.

Contains several references to his views on the question of receiving Genêt as French minister.

Aulard, François V. A., ed. *Receuil des actes du Comité de Salut Public, avec la correspondence officielle des représentants en mission et le registre du Conseil Exécutif Provisoire.* Paris, 1889–1923. 26 vols.

Materials on the missions of both Genêt and Fauchet to the United States.

J. P. Brissot député du département d'Eure et Loire à ses commettants, sur la situation de la Convention Nationale, sur l'influence des anarchistes, et les maux qu'elle a causée, sur la nécessité d'anéantir cette influence, pour sauver la République (Brochures Politiques, 1789–1794, vol. 87). Paris, 1794.

A defense of the Girondist policy both at home and abroad, addressed to the constituents of Brissot's district.

Corbitt, D. C., ed. and trans. "Papers Relating to the Georgia-Florida Frontier, 1784–1800," *Georgia Historical Quarterly*, XX (1936), 356–365; XXI (1937), 73–83, 185–188, 274–293, 373–381; XXIV (1940), 257–271.

Several letters from the Panton and Leslie correspondence containing information on the projected French attack on St. Augustine in 1794.

Coulter, E. Merton, ed. "The Creek Troubles of 1793," *Georgia Historical Quarterly*, XI (1937), 274–280.

Contains a letter from John Twiggs to Jared Irwin written in 1793, giving a fairly complete description of the forts established along the Oconee River.

Thomas Houghton to Governor Mathews, May 20, 1794, *Georgia Historical Quarterly*, XIV (1930), 254–255.

A firsthand account of Elijah Clark's settlement across the Oconee River, indicating the potential danger in permitting this settlement to go unmolested.

Imlay, Gilbert. "Mémoire sur la Louisiane, présenté au Comité de Salut Public par un Citoyen Américain," *American Historical Review*, III (1897), 491–494.

Contains suggestions as to the reconquest of Louisiana by France. This document had great influence on the foreign policy of the Girondist government.

Jefferson, Thomas. *The Writings of Thomas Jefferson.* Paul Leicester Ford, ed. New York, 1892–1899. 10 vols.

For Jefferson's views on Genêt, see his diary in Vol. I. Letters dealing with Genêt's recall and with the problem of hostile Indians in the southeast are to be found in Vol. VI.

McQueen, John. *The Letters of Don Juan McQueen to His Family, Written from Spanish East Florida, 1791–1807.* Walter C. Hartridge, ed. Columbia, South Carolina, 1943.

Contains an account of the seizure and imprisonment of Abner Hammond after his entry into East Florida. McQueen wrote several letters indicating the uncertainty that was felt in St. Augustine in 1794.

Martens, George Friedrich von. *Receuil des Principaux Traités d' Alliance, de Paix, de Trêve ... & c., conclus par les Puissances de l'Europe.* Göttingen, 1791–1801. 7 vols.

Contains the Treaty of Basle of 1795.

Michaux, André. "Portions of the Journal of André Michaux, Botanist, written during his travels in the United States and Canada, 1785 to 1796," Charles S. Sargent, ed. *Proceedings of the American Philosophical Society,* XXVI (1889), 1–145.

Contains an account of the journey made by Michaux to the Kentucky region and his controversial meeting with General George Rogers Clark.

Morris, Gouverneur. *The Diary and Letters of Gouverneur Morris.* Anne Cary Morris, ed. New York, 1888. 2 vols.

An account of Genêt's mission and subsequent recall appears in Vol. II.

Citizen Alexander Moultrie to Citizen Genêt, January 9, 1794, *Franco-American Review,* I (1937), 284–288.

Expresses approval of the mission of Genêt. The writer was the brother of the governor of South Carolina.

Report of the Historical Manuscript Commission of the American Historical Association (1896). Selections from the Draper Collection in the possession of the State Historical Society of Wisconsin to elucidate the proposed French expedition under George Rogers Clark against Louisiana, in the years 1793–1794. American Historical Association *Annual Report* (1896), I.

Contains a large number of Genêt dispatches including the instructions given him before his departure from France for the United States.

Report on Canadian Archives (1890). Lord Dorchester Correspondence, in Reports on the United States after 1783. Ottawa, 1891.

Contains the first hints of a possible French attack on Canada and Louisiana from the Ohio Valley.

Roman Catholic Records, St. Augustine Parish, White Baptisms, 1784–1799. Tallahassee, Florida, 1941. 2 vols.

Contains valuable reference material concerning the early non-Spanish settlers in East Florida.

Serrano y Sanz, Manuel, ed. *Documentos históricos de la Florida y la Luisiana, siglos XVI al XVIII.* Madrid, 1912.

Contains several interesting documents dealing with the Yazoo Land Company and subsequent events.

Spanish Land Grants in Florida. Tallahassee, Florida, 1940. 5 vols.

Among these documents dealing with land titles is to be found material on the early American settlers in East Florida. There are several short excerpts from the proceedings against the rebels in 1795.

Turner, Frederick Jackson, ed. "Correspondence of the French Ministers to the United States, 1791–1797," American Historical Association, *Annual Report* (1903), II.

A very useful collection of documents drawn from the French Foreign Office collections, for the purpose of illustrating the extensive interest that the French government had in both the internal and external affairs of the United States. Correspondence of Ternant, Genêt, Fauchet, and Adet with the minister of foreign affairs is included in this selection. The special instructions handed to Genêt before he left for Philadelphia are included.

———. "Documents on the Relations of France to Louisiana, 1792–1795," *American Historical Review,* III (1898), 490–516.

Contains several documents relating to the schemes to bring about a pro-French outbreak in New Orleans in conjunction with a Franco-American attack on Louisiana. Included are reports on Louisiana by Imlay and Lyonnet, both of which made a deep impression on the Girondist government in Paris.

———. "The Mangourit Correspondence in Respect to Genêt's Projected Attack upon the Floridas, 1793–1794," American Historical Association, *Annual Report* (1897), pp. 569–679.

An extensive selection of documents to illustrate the part played by Mangourit as French consul in Charleston in the Genêt schemes. In addition to official correspondence with the French minister in Philadelphia, there are numerous dispatches to agents in South Carolina and Georgia with instructions and recommendations. Included among these documents is the very interesting "Address to the Floridians to be issued at St. Mary, April 10, 1794."

John Twiggs to Jared Irwin, April 11, 1793, *Georgia Historical Quarterly,* XI (1927), 275–276.

Recommendations for the construction of fortifications along the Oconee and Altamaha rivers to act as protection for the frontier region of Georgia.

United States. Congress. *American State Papers.* J. W. Gales, Jr., and W. W. Seaton, compilers. Washington, 1832–1861. 38 vols.

For a fairly complete collection of the dispatches between the governor of Georgia and the secretaries of state and war, see *Foreign Affairs* and *Indian Affairs.*

For documents dealing with the Georgia land companies, see *Public Lands.*

Reference to service in the federal militia in the campaign to suppress Elijah Clark and the East Florida rebels is to be found in *Claims.*

United States. Presidential Papers. *A Compilation of the Messages and Papers of the Presidents, 1789–1897.* James D. Richardson, ed. Washington, 1896–1899. 10 vols.

Contains Washington's neutrality proclamation of April 22, 1793.

[George] Walker to Mathews, August 30, 1794. *Georgia Historical Quarterly,* XXVII (1943), 285–289.

The highest legal official in Georgia presents his views on the trial of Elijah Clark for his actions west of the Oconee River.

Wharton, Francis, ed. *The Revolutionary Diplomatic Correspondence of the United States.* Washington, 1889. 6 vols.

Contains a report of the debate in the Continental Congress in 1779 over the question of the possible surrender of the Floridas, in the event of a victory over England.

Whitaker, Arthur Preston, ed. and trans. *Documents Relating to the Commercial Policy of Spain in the Floridas with Incidental Reference to Louisiana.* Florida State Historical Society Publications, no. 10. DeLand, Florida, 1931.

Contains Salcedo's suggestion of the surrender of East Florida to England in 1788. Also contains the royal order of June 9, 1793, opening St. Augustine to trading vessels of certain foreign nations.

2. GUIDES TO ARCHIVAL AND DOCUMENTARY COLLECTIONS

There are in existence several excellent guides to assist those who are unable to visit European archives. Although old, these guides to the materials for the history of the United States in French and Spanish archives published by the Carnegie Institution of Washington are extremely useful. It is to be hoped that soon a complete and accurate check list of the materials in the East Florida Papers in the Library of Congress will be added to this collection of invaluable guides.

Bolton, Herbert E. *Guide to Materials for the History of the United States in the Principal Archives of Mexico.* Washington, 1913.

Catálogo de los fondos de las Floridas (Publicaciones del Archivo Nacional de Cuba, III). Guillermo de Zendegui, ed. Havana, 1944.

Hill, Roscoe R. *Descriptive Catalogue of the Documents Relating to the History of the United States in the "Papeles procedentes de Cuba" Deposited in the Archivo General de Indias at Seville.* Washington, 1916.

Leland, Waldo G. *Guide to Material for American History in the Libraries and Archives of Paris.* Washington, 1932–1943. 2 vols.

Manning, Mabel M. "East Florida Papers in the Library of Congress," *Hispanic American Historical Review,* X (1930), 392–397.

Preliminary Check List of Floridiana, 1500–1865, in the Libraries of Florida. Florida Library Association *Bulletin,* No. 2. Jacksonville, Florida, 1930.

Robertson, James Alexander. *List of Documents in Spanish Archives Relating to the History of the United States.* Washington, 1910.

Shepherd, William R. *Guide to the Materials for the History of the United States in Spanish Archives.* Washington, 1907.

Surrey, Nancy N. M., ed. *Calendar of Manuscripts in Paris for the History of the Mississippi Valley to 1803.* Washington, 1926–1928. 2 vols.

Wroth, Lawrence C. "Source Materials of Florida History in the John Carter Brown Library of Brown University," *Florida Historical Quarterly,* XX (1941), 3–46.

3. ARTICLES IN PERIODICALS

Alphonse, Bertrand. "Les États-Unis et la Révolution Française," *Revue des Deux Mondes,* XXXIII (May, 1906), 392–430.

The accepted view that the United States avoided living up to its commitments under the French alliance.

Barthold, Allen Jennings. "French Journalists in the United States, 1780–1800," *Franco-American Review,* (1937), 215–230.

Reveals the names of a number of Frenchmen who traveled in the United States and left impressions in writing.

"Citizen Genêt," *The American Historical Record*, III (1874), 49–52.

A short and uncritical résumé of some of Genêt's activities in the United States.

Corbitt, D. C. "The Return of Spanish Rule to the St. Marys and the St. Johns, 1813–1821," *Florida Historical Quarterly*, XX (1941), 47–68.

Interesting in the comparison of similar situations in 1795 and 1813.

Coulter, E. Merton. "Elijah Clark's Foreign Intrigue and the Trans-Oconee Republic," *Mississippi Valley Historical Review*, extra number, November, 1921.

The first serious effort to delve into the motives behind the activities of the Georgia general.

Desdevises du Dezert, G. "Vice-rois et captaines-generaux des Indes Espagnoles," *Revue Historique*, CXXV (1917), 225–264.

Not as revealing as the title might indicate, but useful for background material on such a person as Las Casas in Havana.

Drumm, Stella M. "Samuel Hammond," *Missouri Historical Society Collections*, IV (1923), 402–422.

Contains some highly interesting information about this very elusive character who caused the Spanish in St. Augustine so much trouble.

Fletcher, Mildred S. "Louisiana as a Factor in French Diplomacy from 1763–1800," *Mississippi Valley Historical Review*, XVII (1930), 367–377.

Gives some indication of the origins of the French schemes to regain control of the Mississippi Valley.

"French Consular Agents in the United States, 1791–1800," *Franco-American Review*, I (1936), 85–90.

A most useful listing of the names and dates of office of all French consular agents during the last decade of the eighteenth century.

Harmon, George D. "Benjamin Hawkins and the Federal Factory System," *North Carolina Historical Review*, IX (1932), 138–152.

Contains a short account of the trading post at Coleraine on the St. Mary's.

Haskins, Charles H. "The Yazoo Land Companies," American Historical Association, *Papers*, V (1891), 59–103.

The accepted authority on this topic.

James, James Alton. "French Diplomacy and American Politics, 1794–1795," American Historical Association, *Annual Report* (1911), I, 151–163.

Gives an indication of the influence that the French alliance question exercised in American politics.

Keller, William F. "The Frontier Intrigues of Citizen Genêt," *Americana*, XXXIV (1940), 567–595.

Gives a sketchy summary of the Genêt projects in the western part of the United States.

Lockey, Joseph B. "The Florida Intrigues of José Alvarez de Toledo," *Florida Historical Quarterly*, XII (1934), 145–178.

Includes some very useful information concerning certain border characters who were present along the Georgia-Florida frontier for some length of time.

———. "The St. Augustine Census of 1786," *Florida Historical Quarterly*, XVIII (1939), 11–31.

Useful in identifying several residents of St. Augustine and in establishing their places of origin.

Murdoch, Richard K. "Citizen Mangourit and the Projected Attack on East Florida in 1794," *The Journal of Southern History*, XIV (1948), 522–540.

A summary of Mangourit's efforts to prepare his part of the attacking force in conjunction with Genêt's broader scheme against the Spanish in Louisiana.

Rives, George L. "Spain and the United States in 1795," *American Historical Review*, IV (1898), 62–79.

A summary of conditions leading up to the Pinckney Treaty.

Turner, Frederick Jackson. "Carondelet on the Defense of Louisiana, November 24, 1794," *American Historical Review*, II (1897), 474–505.

Contains the views of the governor of Louisiana on the possibility of a French attack and on the weakness of the province's defenses.

————. "The Diplomatic Contest for the Mississippi Valley," *Atlantic Monthly*, XCIII (May, 1904), 676–691; (June, 1904), 807–817.

Written for popular consumption, but gives a clear and precise summary of the major issues in this contest.

————. "The Origins of Genêt's Projected Attack on Louisiana and the Floridas," *American Historical Review*, III (1898), 650–671.

One of the first attempts to analyze the motives lying behind the mission of the French minister.

————. "The Policy of France toward the Mississippi Valley in the Period of Washington and Adams," *American Historical Review*, X (1905), 249–279.

An expansion of Turner's views concerning the French schemes to regain Louisiana.

Whitaker, Arthur Preston. "Alexander McGillivray, 1783–1789," *North Carolina Historical Review*, V (1928), 181–203.

Gives an excellent account of the relationship between this leader of the Creek Indians and the Spanish authorities.

————. "Alexander McGillivray, 1789–1793," *North Carolina Historical Review*, V (July, 1928), 289–309.

Continues the career of this Creek leader until his death.

————. "Spain and the Cherokee Indians, 1783–1798," *North Carolina Historical Review*, IV (1927), 252–269.

An excellent survey of the relations between these Indians and the Spanish in New Orleans and St. Augustine.

Wyllys, Rufus Kay. "The Filibusters of Amelia Island," *Georgia Historical Quarterly*, XII (1928), 297–325.

Offers an interesting comparison of the later capture of Amelia Island with the events in 1795.

4. BIOGRAPHIES

Brissot, Jacques-Pierre. *Mémoires de Brissot*. Mathurin François Adolphe de Lescure, ed. Paris, 1877.

A standard work, containing a short but accurate biography of the Girondist leader, and a selection of material indicating his interest in Spanish America.

————. *Mémoires*. Claude Marie Perroud, ed. Paris, 1911. 4 vols.

This item contains several letters to Miranda dealing with the possible freeing of Spanish America.

Caughey, John Walton. *McGillivray of the Creeks.* Norman, Oklahoma, 1938.

An excellent collection of documents dealing with the later phases of the life of this interesting Creek leader.

Godoy, Manuel de. *Cuenta dada de su vida politica por Don Manuel Godoy.* Madrid, 1836–1842. 6 vols.

Offers some background material for the period just before 1795.

Hays, Louise Frederick. *Hero of Hornet's Nest: A Biography of Elijah Clark, 1733 to 1799.* New York, 1946.

A fairly useful biography of Elijah Clark. The author has made use of a large amount of previously unknown material in the Georgia archives.

Robertson, William Spence. *The Life of Miranda.* Chapel Hill, North Carolina, 1929. 2 vols.

By far the best life of this Venezuelan patriot. Especially useful for the period of Miranda's service in the French army.

Sparks, Jared. *The Life of Gouverneur Morris.* Boston, 1832. 3 vols.

Vol. II contains comments on Genêt's mission and on the reaction of the French government to Jefferson's request for the recall of the French minister.

5. GENERAL WORKS

Adet, Pierre Auguste. *The Gros Mousqueton Diplomatique, or Diplomatic Blunderbuss.* Philadelphia, 1796.

An interesting pamphlet in which the French minister attempts to defend himself from charges of having acted in an undiplomatic fashion.

Arthur, Timothy Shay, and William Henry Carpenter. *The History of Georgia from its Earliest Settlement to the Present Time.* Philadelphia, 1852.

Contains a fair summary of the local events in Georgia during the administration of Governor Mathews.

Barbé-Marbois, François, Marquis de. *Histoire de la Louisiane et de la cession de cette colonie par la France aux États-Unis de l'Amérique Septentrionale ...* Paris, 1829.

An excellent and penetrating little work by this well-known traveler.

Bemis, Samuel Flagg. *Jay's Treaty: A Study in Commerce and Diplomacy.* New York, 1923.

The accepted authority on this subject.

———. *Pinckney's Treaty: A Study of America's Advantage from Europe's Distress, 1783–1800.* Baltimore, 1926.

Contains an excellent account of the diplomatic negotiations carried on between Spain and the United States during the fifteen years after the American Revolution.

Berquin-Duvallon [?]. *Travels in Louisiana and the Floridas, in the Year, 1802, giving a Correct Picture of those Countries.* John Davis, trans. New York, 1806.

Excellent for a brief summary of physical conditions in these Spanish provinces at the turn of the century.

Brevard, Caroline Mays. *A History of Florida from the Treaty of 1763 to Our Own Times.* Florida State Historical Society Publications, no. 4. James Alexander Robertson, ed. DeLand, Florida, 1924–1925. 2 vols.

Probably the most useful of the many histories of Florida. Contains valuable information in the appendixes.

Brissot de Warville, Jacques Pierre. *New Travels in the United States of America, performed in 1788.* Translated from the French. Dublin, 1792.

An excellent and penetrating view of America by this famous Girdonist leader.

Brooks, Robert Preston. *History of Georgia,* Atlanta, 1913.

At one time considered the official history of Georgia. Contains a lengthy account of Mathews and the Land Act.

Cable, George Washington. *The Creoles of Louisiana.* New York, 1884.

Contains a few references to the French unrest in New Orleans at the time of the French Revolution.

Carroll, Mary Teresa Austin. *A Catholic History of \Alabama and the Floridas.* New York, 1908.

Contains some useful information on local place names, and on Indian activities at the time of the American Revolution.

Cash, W. T. *The Story of Florida.* New York, 1938. 4 vols.

The official history of the state. It contains some useful material on early American settlers in East Florida.

Chadwick, French E. *The Relations of the United States and Spain, Diplomacy.* New York, 1909.

A brief survey on the relations of the two nations in the hundred years before the Spanish-American War.

Chapman, John Abney. *History of Edgefield County from the Earliest Settlement to 1897.* Newberry, South Carolina, 1897.

Contains genealogical material on several important South Carolina members of Mangourit's group.

Chappell, Absalom Harris. *Miscellanies of Georgia, Historical, Biographical, Descriptive, Etc.* Atlanta, 1874.

Contains one of the earliest descriptions of Elijah Clark's activities along the Oconee River. Unfortunately this work is highly opinionated and laudatory.

Coe, Samuel Gwynn. *The Mission of William Carmichael to Spain.* Johns Hopkins Studies in Historical and Political Science, XLVI, no. 1. Baltimore, 1928.

An excellent account of events leading to the conclusion of the Pinckney Treaty, based on documents from both United States and Spanish archives.

Conway, Moncure Daniel. *Thomas Paine (1737–1809) et la révolution dans les deux mondes.* Felix Rabbe, trans. Paris, 1900.

Contains interesting views of Paine on the introduction of French revolutionary doctrine into Spanish America.

Coulter, E. Merton. *Georgia: A Short History.* Chapel Hill, North Carolina, 1947.

A revision of an earlier work, *A Short History of Georgia* (1933). The accepted standard history of the state.

Curley, Michael Joseph. *Church and State in the Spanish Floridas, 1783–1822.* Catholic University, Studies in American Church History, XXX. Washington, 1940.

An excellent survey of ecclesiastical problems during the second period of Spanish occupation.

Dare, Frederick W. *Florida Old and New.* New York, 1934.

A useful sketch of early Florida.

Davis, Thomas Frederick. *History of Early Jacksonville, Florida....* Jacksonville, 1911.

A very useful description of the St. John's region at the time of the purchase of Florida. Contains several interesting anecdotes about early American settlers, and gives a good picture of Fort San Nicolás.

———. *MacGregor's Invasion of Florida, 1817*. St. Augustine, Florida, 1928.

Useful as a comparison between events of 1795 and 1817.

Dewhurst, William Whitwell. *The History of Saint Augustine, Florida*. New York, 1881.

One of the earliest of the "tourist" histories of the Florida region.

Ellery, Eloise. *Brissot de Warville: A Study in the History of the French Revolution*. Boston, 1915.

Gives a fairly clear picture of Brissot as the leader of the Girondists, but is unfortunately limited in material on the United States.

Evans, Lawton B. *A History of Georgia*. New York, 1898.

Gives the old and accepted account of Governor Mathews and the Land Act of 1795.

Fairbanks, George R. *History of Florida from Its Discovery by Ponce de Leon, in 1512, to the Close of the Florida War in 1842*. Philadelphia, 1871.

Old, but contains an excellent account in brief of the period of Spanish occupation of Florida.

Fauchet, Jean Antoine Joseph, Baron. *A Sketch of the Present State of Our Political Relations with the United States of North America*. Philadelphia, 1797.

A defense of the French arguments in the Franco-American difficulties leading to the "Quasi War."

Forbes, James G. *Sketches, Historical and Topographical of the Floridas; More Particularly of East Florida*. New York, 1821.

One of the earliest descriptions of the physical character of the Florida peninsula, as well as its early history.

Fuller, Herbert Bruce. *The Purchase of Florida, Its History and Diplomacy*. Cleveland, 1906.

Contains excellent accounts of the local frontier problems, but neglects the Spanish side almost completely.

Gaffarel, Paul Louis Jacques. *La politique coloniale en France de 1789 à 1830*. Paris, 1908.

Contains a running account of the general views of the French government on the colonial question during and after the period of the revolution.

Gayarré, Charles. *History of Louisiana*. New Orleans, 1854–1866. 4 vols. in 3.

Vol. III on the Spanish period contains many useful bits of information not to be found in the general histories of the state.

Genet, George Clinton. *Washington, Jefferson and "Citizen" Genêt, 1793*. New York, 1899.

A highly unsuccessful attempt by the author to defend his ancestor and place him on a plane equal to that of George Washington.

Gilmer, George B. *Sketches of Some of the First Settlers of Upper Georgia, of the Cherokees, and the Author*. Americus, Georgia, 1926.

Valuable as a source of local information concerning place names and genealogy.

Harris, Joel Chandler. *Stories of Georgia*. New York, 1896.

Some very interesting local tales about Elijah Clark by the creator of *Uncle Remus*. Also a brief sketch of the career of Daniel McGirt, the outlaw.

Hodgson, Joseph. *The Cradle of the Confederacy; or the Times of Troup, Quitman and Yancey.* Mobile, Alabama, 1876.

Contains a useful account of the life of George Mathews of Georgia, emphasizing the governor's connection with the land schemes.

Imlay, Gilbert. *A Topographical Description of the Western Territory of North America.* 3d ed. London, 1797.

Contains a population table which indicates roughly the number of white settlers living along the St. Mary's River in the 1790's.

Jones, Charles C. *Memorial History of Augusta, Georgia.* Syracuse, New York, 1890.

Contains several anecdotes about Augusta during the administration of Governor Mathews, in addition to statistics on the number of residents about 1790.

Knight, Lucian Lamar. *Georgia's Landmarks, Memorials and Legends.* Atlanta, 1914. 2 vols.

Contains considerable material on Elijah Clark, including what purports to be excerpts from some of his correspondence.

Lanier, Sidney. *Florida: Its Scenery, Climate, and History.* Philadelphia, 1876.

Contains accounts of the St. John's and St. Mary's regions soon after the American Revolution.

Lokke, Carl Ludwig. *France and the Colonial Question: A Study of Contemporary French Opinion, 1763–1801.* Columbia University, Studies in History, Economics and Public Law, no. 365. New York, 1932.

An interesting account of the divergent views in France on the question of regaining lost colonies.

Lyon, E. Wilson. *Louisiana in French Diplomacy, 1759–1804.* Norman, Oklahoma, 1934.

Probably the best basic work on the problems of the Louisiana region.

McCall, Ettie Tidwell. *Roster of Revolutionary Soldiers in Georgia.* Atlanta, 1941.

Contains information on the military careers of several of the Georgia leaders.

McCall, Hugh. *The History of Georgia containing Brief Sketches of the most Remarkable Events up to the Present Day* [1784] (reprinted). Atlanta, 1909.

One of the oldest histories of Georgia, with an excellent account of early Indian treaties and population movements toward the south and west. Also material on the McGirt family.

McQueen, Alexander S. *History of Charlton County.* Atlanta, 1932.

Contains material on early inhabitants and place names.

Mathews, Catherine Van Cortlandt. *Andrew Ellicott, His Life and Letters.* New York, 1908.

Contains excerpts from the letters and diaries of the man who was commissioned to run the southern boundary line of the United States. His personal views on certain of the Spanish officials in Louisiana and the Floridas are enlightening.

Minngerode, Meade. *Lives and Times.* New York, 1925.

Presents the traditional picture of Genêt as a rather evil character determined to involve the United States in the European war, regardless of the expense.

Mohr, Walter H. *Federal Indian Relations, 1774–1788.* Philadelphia, 1933.

An excellent work on the relations between the government of the new republic and the Indians. Much useful background material on the struggle between Georgia and the federal government over the validity of treaties with the Creeks and Cherokees.

Moore, John Bassett. *History and Digest of the International Arbitration to Which the United States Has Been a Party.* Washington, 1898. 6 vols.

Excellent coverage of the arguments between the United States and France leading to the Convention of 1800.

Morse, Jedidiah. *An Abridgement of the American Gazette.* Boston, 1798.

Contains some valuable figures on population and settlement in southern Georgia, as well as interesting descriptions of local physical features.

Moultrie, Alexander. *An Appeal to the People, on the Account of a Certain Public Body in South Carolina, Respecting Col. Drayton and Col. Moultrie.* Charleston, South Carolina, 1794.

A pamphlet in which the author attempted to clear himself and his associate of the charge of having assisted the French consul to raise troops within the boundaries of the United States for service in a foreign army.

O'Neall, John Belton. *The Annals of Newberry.* Newberry, South Carolina, 1892. 2 parts in 1 vol.

Contains some references to participants in the attempt to raise troops for the French cause.

Parra-Pérez, Caracciolo. *Miranda et la Révolution Française.* Paris, 1925.

Contains a short but useful account of Miranda as an officer in the French republican army.

Pickett, Albert James. *History of Alabama and Incidentally of Georgia and Mississippi, from the Earliest Period.* Sheffield, Alabama, 1896.

Contains some useful material on the Indian problem during the Spanish period.

Pitkin, Timothy. *A Political and Civil History of the United States of America, from the Year 1763 to the Close of the Administration of President Washington, in March, 1797.* New Haven, 1828. 2 vols.

Contains an interesting although highly colored account of Genêt's mission to the United States.

Pradt, Dominique G. F. de. *Des Colonies, et de la révolution actuelle de l'Amérique.* Paris, 1817. 2 vols.

A firsthand account of the result of the French Revolution in France's American colonial possessions.

Ramsay, David. *The History of South Carolina from Its First Settlement in 1670, to the Year 1808.* Charleston, 1809. 2 vols.

Old, but contains interesting anecdotes about Genêt's reception after his landing at Charleston.

Rénaut, François Pierre. *Le Pacte de Famille et l'Amérique: La Politique Coloniale Franco-Espagnole de 1760–1792.* Paris, 1922.

A rather careful study of the impact of the close collaboration of France and Spain in Europe on the Spanish-American colonies.

Reynolds, Charles Bingham. *Old Saint Augustine.* St. Augustine, Florida, 1885.

Contains a fairly good account of the arrival of the Minorcan group in Florida during the period of English occupation.

Robertson, James Alexander. *Louisiana under the Rule of Spain, France and the United States, 1785–1807.* Cleveland, 1911. 2 vols.

The accepted authority on this topic. The author made excellent use of all available documentary material and includes some in the appendixes.

Robin, Claude C. *Voyages dans l'interieur de la Louisiane, de la Floride Occidentale, et dans les Isles de la Martinique, et de Saint-Domingue pendants les années 1802, 1803, 1804, 1805, et 1806.* Paris, 1807. 3 vols.

Useful for the abbé's comments on physical features and local anecdotes.

Roselli, Bruno. *The Italians in Colonial Florida.* Florida, 1940.

Useful for genealogical purposes in tracing the ancestry of early settlers in St. Augustine who originated in Italy.

Rosengarten, Joseph G. *French Colonists and Exiles in the United States.* Philadelphia, 1907.

An informative work on French settlers and travelers in the United States, with a useful bibliography.

Rydjord, John. *Foreign Interest in the Independence of New Spain.* Durham, North Carolina, 1935.

Contains some suggestions as to French views on the possession of Louisiana.

Saye, Albert Berry. *A Constitutional History of Georgia, 1732–1945.* Athens, Georgia, 1948.

Contains an excellent account of the development of constitutional government in Georgia and of the Yazoo land frauds.

Sherwood, Adiel. *A Gazetteer of the State of Georgia.* 2d ed. Philadelphia, 1829.

Contains useful statistical information on Georgia at the turn of the century.

Siebert, Wilbur H. *Loyalists in East Florida, 1774–1785.* Florida State Historical Society Publications, no. 9. DeLand, Florida, 1929. 2 vols.

A comprehensive work including much documentary material dealing with the transfer of East Florida to Spain in 1784.

Snowden, Yates, ed. *History of South Carolina.* Chicago, 1920. 5 vols.

The official history of the state with lengthy biographical sketches.

Stevens, William Baron. *A History of Georgia from Its First Discovery by Europeans to the Adoption of the Present Constitution in 1798.* New York, 1847. 2 vols.

The basic history of the state followed by most of the later compilers of Georgia histories.

Swanton, John R. *Early History of the Creek Indians and Their Neighbors.* Washington, 1922.

———. *Indian Tribes of the Lower Mississippi Valley and Adjacent Coast of the Gulf of Mexico.* Washington, 1911.

Together offer background material for the problems of Indian control.

Thomas, Charles Marion. *American Neutrality in 1793.* New York, 1931.

A useful and concise account of the efforts of the United States to remain clear of the European war.

Trescott, William Henry. *The Diplomatic History of the Administrations of Washington and Adams, 1789–1801.* Boston, 1857.

Presents the accepted view of the struggle of both presidents to keep the United States out of the European wars.

Villiers du Terrage, Marc de. *Les dernières années de la Louisiane Française.* Paris, 1903.

Contains a useful summary of the period of Spanish occupation with footnote references to little-known materials.

Vocelle, James Thomas. *History of Camden County, Georgia.* St. Mary's, Georgia, 1914.

———. *Reminiscences of Old St. Marys.* St. Mary's, Georgia, 1913.

Both contain useful information about the old fortifications built by the United States at the mouth of the river. They also include short accounts of several of the American families who moved to East Florida about 1790.

Walton, William. *An Exposé on the Dissentions of Spanish America.* London, 1814.

One of the very earliest accounts of the origins of unrest in Spanish America. The influence of the French Revolution is scarcely recognized.

Whitaker, Arthur Preston. *The Spanish-American Frontier: 1783–1795.* Boston, 1927.

Contains one of the most accurate accounts of the background events leading to the Pinckney Treaty of 1795.

White, George. *Historical Collections of Georgia.* New York, 1854.

Contains a fairly accurate account of some of the activities of Elijah Clark.

———. *Statistics of the State of Georgia.* Savannah, Georgia, 1849.

Contains some useful documentary materials quoted in fragmentary form.

Williams, John Lee. *The Territory of Florida: or Sketches ... of the Country ... from the First Discovery to the Present Time.* New York, 1839.

One of the earliest travel accounts of the Florida peninsula.

Winterbotham, W. *An Historical, Geographical, Commercial, and Philosophical View of the American United States, and the European Settlements in America and the West Indies.* London, 1795. 4 vols.

Contains interesting statements concerning East Florida, as well as a useful map.

CONTEMPORARY NEWSPAPERS

A large number of contemporary newspapers and periodicals were investigated in the preparation of this study. It was found that although there was a dearth of editorial comment in the major northern newspapers on matters pertaining to East Florida and the Georgia frontier, there were printed a large number of letters from travelers or visitors who were either connected with the Franco-American venture or who were at least witness to some phase of the enterprise. In addition, there were several quite violent editorial battles waged in both South Carolina and Georgia newspapers, the first over the Drayton-Moultrie case, and the second over the possible punitive action that the governor of Georgia might take in the case of Elijah Clark and his Trans-Oconee venture. It is of interest to note that the closer the editor was to the St. Mary's River, the more likely he was to trumpet for an immediate war with both Spain and the southeastern Indians.

This newspaper material was used in the original in the following repositories: American Antiquarian Society, Worcester, Massachusetts; Boston Athenaeum; Boston Public Library; Charleston Library Society, Charleston, South Carolina; Georgia Historical Society; Harvard University Library; Henry E. Huntington Library, San Marino, California; Massachusetts Historical Society; and the New York Public Library.

American Apollo (Boston, Massachusetts).

Scattered issues for 1792.

American Minerva and New York Evening Advertiser.

Scattered issues for 1794 and 1795.

The Augusta *Chronicle and Gazette of the State* (Augusta, Georgia).

Complete issues for 1793–1796.

Baltimore *Evening Post.*
    Scattered issues for 1793.
City Gazette and Daily Advertiser (Charleston, South Carolina).
    Complete issues, June, 1793–June, 1795.
Columbian Centinel (Boston, Massachusetts).
    Complete issues for 1792–1795.
Columbian Herald (Columbia, South Carolina).
    Complete issues, July 1794–July, 1795.
Columbian Museum (Savannah, Georgia).
    Scattered issues for 1793.
Federal Gazette and Philadelphia Daily Advertiser
    Scattered issues for 1792 and 1793.
Federal Orrery (Boston, Massachusetts).
    Scattered issues for 1794.
Gazette of the United States (Philadelphia).
    Complete issues for 1790–1796.
General Advertiser (Philadelphia).
    Scattered issues for 1792–1794.
Georgia Gazette (Augusta).
    Complete issues for 1794–1795.
The Herald (New York).
    Complete issues, June–December, 1794.
The Massachusetts Mercury (Boston).
    Scattered issues for 1793 and 1796.
The Mercury (Boston, Massachusetts).
    Scattered issues for 1793.
National Gazette (Philadelphia).
    Scattered issues for 1791, 1792 and 1793.
South Carolina Gazette (Charleston).
    Complete issues for 1794 and 1795.
South Carolina State Gazette (Charleston).
    Scattered issues for 1794 and 1795.
Southern Sentinel and Gazette of the State (Savannah, Georgia).
    Complete issues for 1794.
Virginia Gazette and Weekly Advertiser (Richmond).
    Scattered issues for 1793 and 1794.

INDEX

INDEX

Adet, Pierre Auguste: French minister,
95; on schemes against Amelia Island,
95–96; report to France, 129–130; arrival in United States, 169; report on
Clark, 173
Alforeso, Lieutenant José, commander at
San Nicolás, 89
Aliens. *See* Settlers
Altamaha River, as Indian boundary, 3,
148
Amelia Island: landing of French
agents, 36, 77; presence of privateers,
93; under rebel attack, 93–104 *passim*,
120; location and description, 161
Anastasia Island, 77; location and description, 165
"Anglo-Americans," named by Quesada,
105
Apalachicola River, 67
Ashley, William: listed as rebel, 107;
connection with attack on East Florida, 124
Ashley family, to East Florida, 5, 148
Atkinson, Andrew: captain in Florida
militia, 63; report to governor, 63;
meeting with Mathews, 64; visit to
Georgia, 94; rewards for service, 104;
second visit to Georgia, 108–109, 124–
125, 175; biographical material, 161
Atkinson, Nathaniel: report on Clark,
81; biographical material, 166
Atkinson family, to East Florida, 5
Augusta, 27; no longer capital, 140; location, 160

Bell, William, justice in Wilkes County,
159
Berrein, John, port inspector at Savannah, 74
Berrio, Captain Pedro Diaz: defense of
Amelia Island, 93, 102; member of
governor's council, 168
Bert, Major: as official go-between, 15;
biographical material, 151
Blunt family, to East Florida, 5
Booth, owner of *Mère Mitchele*, 166
Bowles, William Augustus, 162
Branzon, Captain, commander of *Las
Casas*, 13
Burke County, grand jury, 33

Burnett (John or Robert): attack on
Juana, 86; family, 167
Burnt Fort, desertion of militia, 132
Buttermilk Bluff, settlement, 4
Byck, Augustin, burning of plantations
in East Florida, 44

Calle de la Marina, 72
Camden County: laid out, 4, 25, 148; arrival of recruits, 34; Indian threat,
70; renegades, 83
Canada, plans for invasion, 13
Carne, Captain Peter, 86; in militia, 167
Carnes, Thomas P.: meeting with Clark,
59; report to Mathews, 159; biographical material, 160
Carondelet, Francisco Luis Héctor, Baron
de: governor, 8; Indian policy, 65;
attitude toward Clark, 67; view on
Indians, 115; biographical material,
149
Catafal, Subaltern Pablo, 91; in Mountain Fusiliers, 168
Catalan Light Infantry Company, 89,
168
"Cato," editorialist, 57–58
Cattle, sales in East Florida, 70
Céspedes, Governor Vicente Manuel de,
4; admission of settlers, 4
Chappell, Absolom Harris, views on
Clark, 60, 161
Charles IV, King of Spain, 144
Charles IX, King of France, 1
Chatham County, 164
Chattahoochee River, 67
Christmas, Robert, justice in Wilkes
County, 159
Christopher, Sergeant Spicer, 126
Clark, General Elijah: Genêt's plans,
10; with Samuel Hammond, 31; resignation from militia, 31; march to St.
Mary's, 37; new plans against East
Florida, 50; Trans-Oconee settlement,
51–61 *passim;* surrender, 60; Yazoo
land sales, 75; plans for renewal of attack on East Florida, 79; reappearance in East Florida, 114–122 *passim*,
124–138 *passim;* French commission,
114; rumors of payments, 154; visit to
Wilkes County, 159; land purchases,
164

[201]